Leftist Governments in Latin America

Successes and Shortcomings

Can Latin America's new left stimulate economic development, enhance social equity, and deepen democracy in spite of the economic and political constraints it faces? This is the first book to systematically examine the policies and performance of the left-wing governments that have risen to power in Latin America during the last decade. Featuring thorough studies of Bolivia, Brazil, Chile, and Venezuela by renowned experts, the volume argues that moderate leftist governments have attained greater, more sustainable success than their more radical, contestatory counterparts. Moderate governments in Brazil and Chile have generated solid economic growth, reduced poverty and inequality, and created innovative and fiscally sound social programs, while respecting the fundamental principles of market economics and liberal democracy. By contrast, more radical governments, exemplified by Hugo Chávez in Venezuela, have expanded state intervention and popular participation and attained some short-term economic and social successes, but they have provoked severe conflict, undermined democracy, and failed to ensure the economic and institutional sustainability of their policy projects.

Kurt Weyland is the Lozano Long Professor of Latin American Politics at the University of Texas at Austin. He has published *Democracy without Equity: Failures of Reform in Brazil* (1996); *The Politics of Market Reform in Fragile Democracies* (2002); *Bounded Rationality and Policy Diffusion: Social Sector Reform in Latin America* (2007); and many articles and book chapters on democratization, neoliberalism, populism, and social policy in Latin America. His new book project analyzes the wave-like diffusion of political regime changes across countries in Europe and Latin America, starting with the explosive spread of the 1848 revolution in both continents.

Raúl L. Madrid is an Associate Professor in the Department of Government at the University of Texas at Austin. He is the author of *Retiring the State: The Politics of Pension Privatization in Latin America and Beyond* (2003). His articles on economic and social policy reform, elections and party systems, and ethnic politics in Latin America have appeared in *Comparative Politics, Electoral Studies, Journal of Latin American Studies, Latin American Politics and Society, Latin American Research Review*, and *World Politics*. He is currently working on a book on the emergence of ethnopopulism in Latin America.

Wendy Hunter, Associate Professor of Government at the University of Texas, is the author of *Politicians against Soldiers: Eroding Military Influence in Brazil* (1997) and numerous articles and book chapters on the military and social policy issues in Latin America, as well as on the Workers' Party in Brazil. Journals in which her articles appear include *Comparative Politics*, the *American Political Science Review, Comparative Political Studies, World Politics*, and *Latin American Politics and Society*. She is currently finishing a book on the Workers' Party in Brazil.

Leftist Governments in Latin America

Successes and Shortcomings

Edited by

KURT WEYLAND
University of Texas, Austin

RAÚL L. MADRID
University of Texas, Austin

WENDY HUNTER
University of Texas, Austin

CAMBRIDGE
UNIVERSITY PRESS

CAMBRIDGE UNIVERSITY PRESS
Cambridge, New York, Melbourne, Madrid, Cape Town, Singapore,
São Paulo, Delhi, Dubai, Tokyo, Mexico City

Cambridge University Press
32 Avenue of the Americas, New York, NY 10013-2473, USA

www.cambridge.org
Information on this title: www.cambridge.org/9780521130332

First published 2010

Printed in the United States of America

A catalog record for this publication is available from the British Library.

Library of Congress Cataloging in Publication data

Leftist governments in Latin America : successes and shortcomings / edited by Kurt Weyland,
Raúl L. Madrid, Wendy Hunter.
    p. cm.
Includes bibliographical references and index.
ISBN 978-0-521-76220-5 – ISBN 978-0-521-13033-2 (pbk.)
1. Latin America – Politics and government – 1980–   2. Socialism – Latin America.
I. Weyland, Kurt Gerhard.   II. Madrid, Raúl L.   III. Hunter, Wendy.   IV. Title.
JL960.L43   2010
320.53098 – dc22   2010000987

ISBN 978-0-521-76220-5 Hardback
ISBN 978-0-521-13033-2 Paperback

Contents

Acknowledgments

When working on a book, one incurs a number of intellectual, professional, and personal debts. This is even more the case with an edited volume, which is by its very nature a collaborative enterprise.

In many ways, our primary debt of gratitude is to the University of Texas at Austin (UT). Its financial and administrative support and its wealth of superb faculty have made this project feasible, manageable, and even enjoyable. Specifically, we are grateful to Bryan Roberts, Director of UT's Lozano Long Institute of Latin American Studies (LLILAS) at the time, for suggesting the idea of holding the conference on which this book is based. Bryan's backing and support have been crucial. We also thank LLILAS's student interns and especially Paloma Díaz, who, in her usual indefatigable way, did an outstanding job organizing and running the conference. For generous financial support for the meeting and the resulting book, we thank LLILAS; the Department of Government and its chair Gary Freeman; the Office of Development; and the Sterling Clark Holloway Centennial Lectureship in Liberal Arts.

The conference, titled "The Performance of Leftist Governments in Latin America: What Does the Left Do Right?" was held at UT in March 2008 and featured two days of lively, stimulating debates. We thank all the paper presenters, discussants, panel chairs, and audience participants. In addition to the chapter authors featured in this volume, we are particularly grateful to Steve Ellner, Linda Farthing, Ricardo Ffrench-Davis, Benjamin Kohl, Steven Levitsky, and our keynote speaker, Chile's former President Ricardo Lagos.

Riitta Koivumäki did an excellent job helping us put together this volume, and Ruth Homrighaus skillfully smoothed out the prose. The comments and suggestions we received from Cambridge's anonymous reviewers greatly improved the volume. In particular, they helped us to sharpen our central arguments and advance a clear message on a topic that has attracted enormous attention and debate, inside and outside of academia. We are very thankful to our editor Eric Crahan for accompanying this project since its early stages and for shepherding it expeditiously and with exemplary professionalism through the review process. We are grateful to Shana Meyer of Aptara for her excellent organization and oversight of the production process.

Collaborating on a large and difficult project over an extended time frame can be a source of tension, if not conflict. Not in our case! Instead, editing this book has further strengthened the long-standing professional and personal cooperation among the editors, and we are very grateful for that. The resulting volume is dedicated to our children, Andi and Niko Hunter Weyland, and Bela and Nico Madrid.

Acronyms and Abbreviations

ADN	Acción Democrática Nacionalista (Nationalist Democratic Action, Bolivia)
AFP	Administrador de fondo de pensión (Pension fund administrator)
ALBA	Alternativa Bolivariana para los Pueblos de Nuestra América (Bolivarian Alternative for the Americas)
ANC	Asamblea Nacional Constituyente (National Constituent Assembly, Venezuela)
ATPDEA	Andean Trade Promotion and Drug Eradication Act (United States)
BANFOANDES	Banco de Fomento Regional Los Andes (National Bank, Venezuela)
BG	British Gas
BNDES	Banco Nacional de Desenvolvimento Econômico e Social (National Bank for Economic and Social Development, Brazil)
BP	British Petroleum
BPC	Benefício de Prestação Continuada (Continuous Cash Benefit Program, Brazil)
CADIVI	Comisión de Administración de Divisas (Commission for the Administration of Currency, Venezuela)
CANEB	Cámara Nacional de Exportadores de Bolivia (National Chamber of Exporters of Bolivia)
CANTV	Compañía Anónima Nacional de Teléfonos de Venezuela (National Telephone Company of Venezuela)
CNT	Confederação Nacional do Transporte (National Confederation of the Transport Sector, Brazil)
Coca-Cola FEMSA	Coca-Cola Fomento Económico Mexicano, S.A. (Bottler company of Coca-Cola, Mexico)

CPMF	Contribuição Provisória sobre a Movimentação ou Transmissão de Valores e de Créditos e Direitos de Natureza Financeira (Tax on financial transactions, Brazil)
ECLAC	Economic Commission for Latin America and the Caribbean
FA	Frente Amplio (Broad Front, Uruguay)
FONASA	Fondo Nacional de Salud (National Health Fund, Chile)
GDP	Gross domestic product
G7	Group of Seven, meeting of finance ministers from seven leading industrialized nations
IBCE	Instituto Boliviano de Comercio Exterior (Bolivian Foreign Trade Institute)
IBGE	Instituto Brasileiro de Geografia e Estatística (Brazilian Institute of Geography and Statistics)
IBOPE	Instituto Brasileiro de Opinião Pública e Estatística (Brazilian Institute of Public Opinion and Statistics)
ICSID	International Center for the Settlement of Investment Disputes
IDH	Índice de Desarrollo Humano (Human Development Index)
IEDI	Instituto de Estudos para o Desenvolvimento Industrial (Institute for the Study of Industrial Development, Brazil)
IMF	International Monetary Fund
INE	Instituto Nacional de Estadística (National Institute of Statistics, Bolivia)
IPEA	Instituto de Pesquisa Econômica Aplicada (Institute of Applied Economic Research, Brazil)
IPEADATA	Instituto de Pesquisa Econômica Aplicada, Base de Dados (Database of Institute of Applied Economic Research, Brazil)
ISAPRE	Institución de Salud Previsional (Health insurance fund, Chile)
ISI	Import-substitution industrialization
IVA	Impuesto al Valor Agregado (Value-added tax)
MAS	Movimiento al Socialismo (Movement toward Socialism, Bolivia)
MAS	Movimiento al Socialismo (Movement toward Socialism, Venezuela)
MBR-200	Movimiento Bolivariano Revolucionario-200 (Bolivarian Revolutionary Movement 200, Venezuela)
MDG	Millennium Development Goal
MDS	Ministério do Desenvolvimento Social e Combate à Fome (Ministry of Social Development and Fight against Hunger, Brazil)

MERCAL	Mission Mercal (National food distribution chain, Venezuela)
MIR	Movimiento de la Izquierda Revolucionaria (Movement of the Revolutionary Left, Bolivia)
MNR	Movimiento Nacionalista Revolucionario (Nationalist Revolutionary Movement, Bolivia)
MST	Movimiento dos Sem Terra (Landless Movement, Brazil)
MVR	Movimiento V [Quinta] República (Fifth Republic Movement, Venezuela)
NASA	National Aeronautics and Space Administration (United States)
NDP	National Development Plan (Bolivia)
NGO	Non-governmental organization
OECD	Organisation for Economic Cooperation and Development
OPEC	Organization of Petroleum Exporting Countries
PAC	Programa de Aceleração do Crescimento (Growth Acceleration Program, Brazil)
PDC	Partido Demócrata Cristiano de Chile (Christian Democratic Party)
PDVSA	Petróleos de Venezuela, S.A. (Petroleum of Venezuela)
Petrobras	Petróleo Brasileiro S.A. (Brazilian Petroleum)
Plan AUGE	Plan de Acceso Universal con Garantías Explícitas de Salud (Plan of Universal Access with Explicit Guarantees in Health, Chile)
PNUD	Programa de Naciones Unidas para el Desarrollo (United Nations Development Programme)
PODEMOS	Poder Democrático y Social (Social and Democratic Power, Bolivia)
PPD	Partido por la Democracia (Party for Democracy, Chile)
PPI	Programa de Promoción del Investigador (Program for Promotion of Investigators, Venezuela)
PPT	Patria Para Todos (Fatherland for All, Venezuela)
PRN	Partido da Reconstrução Nacional (National Reconstruction Party, Brazil)
PS	Partido Socialista de Chile (Socialist Party of Chile)
PSDB	Partido da Social Democracia Brasileira (Party of Brazilian Social Democracy)
PSU	Prueba de Selección Universitaria (Exam for University Selection, Chile)
PSUV	Partido Socialista Unido de Venezuela (United Socialist Party of Venezuela)
PT	Partido dos Trabalhadores (Workers' Party, Brazil)
RCTV	Radio Caracas Televisión (Private media company, Venezuela)

RN   Renovación Nacional (National Renewal, Chile)
SENIAT   Servicio Nacional Integrado de Administración Aduanera y Tributaria (Integrated National Customs and Tax Administration Service, Venezuela)
SERNAM   Servicio Nacional de la Mujer (National Women's Service, Chile)
SUNACOOP   Superintendencia Nacional de Cooperativas (National Superintendency of Cooperatives, Venezuela)
UDAPE   Unidad de Análisis de Políticas Sociales y Económicas (Social and Economic Policy Analysis Unit, Bolivia)
UDI   Unión Demócrata Independiente (Independent Democratic Union, Chile)
UN   Frente de Unidad Nacional (National Unity Front, Bolivia)
UNDP   United Nations Development Programme
UNT   Unión Nacional de Trabajadores de Venezuela (National Workers' Union of Venezuela)
VENEPAL   (Compañía) Venezolana de Papel (Venezuelan Paper Firm)
YPFB   Yacimientos Petrolíferos Fiscales Bolivianos (Bolivian State Petroleum Fields)

Contributors

Pedro Luiz Barros Silva has been a Professor in the Institute of Economics at the State University of Campinas (UNICAMP), São Paulo, since 1985. His research focuses on the formulation, analysis, and evaluation of public policies and reform of the state. His publications include *Limites e obstáculos à reforma do Estado no Brasil: A experiência da previdência social na Nova República* (2003); and (with Geraldo Biasoto, Jr., and Sulamis Dain) *Regulação do Setor Saúde nas Américas: As relações entre o público e o privado numa abordagem sistêmica* (2006). He is currently directing two major studies on the process of fiscal decentralization in Brazil and is working on a project on poverty reduction and policy regimes.

José Carlos de Souza Braga is Professor in the Institute of Economics at the State University of Campinas (UNICAMP), São Paulo, Brazil, and was the Executive Director of the Institute's Center for Studies on International Economic Relations from 2003 to 2007. He has published *The Temporality of Wealth* (2000), an analysis of the financialization process of capitalism, and many articles on monetary and financial issues in books and journals. His new research project is about the current international transformations and their impact on the stability and development of the Brazilian economy.

Javier Corrales is Associate Professor of Political Science at Amherst College in Massachusetts. He is the author of *Presidents without Parties: The Politics of Economic Reform in Argentina and Venezuela in the 1990s* (2002). His research has been published in *Comparative Politics, World Development, Political Science Quarterly, International Studies Quarterly, World Policy Journal, Latin American Politics and Society, Journal of Democracy, Latin American Research Review, Studies in Comparative International Studies, Current History*, and *Foreign Policy*. He is currently working on a book manuscript on constitutional changes in Latin America and an edited volume on the politics of sexuality in Latin America.

Vera Lúcia Cabral Costa is the Director of the School for Teachers' Professional Development of the Education Department of the State of São Paulo. She was Director of Social Policies at the Administrative Development Foundation (FUNDAP) of the State of São Paulo. She has also worked as a researcher at the Center for Public Policy Studies at the University of Campinas (NEPP-UNICAMP) and as a consultant for the Brazilian Federal Government and the Inter-American Development Bank. Her recent publications include (with Renilson Rehem Souza) *Atenção à Saúde no SUS de São Paulo – Uma perspectiva regional* (2008); and (with Pedro Silva and Geraldo Biasoto) *A Efetividade das Políticas de Saúde na América Latina: Experiências bem-sucedidas* (2008).

George Gray Molina is an Oxford-Princeton Global Leaders' Fellow at the Woodrow Wilson School of Public and International Affairs, Princeton University. He is a Bolivian economist and political scientist. He edited *La economía boliviana más allá del gas* (2005), *El estado del Estado en Bolivia* (2007), and *La otra frontera* (2008) as Coordinator of the Human Development Report at UNDP-Bolivia. He also coedited *Tensiones irresueltas: Bolivia, pasado y presente* (2009) with John Crabtree and Laurence Whitehead, and *The Bolivian Growth Puzzle* (in press) with Francisco Rodríguez and Ricardo Hausmann. He is currently working on a book on Bolivian inequality and on the political economy of growth pockets in Latin America.

Evelyne Huber, Morehead Alumni Distinguished Professor and Chair of the Department of Political Science, University of North Carolina at Chapel Hill, is coauthor of *Capitalist Development and Democracy* (1992) and *Development and Crisis of the Welfare State* (2001); and editor of *Models of Capitalism: Lessons for Latin America* (2002). She is currently investigating the impact of democracy, political power distributions, and transitions to open economies on systems of social protection and investment in human capital in Latin America and the Caribbean.

Wendy Hunter, Associate Professor of Government at the University of Texas, is the author of *Politicians against Soldiers: Eroding Military Influence in Brazil* (1997) and numerous articles and book chapters on the military and social policy issues in Latin America, as well as on the Workers' Party in Brazil. Journals in which her articles appear include *Comparative Politics*, the *American Political Science Review*, *Comparative Political Studies*, *World Politics*, and *Latin American Politics and Society*. She is currently finishing a book on the Workers' Party in Brazil.

Peter R. Kingstone is an Associate Professor of Political Science at the University of Connecticut. He is the author of *Crafting Coalitions for Reform: Business Preferences, Political Institutions and Neoliberal Reform in Brazil* (1999) and coeditor with Timothy Power of *Democratic Brazil: Actors, Institutions and Processes* (2000) and *Democratic Brazil Revisited* (2008). He has published articles on the politics of economic reform in *Comparative Politics*, *Comparative Political Studies*, *Latin American Politics and Society*, and *Political Research Quarterly*. He is currently working on the comparative politics of privatization and pension reform and a study of political institutions and neoliberal economic reform.

Raúl L. Madrid is an Associate Professor in the Department of Government at the University of Texas at Austin. He is the author of *Retiring the State: The Politics of Pension Privatization in Latin America and Beyond* (2003). His articles on economic and social policy reform, elections and party systems, and ethnic politics in Latin America have appeared in *Comparative Politics, Electoral Studies, Journal of Latin American Studies, Latin American Politics and Society, Latin American Research Review*, and *World Politics*. He is currently working on a book on the emergence of ethnopopulism in Latin America.

Aldo F. Ponce is currently a PhD Candidate in the Department of Political Science at the University of Houston. He holds master's degrees in Economics and Latin American Studies from the University of Connecticut and one in Political Science from the University of Houston. He has published articles on free trade agreements in Latin America and the *piquetero* social movement. His current projects focus on elections in countries facing transitions to democracy, legislatures in countries with weakly institutionalized party systems, and political networks under changing trade policy environments.

Jennifer Pribble is an Assistant Professor of Political Science and International Studies at the University of Richmond. Her research interests include Latin American political economy and comparative social policy. She is the author of "Women and Welfare: The Politics of Coping with New Social Risks in Chile and Uruguay," which appeared in *Latin American Research Review*, and is a coauthor of "Political Determinants of Inequality in Latin America and the Caribbean," which appeared in *American Sociological Review*.

John D. Stephens is Gerhard E. Lenski Jr. Professor of Political Science and Sociology and Director of the Center for European Studies at the University of North Carolina, Chapel Hill. His main interests are comparative social policy and political economy, with area foci on Europe, the Antipodes, Latin America, and the Caribbean. He is the author or coauthor of four books including *Capitalist Development and Democracy* (with Evelyne Huber and Dietrich Rueschemeyer, 1992) and *Development and Crisis of the Welfare State* (with Evelyne Huber, 2001) and numerous journal articles.

Kurt Weyland is the Lozano Long Professor of Latin American Politics at the University of Texas at Austin. He has published *Democracy without Equity: Failures of Reform in Brazil* (1996); *The Politics of Market Reform in Fragile Democracies* (2002); *Bounded Rationality and Policy Diffusion: Social Sector Reform in Latin America* (2007); and many articles and book chapters on democratization, neoliberalism, populism, and social policy in Latin America. His new book project analyzes the wave-like diffusion of political regime changes across countries in Europe and Latin America, starting with the explosive spread of the 1848 revolution in both continents.

The Performance of Leftist Governments in Latin America

Conceptual and Theoretical Issues

Kurt Weyland

The first decade of the third millennium has seen a striking move to the left in Latin America. After the victory of Hugo Chávez in Venezuela in December 1998, presidents who identify themselves and are widely seen as part of the left have been elected in Bolivia, Brazil, Chile, Ecuador, El Salvador, Guatemala, Nicaragua, Paraguay, and Uruguay, and leftists in Mexico and Peru came very close to accomplishing the same feat. Moreover, former Argentine president Néstor Kirchner, who represented the center-left wing of the ideologically heterogeneous and amorphous Peronist Party, won in 2003 against the exponent of the party's neoliberal wing, Carlos Menem. The current Argentine president, Cristina Fernández de Kirchner, who took over from her husband in 2007, occupies a similar position on the ideological spectrum. As a result, left-leaning presidents currently govern approximately two-thirds of the region's population.

This shift to the left constitutes a dramatic change from the 1990s, when the left elected barely any presidents in Latin America and when governments of various stripes enacted market-oriented reforms – the economic project of the right – in most countries of the region. At that time, the Washington Consensus on market reform was indeed the consensus approach among high-ranking policymakers, and although there always were organized interests, sectors of the population, and political parties (especially from the left) that rejected it, they were fairly marginalized in many nations and could at best exert defensive veto power. Whereas until the 1980s, the left had claimed the mantle of modernity and structural reform, in the 1990s neoliberals occupied this discourse and redefined its meaning. Rather than spearheading progress, the left was accused of clinging to a failed and untenable status quo. The

I would like to thank Javier Corrales, Gustavo Flores Macías, Evelyne Huber, Wendy Hunter, John Stephens, the anonymous reviewers, and especially Raúl Madrid for excellent comments on this chapter. I am also very grateful to Andrew Stein for a wealth of documents and important research materials.

protagonists of market reform appealed to new winners. By contrast, the left seemed to defend losers, dying sectors, and shrinking constituencies, which did not look like a propitious strategy for gaining power.

How the situation has changed! Discontent with neoliberalism has spread as it has failed to fulfill its promise of enhancing mass prosperity, and as it has exacerbated long-standing problems such as precarious employment. Promoters of the market system have worried about a popular backlash that would reverse the reforms of the 1990s. From the other side of the ideological spectrum, leftists have rejoiced in the hope that the opportunity to enact their long-delayed projects has finally arrived. As radical populists, leaders of contentious mass movements, and representatives of parties with Marxist origins took power in country after country, the time seemed ripe for dramatic change. The question was how far would leftist presidents go? And what would they accomplish on the economic, social, and political fronts?

The present volume seeks to answer these important questions and in this way complement the burgeoning literature on Latin America's "new left." Many scholars have documented the reversal of political trends; proposed classification schemes to make sense of the variety of leftist movements, leaders, and governments; and sought to explain their emergence and rise to power (Petkoff 2005; Castañeda 2006; Cleary 2006; Arnson 2007; Boeckh 2007; Hunter 2007; Roberts 2007; Castañeda and Morales 2008; De la Torre and Peruzzotti 2008; Madrid 2008; Cameron 2009; E. Silva 2009; Weyland 2009; Levitsky and Roberts in press). This book takes the discussion a crucial step further by investigating what left-wing governments have actually done and what they have accomplished. In political science jargon, the chapters analyze the policy outputs and outcomes of the new wave of administrations, focusing on three main spheres: economy, society, and politics. The following questions guide this analysis. First, have leftist governments managed to boost economic growth and upgrade development despite the constraints arising from economic globalization and the legacies of domestic market reform? Second, have they distributed the benefits of growth more equitably and improved the social well-being of the population, especially of previously neglected, poorer sectors – and have they done so in an economically and politically sustainable fashion? And third, have they promoted the political inclusion of marginalized groupings and boosted political participation in general, yet without undermining pluralism and liberal safeguards?

These crucial questions have so far not received the scholarly attention they deserve. Whereas the present volume concentrates on the *performance* of the left, much of the extant literature has discussed the classification of leftist governments and the causes of their assumption of power (cf. Petkoff 2005; Castañeda 2006; Cleary 2006). For instance, controversies have raged on the proper labels for various presidents (e.g., Arnson 2007). Are some of them populists, and if so, based on what definition of populism? Are others social–democratic, and what would that notion mean in contemporary Latin America? Can one even speak of social democracy in a setting in which the "working class" (strictly defined) is small and shrinking, trade unions are weak, and external economic constraints are often tight (Sandbrook, Edelman, Heller, and Teichman 2007; Lanzaro 2008; Roberts 2008)?

Scholars also disagree on whether there are two main groups of leftist movements, parties, and governments, or whether it is useful to design more complex, multidimensional classification schemes (Ramírez Gallegos 2006; Cameron 2009: 334–35; Levitsky and Roberts in press). Simple classification schemes emphasize a basic difference in the political orientation and strategy of Latin America's contemporary leftists, distinguishing a moderate from a more radical grouping. By contrast, multidimensional classifications in addition highlight organizational differences, such as the differential institutionalization of left-wing parties and movements (see Levitsky and Roberts in press). The latter approach may be useful for analyses that investigate leftist forces, their origins, and their rise to power.[1] This volume, however, focuses on policy and performance and examines the decision outputs and outcomes of left-wing governments. For this analytical purpose, the crucial difference concerns the political orientation and strategy of these administrations, not the organizational features of the forces sustaining them. The present book therefore applies a simple, pragmatic ordering scheme that arrays leftist governments on a continuum ranging from moderation to fairly radical contestation, similar to Kaufman (2007: 24) and to Levitsky and Roberts themselves in their concluding chapter (in press).[2]

The moderate current tempers its pursuit of leftist goals prudently, respecting economic constraints and political opposition. When encountering problems and resistance, it negotiates rather than trying to impose its will. By contrast, the more radical wing challenges neoliberalism, defies strictures of globalization, and attacks the political opposition. To maintain and strengthen the loyalty of its mass followers, it feels the political urge to contest with enemies, especially political adversaries, business sectors, or the U.S. government – the favorite target during the presidency of George W. Bush. The present volume therefore calls this current *contestatory*. It avoids the label *radical* because, although clearly more radical than its moderate counterparts, the contestatory left is not nearly as radical as its forefathers in the 1960s and 1970s. Above all, by forgoing a comprehensive, systematic assault on capitalist property relations, it does not go to the root of socioeconomic and political problems in the eyes of true Marxists.

---

[1] In an in-depth conceptual analysis, however, F. Silva (2009) demonstrates that various dimensions along which leftist forces have been distinguished in fact align quite closely; he therefore arrives at two groupings arrayed along a single dimension, very similar to the approach of the present volume.

[2] Such a simple scheme also has the advantage of yielding a reasonable number of cases per category. By contrast, Levitsky and Roberts' two-dimensional scheme ends up with an average of only two cases per cell. As a result, causal analysis runs a greater risk of getting confounded by the idiosyncratic characteristics of a single case, which are more likely to cancel out if scholars use a one-dimensional distinction that groups together more cases.

Virtually all observers agree that in rhetoric and action (though more in rhetoric than in action), Venezuela's President Hugo Chávez is charting a fairly radical and contestatory political and policy course for contemporary Latin America. Although not pursuing a total transformation of the socioeconomic and political order as earlier generations of leftist radicals did in revolutionary Cuba and Salvador Allende's Chile, Chávez's proposals and programs deviate starkly from the market orientation that became predominant after the global collapse of communism and the enactment of economic liberalization in Latin America. Chávez's efforts to contest the hegemony of neoliberalism and move toward twenty-first-century socialism are quite radical in the current world-historical setting. The Bolivarian leader's approach is clearly more defiant than the projects pursued by Socialist presidents Ricardo Lagos (2000–06) and Michelle Bachelet in Chile (2006–2010), who are – among the administrations under investigation – furthest toward the moderate pole.[3] On this continuum, Bolivia's Evo Morales (2006–present) is in the eyes of many observers closer to the Venezuelan leader. By contrast, the orientation of Brazil's Luiz Inácio Lula da Silva is fairly similar to that of the Chilean Concertación. In fact, the social policies of the Lula government are more timid than Chile's, which has promoted an ambitious health reform (Plan AUGE) and an overhaul of the pension system. But Lula faces more pressure and independent action in some areas, especially land reform. Based on the classification of policy stances, the present volume identifies and examines two groups of leftist governments, exemplified by Chávez's Venezuela on the contestatory pole and by the Chilean Concertación and Lula's Brazil on the moderate end of the spectrum.

This distinction of two groupings also reflects mutual influence inside each camp and a certain degree of tension between them. Clearly, Chávez has served as an important source of inspiration and of political and financial support for Bolivia's Morales (and Ecuador's President Rafael Correa), whereas the Chilean model and its socioeconomic accomplishments have influenced the center-left and left in Brazil. At the same time, Chávez has challenged Brazil's claim to South American leadership, and Morales' hydrocarbon nationalization of May 2006 affronted Brazil by hurting its national oil company Petrobras. In turn, Lula da Silva has countered Chávez's influence in Central America by assiduously courting El Salvador's new left-wing president, Mauricio Funes ("Modelo Importado do Brasil" 2009). As a result, underneath the diplomatic surface of leftist brotherhood there has been unease and tension between the two camps. The moderate and contestatory lefts are not only conceptual constructions but also act as loose coalitions in the real world. The distinction of two policy approaches therefore seems to be valid and useful for this book's analytical purposes.

---

[3] With deliberate exaggeration, a leading figure in Lagos' and Bachelet's Socialist Party told me during an interview in Santiago in July 2007 that "President Lagos led Chile's best government ever – of the right."

This volume avoids another tricky conceptual issue by concentrating on Bolivia, Brazil, Chile, and Venezuela, whose current presidents indisputably are leftists in extraction and orientation. The left is defined in ideological terms, characterized by the determined pursuit of social equity, justice, and solidarity as an overriding priority. Although historically focused on reducing or eliminating socioeconomic class differences, this egalitarian, antihierarchical approach has been broadened in recent decades to oppose any kind of status difference, especially those based on ascriptive criteria such as gender, race, and ethnicity. The left is driven by the optimistic belief that equity and nondiscrimination are attainable. The hope that "a new world is possible!" drives the left, whereas the right highlights obstacles and constraints and claims that reform tends to have counterproductive, perverse effects (Hirschman 1991). The left pursues its goal of egalitarian transformation through deliberate political action, relying on the state as a principal instrument for reshaping the economy and society. Critical of the anarchy of the market, where actors are driven by private profit motives and exposed to the vagaries of supply and demand, the left enlists the visible hand of the state, which – especially if it is democratically legitimated – is seen as pursuing collective, social rationality, that is, the common good. Whether more moderate or more radical and contestatory in orientation, the governments under investigation all embrace these typically leftist beliefs and goals.

By featuring case studies of administrations that clearly qualify as leftist, the present volume avoids grappling with borderline cases, such as Argentina's Kirchner or Peru's born-again Alan García, who is trying to make up for his catastrophic first term by charting a "responsible" nonleftist course. Instead, the chapters focus on unambiguous and exemplary cases.[4] To ensure proper balance, they examine two administrations close to the moderate pole and two governments that tend toward the more radical, contestatory side of the spectrum. The effort to undertake a systematic and thorough examination of four paradigmatic experiences is particularly important because the recent rise of the Latin American left – especially the emergence of a more radical, contestatory left – has evoked a good deal of passion from different academic and ideological camps. But both the fears of the right and the excitement among the left can become obstacles to scholarly analysis, which benefits from neither panic nor wishful thinking. Instead, the best understanding of past experiences and future prospects arises from studies that bring a wealth of empirical information and data to bear.

---

[4] But of course, in analyzing the real world, the project does encounter some gray zones. For instance, Chilean Socialists only captured the presidency in 2000, but played a decisive role in government as part of a center-left coalition from 1990 onward. And although Lula's predecessor, Fernando Henrique Cardoso (1995–2002), enacted market reforms in an alliance with a center-right party, his own Party of Brazilian Social Democracy claimed a center-left orientation, and the president himself had, in his earlier incarnation as a sociologist, professed a commitment to socialism (see Power 2001).

To explain the parameters under which the two currents of leftism oper-
ate and the distinctive strategies they pursue, the following section provides a
broader perspective on the historical evolution of the left. The subsequent
three sections discuss the guiding questions examined in this volume and
summarize the main conclusions arising from the case studies. Specifically,
they focus on left-wing efforts to stimulate economic development under the
strictures of globalization, to enhance social justice in spite of resource constraints, and to deepen democracy without undermining it. In all three areas,
the moderate left has arguably attained better performance than its contestatory counterparts. The sixth section highlights the limits that democracy
itself, with its insistence on checks and balances and liberal safeguards, sets
to radical efforts at producing socioeconomic and political change. The subsequent section accounts for the emergence of moderate-left governments in some
countries, whereas contestatory leftists capture power in others. The penulti-
mate section discusses the book's contributions to important substantive and
theoretical themes, such as the impact of the two lefts on the fate of Latin
America's market system and the abstract question of political agency versus
structure. A final section briefly summarizes the case studies and the concluding
chapter.

THE CENTRAL TASK AND DILEMMA OF THE LEFT

To situate Latin America's contemporary left, clarify the difference between
its two main wings, and examine the opportunities and constraints facing
them, it is useful to start from a broader reflection on the main task the left
has historically set for itself and the obstacles it has faced in fulfilling this
task. Essentially, the left has always sought to attain a structural transformation designed to guide economic activities toward fulfilling the social needs of
the popular majority and to advance its political participation. Long crystal-
lized in the demand for socialism, this quest encompasses economic and social
redistribution and the revamping of power relations in economy and society
through the full incorporation of poorer, excluded sectors. Thus, the left has
promoted profound change. Yet these transformative efforts have faced serious constraints arising from the existing organization of economy, society, and
politics. Resource limitations and opposition from socioeconomic and political
elites have posed particular obstacles. As a result, how many of its goals can
the left actually accomplish? And how does it best pursue its agenda? Should
the impulse toward activism or the need for realism prevail?

Thus, leftists face the quandary of how best to cope with the obstacles they
confront, increase their chance of success, and avoid a backlash. When, how,
how far, and how fast should they push for their goals? How bold or how cautious should they be? Throughout history, leftists have differed on these questions. Their approaches have ranged from radical efforts to smash constraints
in a revolution to reformist strategies of transforming existing structures from
within through gradual change. The radical position cuts the Gordian knot

of economic and political constraints with the sword of revolutionary violence. By sweeping away the old order, it seeks to create ample opportunities for rebuilding economy, society, and politics anew and quickly attaining economic solidarity, social justice, and political participation. The moderate position embraced by social democracy, by contrast, fears the costs and risks of such voluntaristic activism and therefore places priority on realism. To bring progress in a nonconfrontational fashion, it takes advantage of any opening in the existing order – especially the political influence granted to the working class via universal suffrage – to enact reforms step by step in a determined, cumulative strategy. It plays by the rules of the game to better the game's outcomes and, eventually, alter the rules and nature of the game itself. In sum: the radical position privileges ambition, boldness, and activism; the moderate position, prudence, gradualism, and realism.

Even inside the revolutionary and moderate poles, debates have raged on the relative importance of activism versus realism. Among Marxists, for instance, Friedrich Engels emphasized the need to wait for the right socioeconomic preconditions for revolutionary change, whereas Lenin adopted a voluntaristic position and took advantage of a unique political opportunity. In a similar disagreement, orthodox communists in Latin America during the 1950s and 1960s advocated waiting for the full development of capitalism and rejected any immediate transition to socialism, which young firebrands Fidel Castro and Ernesto Che Guevara sought. Equivalent discussions occurred within European social democracy. Some sectors believed that each reformist success would enhance working-class power and facilitate further advances, eventually allowing for a peaceful transition to socialism (Stephens 1986). But others argued that the transitional costs of a structural transformation and the incentives of democratic competition would limit social democracy. While achieving immediate improvements inside the existing order, it would refrain from overcoming capitalism (Przeworski 1985).

These old debates between voluntaristic activism and prudent realism play out in Latin America's contemporary left and underlie the difference between its contestatory and moderate wings (Weyland 2009: 148–49). The more radical sectors led by Hugo Chávez invoke some of the slogans and symbols of the revolutionary tradition, put ambition ahead of prudence, and pursue fairly far-reaching goals under current circumstances. By contrast, moderate leaders and governments avoid revolutionary rhetoric, insist on realism, and adopt a gradualist approach. Specifically, the contestatory left rejects neoliberalism, challenges the constraints arising from economic globalization, pursues determined social change, and pushes through political reforms that strengthen the participatory, majoritarian features of democracy at the expense of political pluralism and liberal safeguards. Moderate leftists refrain from such controversial measures and negotiate reform with the domestic and international stakeholders of the established order. So the old disagreements inside the left on how to tackle the dilemma of transformation under constraints continue to reverberate in present-day Latin America.

But of course, times have changed. The range of options available to all of the region's leftists has narrowed greatly in recent decades. Both extremes, especially the revolutionary pole, have lost appeal and run into serious feasibility problems. The collapse of communism has deprived the radical left of an alternative to global capitalism and a source of economic and political support for its own efforts. Who still believes that socialism as a truly new mode of production is an attainable and desirable goal? The dysfunctionalities of import-substitution industrialization also raised doubts about the capacity and rationality of Latin American states. And determined market reform and integration into the global economy have created powerful stakeholders that make any frontal attack on the capitalist system prohibitively costly. The failed and counterproductive attempts of the 1960s and 1970s to start revolutions in Latin America also fueled a profound rethinking among the Latin American left (Castañeda 1993). For these reasons, the basic outline of the socioeconomic order does not face radical challenges any longer. The left now also places much greater value on political democracy, an additional reason to forswear extra-constitutional assaults on power. The experience of brutal authoritarian rule demonstrated the importance of liberal safeguards, which radical leftists used to denounce as bourgeois formalities or obstacles to revolution. The international regime for protecting democracy, especially its electoral rules, has raised another obstacle to revolutionary efforts.

For all of these reasons, no significant force in contemporary Latin America advocates a full-scale revolution. The hope to remove constraints and realize ambitious goals in one fell swoop has evaporated. By historical standards, even the advocates of twenty-first-century socialism are much less radical than their forefathers from the second millennium, such as the Chilean Socialists of the 1960s and early 1970s. But given the tighter constraints and the reduced room for activism, they are still significantly more radical than their moderate contemporaries.

At the other end of the spectrum, space for social democracy has shrunk as well. Rather than breaking through constraints, social democracy sought to bend them. Keynesian economics provided the cornerstone for this strategy (Przeworski 1985: 36–38). It depicted demand management by the state, which could be used to pursue social justice via redistributive reforms, as crucial for the proper functioning of a market economy. Accordingly, the profit interests of capitalists and the consumption interests of workers overlapped substantially. This compatibility claim eased the socioeconomic and political obstacles facing social–democratic reforms and allowed for negotiated advances. Yet with the decline of Keynesian economics and the rise of globalization, which tipped the balance of power toward mobile capital holders and weakened workers and governments, this synergy faded. Social democracy has faced increasing financial pressures even in northwest Europe (Lange and Garrett 1991: 548–55; Lemke and Marks 1992; Sassoon 1996: chaps. 16, 22, 24; Huber and Stephens 2001: chaps. 6–7). In a dependent region suffering from unfavorable starting chances in the global economy such as Latin America, social democracy's historical accomplishments cannot be replicated in the foreseeable future. An underdeveloped productive apparatus, deep social segmentation due to the exclusion of many workers from the formal economy, and the organizational weakness and shallow societal roots of many political parties and trade unions preclude a determined reform strategy that could profoundly alter the distribution of socioeconomic benefits in society. Gradualist efforts nowadays face tighter constraints, especially in the Third World.

Therefore, the northwest European experience cannot be replicated in present-day Latin America. Trying to attain a semblance of mass prosperity in the first place, Latin American countries put special emphasis on economic growth and development. Because domestic business alone cannot spearhead this process, foreign capital is needed. But a recent history of political instability and severe economic turmoil makes investors worry about a much wider range of issues than in stable northwest Europe (Mosley 2003). Because investors may withdraw their capital at will, the bargaining power of workers and governments on a host of important issues has diminished. Therefore, the balance between different social forces that underlay European social democracy is unlikely to emerge. The socioeconomic improvements that Latin America's moderate leftists can attain are likely to be much more limited than the accomplishments of their European comrades. The reformist option has lost a good part of its luster as well.

In sum, leftists in contemporary Latin America can neither smash constraints through a revolution nor evade them through social–democratic synergies between economic growth and social justice. Therefore, they face the classical dilemma of leftism in an especially stark fashion: how to bring about change despite obstacles. Although the bounds of feasibility have tightened and their range of options has narrowed, they still have to make a choice on whether to put activism or realism first. Should they challenge the socioeconomic and political constraints they face, even at the risk of provoking reactions such as capital flight or strenuous political opposition? Or should they seek modifications via negotiation within the confines of the established system, even at the risk of making painfully slow progress and leaving the root causes of problems in place? Should they be bold and make a determined push for their goals, yet incur the danger of a backlash? Or should they prudently take step after step and embark on a long march, which may never reach its goal?

The contestatory and moderate lefts in present-day Latin America diverge in their strategic choices. Among the four cases under investigation, Evo Morales in Bolivia and especially Hugo Chávez in Venezuela have tended to prefer ambition over caution, whereas Ricardo Lagos and Michelle Bachelet in Chile and Luiz Inácio Lula da Silva in Brazil have adopted the inverse priority. For reasons to be explained later, more radical leftist governments have often defied the forces empowered by economic globalization and domestic market reform and have enlisted inclusionary mass mobilization to put pressure on the political opposition and bend checks and balances. In these ways, they have sought to reorient the economy toward fostering popular well-being, push through ambitious social programs, and refound the political system with new constitutions. By contrast, moderate leftist administrations have tried to improve the operation of the new market model to produce more dynamic growth, use the proceeds to fund social initiatives sustainably, and negotiate these reforms with the opposition in a setting of liberal pluralism. When facing resistance, they have usually made concessions – whereas the contestatory left has tried to break resistance with ever more forceful means. Thus the moderate and contestatory lefts have navigated the dilemma of change under constraint in distinct ways.

This difference has characterized leftist efforts in the three spheres that the present volume investigates: economy, society, and politics. The following sections examine the specific issues and problems that leftist administrations have confronted in each of these areas and briefly present the main findings of the case studies.

EFFORTS TO STIMULATE ECONOMIC DEVELOPMENT DESPITE THE
STRICTURES OF GLOBALIZATION

Guiding Question 1: Have the efforts of the moderate left to modify the market system and bend the strictures of economic globalization or the radical attempts to challenge domestic neoliberalism and international constraints stimulated more dynamic economic development and opened up more promising prospects for the future?

Given their materialist orientation, leftists have long attributed particular importance to efforts to stimulate economic development and guide it toward the needs of the majority, rather than the profit interests of a minority. The desire to increase economic well-being is especially strong in a region where millions of people – majorities in some countries – suffer from poverty. But economic globalization and the outcomes of market reform have tightened constraints on political efforts to promote development by transferring assets from the public to the private sector, by empowering domestic and foreign businesses that control mobile capital, and by limiting state interventionism. How can leftist governments induce these economic forces to contribute to their developmental efforts or at least not block them? Whereas the contestatory left is willing to apply forceful pressure, the moderate left embraces negotiation to effect gradual reform. Which one of these strategies yields greater success in a sustainable fashion? The question of sustainability is particularly important because governments can use the power of the state to confiscate resources from business in the short run, but they may pay a heavy price by scaring off investors and diminishing development prospects for years to come.

Impressed by these risks, the moderate left has accepted the basic framework of Latin America's new market model and has made modifications step by step, for instance through new industrial policy initiatives and public investment programs in Brazil and through better, firmer regulation of business activities as well as attempts to boost human capital and improve worker training in Chile. They have negotiated these changes with business, driving a harder bargain than their centrist or right-wing predecessors but avoiding any attack on the private sector's main interests. As the case studies of Brazil and especially Chile show, these attempts to guide the market, improve the operation of the new development scheme, and make it produce benefits for broader sectors of the population have been quite successful. Although the moderate left has been constrained by the imperatives of globalization, the need to maintain fiscal equilibrium and make concessions to business, it has nevertheless managed to achieve considerable growth that has helped a majority of the people by boosting employment and raising income levels even among poorer groups. Thus, leftist governments in Brazil and Chile have made a difference. Economic constraints have not imposed virtual policy convergence with the neoliberal right (*pace* Kingstone and Young 2009), as more radical critics have charged. Though not achieving a dramatic turnaround in their countries' economic fate, moderate-left governments have attained steady, sustainable progress.

Rejecting this gradualist approach as excessively cautious and too slow in lifting the living standards of underprivileged sectors, leaders of the more radical left have challenged important constraints arising from globalization and have put significant and increasing pressure on business, especially foreign investors. Most importantly, they have pushed for higher tax and royalty payments and decreed more stringent controls, especially through forced government participation in enterprise management and other steps toward nationalization. The state has tried to use the resulting increase in resource extraction and the greater control over the economy to direct development toward national and popular needs. Yet although these efforts have been quite successful in the short run, their prospects for stimulating economic development over the long run are questionable, as the case studies of Bolivia and especially Venezuela demonstrate. Contestatory left governments have had difficulty managing the increased revenues responsibly without producing an overheating of the economy and inflation. Above all, they have had little success investing in productive ventures that diversify the economy.

Contestatory leftism has prevailed in countries that have relied heavily on oil or gas exports, that benefited tremendously from the international price boom of recent years, and that therefore saw fiscal constraints temporarily loosened (Weyland 2009). This windfall carries great risks, however, as suggested by Venezuela's experiences under Chávez's nemesis, Carlos Andrés Pérez (1974–79; see Karl 1997). Governments often mismanage the exceptional revenues produced by booms, go on ill-considered spending sprees, fail to broaden the economic base, and do not prepare for the subsequent bust bound to occur sooner or later. The analyses in this book offer a good deal of evidence that the more radical leftist governments have not avoided these dangers but have indeed fallen prey to the resource curse. In Venezuela, in particular, the economy has concentrated even more exclusively on one predominant sector while other ventures have atrophied, and Bolivia seems to be heading into the same

cul-de-sac. Moreover, the acrimonious relationship of contestatory left governments with domestic and foreign business has triggered capital flight and dried
up investments, raising further obstacles to the diversification of the economy
and potentially stifling development in the long run. A closer inspection that
looks beyond the short-term successes driven by the recent international commodity boom suggests that radical-left ambition has produced a number of
worrisome trends.

In a nutshell, the moderate left strategy of modifying established constraints
rather than challenging them has achieved better, more solid economic results
and has charted a more promising course for the long run.

EFFORTS TO PROMOTE SOCIAL JUSTICE DESPITE
RESOURCE CONSTRAINTS

Guiding Question 2: Which current of leftism has been more successful in designing
and implementing social policies that boost especially the well-being of poorer groups
and enhance social equity on a solid fiscal and institutional base?

The promotion of social equity has always been a core goal of the left. In fact,
tightening constraints in the economic sphere have given determined efforts to
enhance social justice even greater importance as distinguishing planks of the
left (Maravall 1995: 183–84). However, the limitations exacerbated by domestic market reform and economic globalization have created further obstacles
to social progress. Radical rhetoric and efforts at redistribution raise concern
among investors and thus carry risks for economic development. Also the need
for a responsible economic policy that guarantees budget balance and other
macroeconomic equilibria limits the resources available for new social programs. How, then, can Latin America's contemporary left best seek to attain
social improvements for the less well-to-do majority of the citizenry?

Once again, the moderate and contestatory lefts have pursued distinct strategies. One main reason why the moderate left has acquiesced in the fundamental
framework of the market system and has sought economic reforms inside these
confines has been the hope to stimulate lasting economic development and
thereby lay a sustainable foundation for social progress – directly by boosting employment and income growth among poorer sectors, and indirectly by
increasing tax revenues. The growth in fiscal resources can fund upgrades in
existing social programs and new initiatives to increase human capital and
provide some degree of income security to poorer segments. In these ways, the
moderate left has hoped to alleviate one of the major gulfs in Latin American
societies, namely to allow more and more people to move from the informal
sector of precarious, often low-paying work to the formal sector of steady,
well-remunerated employment coupled with social benefits.

As the experiences of Brazil and Chile show, this gradualist strategy has
indeed produced substantial reductions in poverty (especially impressive in

Chile), important equity-enhancing extensions in the coverage of social transfers and services, and a slight diminution in inequality (especially in Brazil). It is important to highlight that the expansion and reform of social programs has had a solid fiscal foundation, fairly efficient administration, and the necessary level of institutionalization to make progress sustainable. Specific social measures have not just been ad-hoc expedients (driven for instance by narrow electoral goals) but have added up to a systematic approach to overhaul the framework of social protection, especially in Chile, where the moderate left has held government power for almost two decades and thus has had time to unfold its program.

As in the economic sphere, the contestatory left discards this gradualism as painfully slow, criticizes its dependence on economic growth – including the autonomous investment decisions of business – and doubts that it can make a significant dent in social inequality. It therefore traces a bolder strategy that combines some redistribution of assets with major new social programs. Accordingly, it advocates a reallocation of rural property to help the long-neglected rural poor. It also seeks to benefit destitute citizens in general through the creation of generous social programs that provide cheap access to food, income support, and a range of social services. Because even contemporary radicals shy away from confiscatory taxation or massive expropriation of domestic business, they finance these massive new initiatives with revenues produced by resource booms and extracted from foreign investors. This funding mechanism raises serious questions about the financial sustainability of the new social programs. Moreover, the perceived urgency that drives these novel initiatives has also hindered their rational organization, efficient administration, immunization against corruption, and firm institutionalization. Therefore, it is doubtful whether the ambitious programs created by the contestatory left will achieve their social goals effectively and to what extent the greatly increased resource investment will yield actual social progress. Moreover, given their funding mechanism and rushed implementation, these programs do not seem to be well protected against shifting economic conjunctures and political alignments.

Thus, as in the economic sphere, the social achievements that the contestatory left has attained so far seem to rest on quicksand. By contrast, the accomplishments of the moderate left stand on a more solid foundation and therefore accumulate over time – producing substantial, lasting social progress.

ATTEMPTS TO DEEPEN DEMOCRACY WITHOUT UNDERMINING IT

Guiding Question 3: Have moderate or contestatory left-wing administrations better managed the tension between efforts to combat exclusion and discrimination, broaden effective citizenship, and promote political participation, on the one hand, and the preservation of political pluralism and liberal safeguards, on the other?

To guarantee disadvantaged sectors full citizenship and promote their economic and social goals, left-wing forces also seek to enrich established democratic systems. In particular, they intend to eliminate barriers of social class or other bases of discrimination, such as gender and ethnicity, which have structurally excluded underprivileged sectors from full political participation. The contestatory left, in particular, also tries to strengthen the participatory aspects of democracy by calling frequent elections and plebiscites, introducing novel institutions for consultation with society and the recall of representatives, and overhauling the constitutional design of the political system. In these ways, more radical leftists intend to complement or transform the predominantly representative character of the established institutional framework and deepen democracy. They invoke popular sovereignty to remove the constraints arising from established checks and balances and create a new institutional framework that concentrates power in a president legitimated through his direct connection to the people.

How have these participatory efforts played out in political practice? Have the new mechanisms and institutions allowed common people to articulate their interests and demands in an autonomous fashion and attain effective influence over their leaders? Has the citizenry gained an effective voice in decision making and has it felt better represented by its leaders? As the case studies of Venezuela and Bolivia show, the contestatory left has indeed boosted people's subjective satisfaction with the operation of democracy. But these participatory efforts have also had problematic repercussions, bringing the mobilization of followers from the top down and allowing leaders to engineer plebiscitarian acclamation for their decisions, especially in Venezuela (see in general Lijphart 1984: 203–4). Moreover, strengthening of the direct connection between the leader and the masses has led to a bypass of established institutions of consultation and deliberation, further diminishing political accountability and, arguably, the substantive quality of decisions.

Contestatory left efforts have also reduced the space for political pluralism and put pressure on liberal safeguards by strengthening the majoritarian aspects of democracy. Thus, they have run the risk of undermining rather than deepening democracy. This danger is particularly acute because the inclusionary, participatory initiatives of the contestatory left often face political opposition from actors that benefit from the status quo and that worry about the hegemonic repercussions of mobilizational efforts. By incorporating new mass sectors into the political system, more radical leftists seem to use the power and resources of the government to attain and cement a degree of electoral support that may unbalance democratic competition and threaten pluralism. Concern about these tendencies has triggered a great deal of political polarization in Venezuela and Bolivia, which has done further damage to democracy and weakened economic and social development prospects as well.

Seeing these risks and the distrust and opposition that participatory initiatives and institutional reform efforts therefore elicit, the moderate left prefers caution. It concentrates its attempts to stimulate citizen participation at the local level, where decision making operates at the proper scale for effective popular involvement, for instance via participatory budgeting (Baiocchi 2005).

At the national level, by contrast, the moderate left is content with the predominance of representative principles and procedures, which avoid the risk of populist mass manipulation. Therefore, it merely tempers representation through regular consultation with interest associations and other corporatist mechanisms. Furthermore, the moderate left seeks to democratize the established institutional framework by eliminating distortions inherited from the authoritarian past (such as designated senators in Chile). Yet rather than imposing these reforms, for instance by fomenting mass demonstrations, it prefers to negotiate them with the opposition.

This cautious approach fully respects and further strengthens democratic principles and institutions, but it also has a downside. It fails to combat the disappointment with the operation of democracy prevalent in present-day Latin America. Although citizens in many countries maintain a fairly high level of principled commitment to democracy, they are discontented with the way decisions are made and hold crucial mechanisms of representative democracy, especially political parties and parliaments, in dangerously low esteem (Corporación Latinobarómetro 2008: 85–88, 104–9). Whereas the mobilizational efforts and participatory reforms of the contestatory left promise to combat this malaise and reinvigorate democracy, the moderate left chooses to forgo the chance to make such progress for the sake of preserving the political accomplishments that the democratization wave of the 1980s achieved.

On balance, however, the case studies show that the moderate left has attained greater political success in tending to the fragile flower of democracy. Although citizen malaise is problematic, the increasing strangulation of political pluralism and growing infringement on liberal rights and safeguards in the countries governed by the contestatory left are much more problematic. They constitute threats not just to the quality of democracy, but to its very survival. The moderate left's sins of political omission do not prevent the correction of these problems in the future, yet the contestatory left's sins of political commission are threatening to lock in an imbalance of power and hegemonic predominance that make an eventual change of course very difficult and costly. Because democracy recognizes human fallibility and therefore seeks to institutionalize openness, it abhors the closure that the mobilizational tactics and hegemonic tendencies of the contestatory left threaten to produce.

DEMOCRACY AS THE MOST FUNDAMENTAL CONCERN

The relevance of democracy for the debate between moderate and contestatory leftism goes beyond the tension between its participatory and liberal aspects. In a broader perspective, there is a clear friction between more radical leftist efforts at transformation and the pluralism and competitiveness constitutive of democracy. Profound socioeconomic and political change usually faces determined opposition, which takes advantage of the institutions of democracy. Contestatory governments respond to such resistance by concentrating power and whipping up mass support. These efforts raise the specter of left-wing hegemony and infringements on political pluralism and liberal safeguards. The more ambitious and determined the efforts at transformation are, the more acute the risks to democratic competitiveness can become. Democracy inherently hinders change by dispersing power and protecting dissent and opposition. Attempts to push through transformations despite these obstacles can undermine democracy.

If change is supposed to benefit the citizenry and if protagonists seek to minimize the risk of failure, then democratic competitiveness fulfills an essential role in holding current power holders accountable, stimulating public debate, and allowing for learning and corrections along the way. In these ways, democracy fulfills an indispensable control function. For instance, it prevents the perpetuation in power of leaders who win office with popular campaign pledges but then use their new position to pursue other ends, such as ideological pet projects or sheer self-promotion. Democratic pluralism embodies a healthy dose of skepticism, monitors ongoing reform efforts, and prompts the design of better alternatives. Through these mechanisms, it tends to improve decision quality. Although the constant criticism that democracy fosters hinders the pursuit of grand transformatory projects, it reduces the risk of disasters and enables citizens to cut their costs by throwing out ill-performing administrations. Political leaders who push aside democratic constraints can get things done, but they run the risk of doing the wrong things and doing things badly. For the sake of the citizenry, these risks are not worth running. Unbounded political agency can effect socioeconomic and political change, but often tramples on useful boundaries, such as liberal safeguards, and risks having more destructive than constructive repercussions by dismantling the old edifice without rebuilding and institutionalizing a better alternative. With its checks and balances, democracy minimizes this danger, avoids grand yet unpredictable wagers on a total overhaul, and pursues improvements step by step. In this way, the repercussions of each reform are more foreseeable and corrections are feasible along the way. Moreover, democracy gives the beneficiaries of reform a greater capacity to defend accomplishments against reversals, political competition stimulates organizational efforts, and the centrality of elections assigns special importance to the most important power capability that poorer people in Latin America command – their large numbers.

For these reasons, democracy arguably has normative priority over substantive efforts at change. Substantive reform goals cannot justify its abandonment or permanent involution. Instead, democracy is nonnegotiable by enshrining the basic procedural principles that any legitimate decision making on substantive issues must uphold. The present volume therefore places particular weight on democracy in evaluating the performance of the two currents of leftism in contemporary Latin America. Although attempts to bring economic and social improvements are urgent in a region plagued by extensive poverty and deep inequality, they must not infringe on political pluralism and liberal safeguards. And efforts to deepen democracy must not undermine it. Even more fundamental than performance assessments on specific aspects of socioeconomic and political change, the question of democracy constitutes the overarching issue and concern that ties together the three topics examined in this book.

CAUSES OF MODERATION VERSUS CONTESTATORY POSTURES

This introduction has examined the dilemmas facing leftists in contemporary Latin America, highlighting the conflict between activism and realism. It has also previewed the volume's main finding, namely that on balance, the moderate left has performed better in economic, social, and political terms than the contestatory left, especially in a long-term perspective. What remains to be explained is why some of the governments under investigation have pushed hard for leftist goals and challenged constraints, whereas others have worked inside these confines and pursued gradual reforms. Specifically, why have Hugo Chávez, Evo Morales, and the movements supporting them adopted a fairly radical posture, yet Lula da Silva's Workers' Party (Partido dos Trabalhadores – PT) and the Chilean Socialist Party (Partido Socialista de Chile – PSCh), an integral part of the Concertación coalition, have proceeded with caution?

The main answer is that left-wing forces, parties, and governments in Brazil and Chile themselves have been deeply shaped by organizational, institutional, policy-regime, and resource constraints, which have made much less of an imprint on Chávez, Morales, and their supporters. Governing leftists in Brazil and Chile have internalized these constraints and therefore have respected them in their policy and politics. By contrast, the Venezuelan Fifth Republic Movement (Movimiento Quinta República – MVR) and the Bolivian Movement toward Socialism (Movimiento al Socialismo – MAS) emerged out of a repudiation of constraints, especially neoliberalism and representative democracy. After taking power, they have therefore continued to defy constraints and placed boldness ahead of prudence.

Interestingly, major left parties in all four countries were quite radical until the 1980s or 1990s, namely, the PT in Brazil, the PS in Chile, the MIR in Bolivia (Movimiento de Izquierda Revolucionaria – Movement of the Revolutionary Left), and the MAS in Venezuela (Movimiento al Socialismo – Movement toward Socialism). All of those parties moved markedly to the center under the pressures of market reform and associated electoral incentives in the 1990s. In Brazil and Chile, the left that eventually won the presidency was very much shaped by the context of the 1980s and 1990s, especially market reform and consolidating democracy, and the moderating incentives that those economic and political–institutional constraints created.

In Bolivia and Venezuela, by contrast, the left-wing parties that underwent a similar process of moderation foundered on the shoals of an aborted process of market reform (Venezuela) or the disappointing outcomes of structural adjustment (Bolivia). The decline of these center-left forces opened up space for the rise of much more radical left-leaning movements, which cut their teeth in an era in which the market model was subject to far greater questioning and the established party system was unraveling. As economic and political constraints were losing force, contestatory movements emerged. Due to the different historical setting, the two kinds of left-wing forces therefore diverge in their levels of organization, in the degree of institutionalization of the party system in which they arose, and in their orientation toward market economics. Due to the economic structure of their countries, they also encountered different resource constraints.

Organizational Characteristics of Governing Parties

The Workers' Party in Brazil and the Socialist Party in Chile formed much earlier than Chávez's political–electoral movement in Venezuela and the MAS in Bolivia. Correspondingly, the PT and the Chilean left, especially the PS, have a higher level of institutionalization than the MAS and especially the Bolivarian movement. As a result, the PT and PS have followed a steady trajectory of long-term development, whereas the Chávez movement and MAS have pursued a much less predictable course.

The Socialist Party of Chile was founded in the early 1930s (Drake 1978), flourished during the long stretch of democracy that Chile enjoyed until 1973, and managed to survive the highly repressive rule of dictator Pinochet, despite factionalism and divisions. The party reunified upon the reinauguration of democracy in 1990, but the front organization that it had created in 1988 to run in the plebiscite against Pinochet surprisingly established its own identity and survived as a separate party, the Party for Democracy (Partido por la Democracia – PPD). Whereas the PS retained its firm organization and preserved its roots in long-standing traditions, the PPD is a looser, political–electoral party that has positioned itself closer to the ideological center than the PS with its stalwarts. In its almost thirty years of existence, the Brazilian PT has also built up an institutionalized apparatus. Created by labor unions, social movements, and Catholic base activists in 1979/80, the party used the 1980s to forge organizational unity and solidity rather than make an immediate bid for government power. Additional long years in the opposition during the 1990s, which limited the party's access to patronage resources, and the need to integrate gradually growing numbers of cadres, members, and voters further strengthened party institutionalization (Hunter 2007).

By contrast, Venezuela's Bolivarian movement and the Bolivian MAS are much more recent creations that have not attained much organizational solidity. Based on a clandestine conspiracy inside the Venezuelan military, Chávez created an electoral vehicle for the 1998 institution, but never allowed it to gain institutional autonomy and strength. Instead, his overbearing personalistic leadership has engineered and dropped organizational instruments at will: The Fifth Republic Movement, the Bolivarian Circles, the Unified Socialist Party of Venezuela, etc. The Bolivian MAS differs in not being a top-down creation; instead, it emerged from bottom-up mobilization by contestatory movements, especially peasant and indigenous associations. But that movement nature has so far precluded the construction of firm institutions, and the growing projection of Evo Morales' personal leadership has the potential of forestalling institutionalization. Being new and fluid, the MAS is also fragmented and incoherent, and it faces many cross-pressures from the different sectors of its associated popular base (Madrid 2008). For these reasons, both the Bolivarian movement and the MAS have followed much less predictable organizational trajectories than the solid – if not rigid – PT and PS. The latter parties' institutionalization allows and induces leaders to focus on long-term goals, whereas Chávez and Morales face greater incentives to motivate and mobilize their potentially more fleeting following with promises of immediate material benefits and the symbolic rewards of radical rhetoric. Also, by contrast to Lula da Silva and the presidents of the Concertación, Morales and especially Chávez face few constraints from their weakly organized followers. Their moves toward further radicalization, as Chávez has undertaken them in recent years, go unchecked.

Institutional Setting and State of Party System

The PT and the Chilean left have also established themselves as parts of more highly institutionalized party systems, whereas the MAS and the Chávez movement have attained a fairly hegemonic position on the ruins of collapsing party systems. Thus, the PT and the Chilean Socialists face clear political constraints, arising from a consolidated framework of institutional and electoral rules and from the competitive pressures of an active, dynamic opposition that can hold the current government accountable and has a very realistic chance of taking over the executive office at the next election. By contrast, the Bolivarian movement and MAS were catapulted to power in brittle institutional systems that invited efforts at drastic change, and they have confronted an opposition that has been largely moribund in Venezuela and has mustered only defensive veto power in Bolivia. The chances for these adversaries to dislodge Chávez and Morales have been slim. Therefore, those two leaders command much greater institutional room for maneuvering than do Lula da Silva, Lagos, and Bachelet (Flores Macías 2008; Lanzaro 2008).

By Latin American standards, Chile and increasingly Brazil have had well-institutionalized party systems, which make it more difficult for new parties to emerge and capture a large vote share (Mainwaring and Torcal 2005). In Chile the same parties and especially coalitions have dominated since the return to democracy, whereas in Brazil the party system has stabilized since the early 1990s. The existing parties in these countries have deeper roots in society, which has generated stronger and more stable voter attachments. In particular, the PT and PS have long enjoyed close ties to labor unions and a variety of civil society organizations. As a result, no major new contestatory left party has managed to arise and rally large numbers of disgruntled voters. In the absence of significant threats to their left, the moderate left parties have had little reason to move significantly leftward even though opposition to neoliberal policies had risen.

In Bolivia and Venezuela, by contrast, the existing party systems had begun to fall apart by the late 1990s, which made it easier for contestatory left parties to emerge (Domínguez 2008: 335–40). As the old left that had moderated during the 1990s, such as the Bolivian MIR and the Venezuelan MAS, became increasingly discredited, the opportunity arose for new radical movements to capture the growing discontent among the citizenry. Established parties saw their roots in society atrophy, allowing new leaders and movements to garner support with fiery rhetoric and ambitious promises.

The Impact of Market Reform

The Chilean Socialists and later the PT went through the crucible of market reform, which due to its initial accomplishments ended up exerting a deradicalizing effect. By contrast, the Bolivarian movement and the Bolivian MAS emerged in a conjuncture when more and more people became critical of neoliberalism. In Bolivia, the early and always limited success of market reform had faded by the late 1990s, and further-reaching neoliberal promises and hopes of a significant, broad-based diminution of poverty had gone unfulfilled (Grindle 2003). In Venezuela, the very efforts to enact orthodox adjustment had elicited strong rejection and never allowed neoliberalism to be fully implemented. Therefore, the new left arising in those countries was born out of discontent with market economics.

In Chile and Brazil, where market reform had unfolded in the broader context of a state that functioned with reasonable efficiency and effectiveness, existing parties and party systems retained a degree of institutionalization and political support from citizens that precluded the successful rise of outsiders promising radical change. As structural adjustment produced relief for the population and lasting economic results, left parties felt compelled to moderate their initially radical programs and slowly accept the basic outlines of the new market model. Even with the economic downturns affecting these countries in the late 1990s, well-established left parties like the PS in Chile and the PT in Brazil remained within or moved further toward the center left of the political spectrum. They advocated modifications but not a complete overhaul of the newly established economic model. These older left parties and their leaders had reason to stay anchored within the center left in the late 1990s. Public opinion indicated general satisfaction with governance and principled commitment to a market economy (Weyland 2004: 296–312; see Baker 2009: chaps. 4, 7). Moreover, party leaders had the organizational capacity to discipline party activists, who tend to cling to the original leftist ideology, and coax them to acquiesce in the march toward moderation.

By contrast, in Venezuela and Bolivia the established parties were victims of poor governance in the 1990s. In particular, market reforms advanced in a stop-and-go process that never attained convincing results in Venezuela (Weyland 2002: chap. 8), and they disappointed popular expectations in Bolivia by failing to produce sustained growth, increase mass prosperity, and diminish poverty.

Moreover, weak state functioning compounded problems that ranged from rising corruption to escalating crime. Massive societal dissatisfaction with the venality and poor performance of existing leaders and their parties opened the way for the ascendance of the leftist movements led by Hugo Chávez and Evo Morales starting in the mid-1990s (E. Silva 2009). Because at that time, market economics had lost its luster, the new forces adopted a much more radical posture than the PT and the Chilean Socialists. They categorically rejected neoliberalism and called for a more radical transformation of economy, society, and politics. To signal their contestatory intentions, they established friendly relations with the lonely bulwark of state socialism in Latin America: Fidel Castro's Cuba. They then consciously positioned themselves outside the ideological mainstream, in stark contrast to their moderate counterparts.

Natural Resource Endowments

Countries' resource endowments also matter by conditioning how tight immediate economic constraints are. It is no coincidence that the contestatory left emerged in countries and time periods when there happened to be greater economic latitude for pursuing its ambitious goals. Venezuela's well-developed oil industry and Bolivia's recently discovered gas deposits yielded rapidly increasing revenues during the international energy price boom of the mid-2000s. This striking windfall eased economic and fiscal constraints and allowed for significant spending increases – at least in the short run. More broadly, this bonanza seemed to suggest the economic feasibility of a more radical transformation of economy, society, and politics. Returning to the hopeful activism of the old, radical left, the Bolivarian movement and the Bolivian MAS came to believe that "a new society is possible!" (Weyland 2009). The resource bonanza tempted them to reject the constraints highlighted by neoliberalism and to put pressure on domestic, and especially transnational, businesses and international financial institutions.

By contrast, the newly moderate PT and the renovated Chilean left faced continuing economic constraints and resource limitations. Brazil's and even Chile's complex economies are not centered around one commodity as much as Venezuela's, so international supply shortages of that commodity did not suddenly give them dramatically increased bargaining leverage. Brazil's new oil reserves remain undeveloped, and Chile's copper wealth produces only limited revenue increases due to a well-institutionalized, technocratically administered, and reliably implemented stabilization fund, which sterilizes windfall rents (under the vigilant eyes of the right-wing party opposition) and saves these extraordinary resources for lean years (Arellano 2006). Brazil and Chile therefore did not enjoy a sudden bonanza in expendable funds. State revenues increased at rates far below the torrent of petrodollars flowing into Chávez's coffers. Therefore, the PT and the Chilean Socialists saw themselves as subject to real constraints that did not allow for a dramatic transformation. Instead, this setting made the moderate strategy of a long cumulation of small, gradual steps look more promising.

Consequences for Leftist Policy Orientations

For all of these reasons, the contestatory left has enjoyed much greater economic and political latitude (at least in the short run) than the moderate left, which has faced and accepted a range of economic, political, and institutional constraints. Since the leftist forces that captured government power in Brazil and Chile emerged in the context of organizational, institutional, policy, and resource constraints, they ended up adapting to and internalizing these constraints. Therefore, they have pursued a moderate program, seeking reforms inside the confines of the existing socioeconomic and political system. By contrast, the movements taking control of the state in Venezuela and Bolivia arose in wide-open, fluid settings in which established structures were under challenge. After emerging as renovating forces that would wipe the slate clean and refound the country in socioeconomic and political–institutional terms, these forces attained success by repudiating constraints and persisted with this more radical posture while in office. Born radical, they have remained contestatory. Thus, the preference for activism versus realism has systematic roots.

CONTRIBUTIONS OF THE VOLUME

Comparing and evaluating the accomplishments of the two currents of left-wing governments in contemporary Latin America is of particular theoretical and substantive relevance. The market reforms of the 1990s brought profound economic, social, and political change to the region. Many countries dismantled the inward-looking, state-interventionist development model they had applied for decades. As a result, the social structure changed. The formal working class and middle class shrank, whereas the informal sector expanded further (Portes and Hoffman 2003). Politics changed as well, as many established interest associations and political parties decayed and new forms of leadership – such as neopopulism – arose (Hagopian 1998). According to some observers, therefore, the neoliberal wave constituted a critical juncture in Latin American development that is as momentous as the Great Depression of the late 1920s and 1930s (Smith and Korzeniewicz 1997; Roberts in press).

The policies and accomplishments of the Latin American left will have a decisive impact on the fate and significance of the changes triggered by neoliberalism. If the more radical left were to design a promising alternative to the new market model; if Hugo Chávez's twenty-first century socialism, in particular, managed to trace a novel course that performed better than the market model in producing economic prosperity, social well-being, and high-quality democracy; and if the more radical experiments of Chávez and Morales were to attain lasting success, then market reform might end up being a temporary interlude. Of course, even if such successes were achieved in Bolivia and Venezuela, they might not spread to the rest of the region, given that they seem to rest on preconditions – such as huge natural resource rents – that limit the chances for their diffusion.

On the other hand, if the moderate left can introduce sufficiently substantial and beneficial modifications inside the basic outline of the new development scheme, it may succeed in making the market system palatable to large sectors of the population and guaranteeing it lasting political sustenance. Neoliberalism certainly failed to fulfill the promises made by its advocates and the expectations that important sectors of the population initially attached to it. Above all, employment creation remained meager, poverty diminished little if at all, some business sectors reaped tremendous gains without sharing them equitably with workers and consumers, and governments failed to regulate many markets distorted by monopolies and oligopolies. Interestingly, the moderate left is best positioned to rectify these imbalances, rein in domestic and foreign entrepreneurs, and spread the benefits of reform more broadly (cf. Smith and Korzeniewicz 2000). Since the governments of the Concertación in Chile and of Lula da Silva in Brazil have taken a number of promising steps in this direction, the new market model may regain its legitimacy, withstand the criticisms of the more radical left, and prevail for years to come. In sum, the governmental performance of the Latin American left has enormous implications for the economic, social, and political fate of the region.

The present volume also speaks to broader theoretical issues in political economy and political science. As many scholars have emphasized, the left worldwide, even in its European home, has run up against the constraints of economic globalization, especially the voluminous and almost instantaneous movements of liquid capital, which have enhanced the exit options of business and tied the hands of governments. As a result, many instruments and policies traditionally used by the left, such as Keynesian demand stimulation and steeply progressive taxation, now carry prohibitive costs. As mentioned previously, influential studies argue that due to economic and political instability, which makes investors jittery, Third World countries face especially tight constraints (Mosley 2003; Wibbels 2006).

Do Latin America's recent experiences disprove these analyses? Perhaps the left has more room to maneuver than is commonly postulated. Observers had certainly not expected that a developing country would emerge virtually unpunished from the kind of debt default and "haircut" that Argentina imposed on the international financial community. And many oil and gas companies have meekly accepted the much tougher terms that the more radical left in Venezuela and Bolivia has decreed. In the short run, external constraints seem to be less confining than observers believe. But the case studies in this volume suggest that the latitude extended to the more contestatory left by the recent international commodities boom was a short-term respite that is unlikely to last; and the bold initiatives taken during this interlude have had serious costs, for instance in deterring investors, that may haunt these countries for years to come. Sooner or later, external economic constraints will reassert themselves.

On the other hand, new lines of scholarship claim that globalization, despite its strictures, does not preclude egalitarian redistribution. Instead, the global economy leaves many opportunities for equity-enhancing change. Although international capital mobility undermines and precludes a number of traditional left-wing policies, new approaches, such as investment in human capital and other capability-building reforms, can boost economic growth and social justice simultaneously (Bardhan, Bowles, and Wallerstein 2006). Because the moderate left has systematically pursued a reform strategy that takes advantage of this room for maneuver and gradually widens it while avoiding confrontation and backlash, it may be particularly well positioned to bring sustainable improvements. Although full-scale social democracy does not seem to be attainable in the global periphery (*pace* Sandbrook et al. 2007), persistent steps in this direction may end up making a significant difference in popular well-being.

This recent emphasis on the room left by structural constraints raises the question about the political forces that can best use this latitude – another instance of the age-old structure/agency issue. The very experience of the neoliberal populists of the 1990s suggests that charismatic plebiscitarian leaders have a particular impetus and capacity to break through structural impediments and institutional deadlocks: They simply cut the Gordian knot and effect dramatic change in unpropitious situations (Roberts 1995; Weyland 1996). But these transgressive and destructive tendencies make it difficult for such leaders to consolidate their gains, institutionalize their achievements, and thus give them lasting stability. The haphazard nature and precarious accomplishments of plebiscitarian leadership are among the reasons for the failure of the market system to take firm root in a number of Latin American countries.

To avoid this fluidity and the resulting risk of reversal, the left has traditionally preferred well-organized, programmatically oriented parties – aligned with broad-based societal associations such as trade unions – as the main protagonists of change (Huber and Stephens 2001). Through their more rational procedures and longer time frame, such cadre or mass parties can design and pursue a systematic plan for structural change and sustain their advances despite temporary setbacks. But those organizations also have potential downsides, as authors since the times of Robert Michels (1915/1959) have pointed out. They can turn heavily bureaucratic, lose touch with their base, and see their capacity for mobilization and activism atrophy. And during their long march through the institutions, they may end up accommodating to the established system rather than transforming it.

Because leftist governments in contemporary Latin America display very different styles of leadership and bases of organization, they offer an excellent opportunity to revisit this theoretical issue. Among the four cases under investigation, Venezuela under Chávez represents a clear-cut case of charismatic plebiscitarian leadership with a weak and shifting organizational base (outside the military), Bolivia under Morales combines this type of leadership with an activist social movement base, Brazil under Lula da Silva is governed by a well-organized programmatic party that retains a strong societal base but also has a high-profile leader, and Chile's Concertación constitutes a programmatically based alliance of well-organized parties that have turned more electoral–professional as their societal roots have weakened. As the case studies in this volume suggest, better-organized political forces tend to attain greater, more lasting socioeconomic success and to govern in more democratic ways. Although the unfettered leadership of the contestatory left can push through more change, its confrontational approach has important downsides and its weak institutionalization does not create a sustainable foundation for progress.

In conclusion, the present volume not only addresses crucial substantive questions about Latin American development but also speaks to fundamental theoretical topics that arise from the long-standing structure/agency debate. In this way, this book hopes to make a contribution that goes beyond the conjunctural analysis of a few governments that will sooner or later fall from power, as for instance, the increasing malaise and infighting in Chile's Concertación suggest. Above all, it seeks to answer how the core dilemma of the modern left, namely the tension between ambition and realism, plays out in the era of globalization. The case studies presented in the following chapters suggest that it makes little sense to cut the Gordian knot of economic and political strictures yet end up with useless snippets of rope and trample on democracy in the process. It seems more promising to loosen and gradually untie the knot and use the string for new ventures, while preserving democracy along the way.

THE ORGANIZATION OF THE VOLUME

The book addresses the theoretical issues discussed so far through in-depth case studies of the four most prototypical leftist governments in Latin America. This examination starts with the most exciting yet also most controversial experiment undertaken by Latin America's new left – the Bolivarian revolution in Venezuela. In Chapter 2, Javier Corrales offers a wide-ranging analysis and interpretation of the economic and political initiatives of the Chávez government. Although acknowledging some accomplishments, especially a range of new social programs, he voices the concern that the hegemonic tendencies of Chavismo and its marginalization of the opposition have led Venezuela in a semiauthoritarian direction. He also argues that the economic and social policies of the Chávez administration are much closer to returning to Venezuela's old nationalist, state-interventionist development model than realizing a new vision of twenty-first century socialism. These policies, he suggests, are again fueled by a temporary oil boom and therefore unsustainable in economic terms, although renewed economic problems may not necessarily end up undermining Chávez's political predominance.

In Chapter 3, George Gray Molina examines the reform initiatives of the Morales government in Bolivia from a broadly similar perspective. Analyzing the MAS' efforts to transform Bolivian politics, he acknowledges that a contestatory approach can effect significant socioeconomic change, but highlights that it also risks producing political polarization and a stalemate that could potentially erupt in serious conflict. He warns that in its policy approach, which focuses on overcoming neoliberalism and strengthening the role of the state, the new administration may be basing its developmental efforts too exclusively on the recently discovered gas deposits. This strategy risks repeating the cycles of mono-export boom and bust that Bolivia has experienced over the centuries – and that have always left the country impoverished.

Chile has experienced important, lasting successes, such as an unusual stretch of economic growth and a substantial reduction in poverty, but also striking limitations, such as persistent social inequality and a fairly rigid institutional setup. Evelyne Huber, Jennifer Pribble, and John Stephens capture both of these sides of the Chilean experience in Chapter 4. They analyze the political–institutional and economic constraints facing the Concertación coalition, which have precluded any dramatic breakthroughs. Yet the center-left governing alliance, led since 2000 by Socialist presidents, has over time managed to advance its reform agenda through prudent measures to extend state intervention in the economy, strengthen social protection for poorer citizens, and eliminate authoritarian relics from the constitution – and it has done so in an economically and politically sustainable fashion.

In Chapter 5, Peter Kingstone and Aldo Ponce demonstrate that the Lula da Silva administration in Brazil has maintained a high degree of continuity with the economic and social policy approach of its predecessor and has assimilated to the traditional style of politics as well, including patronage and corruption. Although this pragmatic orientation and cautious reform path have guaranteed economic stability, moderate growth, and some reduction in poverty and social inequality, they have not initiated the major transformation of Brazil's unjust economy and society and its elitist political structure that many observers had expected, given the much more ambitious goals pursued for many years by the Socialist Workers' Party. Complementing this interpretation in Chapter 6, Pedro Luiz Barros Silva, José Carlos de Souza Braga, and Vera Lúcia Cabral Costa highlight the paradox that the Lula administration has attained impressive levels of popularity and support despite the absence of comprehensive policy innovation and the failure to put Brazil on track toward true development. They attribute this feat to compensatory social programs for poor sectors of the population that ensure their political consent and in this way reassure better-off sectors that Brazil's skewed development model, which offers them disproportionate gains, will not face popular challenges.

The editors' conclusion uses the rich findings of the case studies for a comparative assessment of the experiences of contestatory and moderate left governments. The discussion first examines the differences in their political strategies, which revolve around the trade-off of participatory majoritarianism versus political liberalism and the potential risks for democracy. The focus then turns to the divergences in economic and social policy, with special attention to the question of sustainability. Thereafter, a comparative section investigates the experiences of other left-leaning governments in the region, namely the moderate administration of Tabaré Vázquez in Uruguay, the more radical governments of Rafael Correa in Ecuador and Daniel Ortega in Nicaragua, and the intermediate case of Néstor Kirchner and Cristina Fernández de Kirchner in Argentina. The last section returns to the guiding questions raised in this introduction and ends with a final evaluation of leftist performance in contemporary Latin America.

2

The Repeating Revolution

Chávez's New Politics and Old Economics

Javier Corrales

This chapter addresses two questions. First, how "revolutionary" is the Hugo Chávez revolution (1999–present) in Venezuela; that is, how much of a departure from the past does the Chávez administration represent? Second, how sustainable are Chávez's economic policies?

On the first question, I will argue that the Chávez administration does represent a clear break from the past at the level of politics, but less so at the level of economics. Politically, the Chávez regime changed Venezuela from a system in which incumbent and large opposition forces shared the spoils of office into a system of reduced political sharing with, and constrained space for, opposition forces. This is not so much because the opposition has retreated voluntarily (as in fact it did in 2005 by refusing to compete in midterm elections) but mostly because the executive branch has concentrated power, eroded the autonomy of checks and balances, reduced press freedoms, imposed costs on actors situated in the opposition, and – since 2008 – failed to recognize the authority of elected opposition officials. In the introductory chapter, Weyland discusses the democratic trade-off faced by the left between mobilizing new, disenfranchised political actors and preserving pluralism. Under Chávez, this trade-off has been rejected, with the government showing little interest since 2005 in guaranteeing pluralism. Of all the elected governments in Latin America since the 1980s, not just those on the left, the Chávez administration has undermined liberal institutions of democracy the most, to the point where it makes sense to speak of a transition to some form of autocracy.

Economically, on the other hand, Chávez's model represents more continuity than originality. Since 2003, the Chávez model has been privileging state control over the economy and reliance on oil. Across a great number of economic policies, the regime resembles the high point of import-substitution industrialization (ISI) of the 1970s, also a time when Venezuela experienced a spectacular oil boom. What has changed this time is the magnitude and duration of the oil boom (by far, the post-2003 oil boom is the largest), more so than the state's economic policies.

This combination of new politics (concentration of power in the executive branch and constraints on the opposition) with old economics (statism and oil dependence) is producing an aggravation, rather than a correction, of some of Venezuela's worst historical economic maladies. On the question of sustainability, one might be tempted to believe that because the Chávez regime is repeating economic mistakes similar to those of the past, the regime is likely to crumble, much like the previous political regime unraveled in the 1990s, arguably a casualty of economic mismanagement. This time around, however, the regime might prove to be more resilient.

Exploring this resilience hypothesis requires addressing the question of the impact of oil booms and busts on regime type. In the third part of this chapter, I offer a theory of how boom and bust cycles affect regimes differently. In a democratic regime based on party cohabitation like the one that prevailed in Venezuela until the 1980s, oil booms and busts can be hypothesized to be far more damaging for the regime than they are in a semi-authoritarian regime such as Chávez's. In other words, the effects of oil booms and oil busts are different depending on regime type. They are more likely to weaken and even kill democracies than nondemocracies. If so, then the Chávez regime may not be as endangered by its economic mistakes as were its predecessors.

NEW POLITICS: INCREASING THE COSTS OF BEING IN THE OPPOSITION

The Chávez administration claims to be fundamentally revolutionary. After eleven years in office as of 2010 (the longest tenure in office of any contemporaneous democratically elected president in Latin America), it is possible to assess this claim. Does the Chávez administration represent a break from the past? I will divide my answer into two parts: one focusing on politics, the other on economics.

Politically, there has been an unquestionable, fundamental break from the past. Venezuela switched from a system of political coexistence, in which large and medium-size parties competed politically (see Levine 1973; Levine 1978) and simultaneously shared access to the spoils of office, to one in which only one party (in alliance with smaller parties) reserves for itself the rights to the spoils of office. To use language from North, Summerhill, and Weingast (2000), Venezuela's regime changed from one in which both the advantages of being in office and the costs of being in the opposition were limited to a system in which the advantage of being in office and the costs of being in the opposition are profound. Elsewhere (Corrales 2005; Corrales 2006; Corrales and Penfold 2007; Corrales 2008), I have applied the term "competitive authoritarian" to describe Chávez (from Levitsky and Way 2006), but my focus was mostly on what made the regime competitive – that is, what allowed it to win elections. In this essay, my focus will be on the authoritarian side – the aspects of the regime that disqualify it from being called a democracy. In a nutshell, the regime has expanded presidential power vis-à-vis other state powers constitutionally mandated to exercise checks and balances (thereby reducing horizontal accountability). It has also reduced the institutional spaces available to the organized opposition (thereby reducing vertical accountability). In addition, the regime has empowered the military like no other contemporary elected government in Latin America.

Formal Expansion of Presidential Powers: The 1999 Constitution

The Chávez regime started out with a dramatic expansion of formal presidential powers. This expansion was accomplished through the Constituent Assembly of 1999, which approved a new constitution less than a year after Chávez took office. The new constitution expanded presidential powers both in comparison to the preceding constitution but also to most other constitutions in Latin America. Table 2.1 lists a number of crucial presidential powers that any given constitution may contain, based on criteria drawn from theoretical works on presidential powers (Shugart and Carey 1992; Carey 2003; Alberts 2006; Hartlyn and Luna 2007). The table shows that no other Latin American constitution approved via a Constituent Assembly since the transition to democracy and until 1999 assigned as many formal powers to the president as the 1999 Venezuelan constitution does.

This constitution is not exactly authoritarian. In some areas, it creates new rights for citizens and sets new limits on presidential power (Wilpert 2003; Hartlyn and Luna 2007). But the net balance is clearly in the direction of empowering the president above any other entity in the political system – certainly far more than the other branches of government and, many would say, most citizens and citizen groups.

Postconstitutional Informal Expansion of Presidential Powers

Presidential powers expanded also through informal mechanisms. Shortly after the enactment of the new constitution in 1999 and up to 2003, the president used the existing formal powers granted by the constitution, together with informal channels, to accumulate further power in the executive branch. First, Chávez eroded horizontal accountability (Coppedge 2003) by enacting a new Supreme Court law that expanded the number of justices from twenty to thirty-six and staffed the new posts with die-hard loyalists, thereby eroding the Court's autonomy. He also compromised the autonomy of the electoral supervisory board, which led to irregularities and mistrust in the electoral process (Kornblith 2005; Kornblith 2006). He purged the military and made military appointments without consultation with Congress. He illegally fired key board members of the state-owned oil company, PDVSA, which produced a widespread labor and business strike, prompting Chávez to fire an additional twenty thousand staff, completely eroding the autonomy of the fattest milk cow in the entire country and the most profitable of Latin America's state-owned enterprises. He conducted a purge of the foreign corps, removing career

TABLE 2.1. *Presidential Powers in Latin America's New Constitutions, 1988–1999*

Category	Ven 1999	Arg 1994	Bra 1988	Col 1991	Ecu 1998	Gua 1985	Nic 1987	Par 1992	Per 1993	Ven 1961
President can set upper limit for budget	Y			Y	Y		Y		Y	Y
Recall referendum possible for legislators	Y			Y	Y				Y	Y
Executive can enter into some treaties without legislative approval	Y			Y					Y	Y
President has some legislative powers during legislative recess	Y									
Enabling law possible in many areas	Y			Y	Y				Y	Y
No legislative oversight of cabinet formation	Y	Y	Y	Y	Y	Y	Y	Y	Y	Y
No censure of executive possible	Y	Y	Y	Y				Y	Y	
Executive can dismiss cabinet at will	Y	Y	Y		Y	Y		Y		Y
Dissolution of assembly possible by executive	Y								Y	
Immediate executive reelection possible	Y	Y	Y		Y		Y		Y	
Six-year executive term length	Y						Y	Y	Y	
Executive can initiate constitutional amendments	Y		Y	Y	Y	Y	Y	Y	Y	Y
Executive can initiate constitutional rewrites	Y		Y	Y		Y	Y		Y	
No legislative approval required for military appointments/promotions	Y		Y		Y	Y		Y	Y	
Unrestricted executive proposal of referenda	Y				Y	Y			Y	
Some executive power to declare state of exception/emergency	Y								Y	
No impeachment of executive possible by legislature	Y			Y	Y	Y	Y			Y
Only Supreme Court has judicial review powers	Y	Y	Y	Y		Y	Y	Y		Y
Prosecutor general primarily dependent on the executive	Y	Y	Y	Y	Y	Y	Y	Y	Y	Y

Note: The table includes all Latin American constitutions approved by Constituent Assemblies between 1988 and 1999 (as well as Venezuela's 1961 constitution, replaced by the 1999 constitution).

Source: Author's compilation.

diplomats in favor of political appointees (Jatar 2006; Boersner 2007). He also eroded the autonomy of the Central Bank and illegally sacked a supposedly congressionally controlled savings fund.

During this second phase of power concentration, Chávez made use of two *Leyes Habilitantes* (Enabling Laws of 2000 and 2001). There was another one in 2007–08, but these two alone led to a dramatic expansion of executive powers. The 2001 Enabling Law, for instance, culminated in the approval of forty-six new decrees on a broad set of topics. These decrees triggered massive protests.

Chávez also obtained legislative approval to transfer resources from both the Central Bank and PDVSA to a special National Development Fund (FONDEN). In 2005, for example, US$6 billion were transferred from international reserves to FONDEN; in February 2006, US$4 billion were transferred from the Central Bank and $6.8 billion from PDVSA. Only the president gets to monitor and draw resources from FONDEN.

In addition, Chávez eroded vertical accountability during this second phase. A new penal code limited the rights to expression of protest. Efforts were made to first avoid, then delay the opposition's call for a recall referendum. He created a special set of forces (e.g., *Círculos Bolivarianos*) together with armed guards (e.g., the reservists) to defend the administration against critics and intimidate opponents. Following the 2004 recall referendum, in which the government prevailed, the government used the lists of signatories (*Lista Tascón* and *Lista Maisanta*) to deny jobs and government contracts to those on the list (Jatar 2006). In 2009, there were reports of approximately 800 citizens placed under investigation for political treason for participating in protests. There are allegations that the government relies on citizen groups that use pressure tactics to harass critics, especially in low-income neighborhoods.

As if this erosion of accountability were not enough, *Chavismo* won twenty of twenty-two governorships in 2004 and obtained 100 percent control of the National Assembly because the opposition boycotted the 2005 election for legislators. In retrospect, this withdrawal was the opposition's most serious tactical mistake, because it amounted to ceding to progovernment forces the only institutional space available to the opposition. But back then, the boycott had a logic. The opposition thought that it would lead to international condemnation of persistent electoral irregularities, which would then force the government to postpone the election and correct the irregularities. But international reaction was tame, and the government proceeded with the elections without opposition participation.

Following the 2005 election, Venezuela's National Assembly became a mere rubberstamp of presidential bills, rather than a bargaining actor. In terms of Cox and Morgenstern's (2002) famous typology of executive-legislative relations, Venezuela became Latin America's preeminent case of "dominant president, subservient legislature," a position famously occupied by Mexico between the 1940s and 1960s and by no other Latin American electoral democracy.

In short, between 1999 and 2003, the formal and informal powers of the president vis-à-vis other state institutions and the citizenry expanded beyond what the 1999 constitution allowed.

Military Government

In terms of appointments and spending, the Chávez administration is the most militaristic Latin America has seen in decades. Since its inception, the Chávez administration has relied on military figures to run key government programs (Trinkunas 2004). Almost a quarter of pro-Chávez forces at the 1999 Constituent Assembly had a military background. Chávez then relied on the military to provide social services (briefly in 2000–01), to staff the bureaucracy (since 2001), to administer the oil sector (starting in 2003), and to handle the booming trade with Colombia (2005–present). In 2008, eight of twenty-four governorships and nine of approximately thirty cabinet positions were controlled by active or retired career officers. In addition, the military is being allowed to conduct illicit business with impunity.

In terms of spending, the expansion of military influence is also conspicuous. Military spending under Chávez has increased sevenfold. Venezuela is today one of the largest arms buyers in the world (*Versión Final* 2008a). Between 2005–07, the government spent an extraordinary $4.4 billion on arms imports (*El Universal* 2 June 2008). This is equivalent to the expense required to build 300 new Bolivarian schools, nineteen superhospitals, thirty-four medical schools, and two sports stadiums (*Versión Final* 2008a). This expansion in military spending has occurred despite the absence of any existing or imminent military conflict, domestically or abroad.

Paradoxically, Chávez's initial strategy was to bolster military powers as a way to bolster presidential powers, but he has now discovered that he might have created a sort of Frankenstein monster. The military apparatus is becoming an uncontrollable beast that has begun to assert itself more forcefully in politics. There are credible rumors, for instance, that key decisions to accept defeat in the 2007 referendum to change the constitution or to make peace with Colombia after the March 2008 Colombia-Ecuadorian conflicts, occurred as a result of military pressure. Today, the military seems to be the only actor capable of exercising veto power over the president – a testament to the erosion of military subordination to civilian power that is expected in democracies.

Freedom of Expression

Freedom of expression has continued to exist under Chávez, but there are fewer means of expression than ever. This is because the government has curtailed the size and overregulated the content of private media. In 2007, the government shocked international observers by refusing to renew the operating license of

RCTV, a leading TV channel and media firm. The government also confiscated RCTV's assets without compensation. This was a new high point in a campaign, begun in 2003, to expand the government's share of media outlets in the country by acquiring small operations such as radio stations and local newspapers.

At the start of the Chávez administration, the Venezuelan state controlled only one television station, one AM radio station, and one FM station. As of 2007, the government controlled 85 percent of all television signals (six channels), two national-level radio stations, a news agency, three thousand community radio stations, three printed media companies, seventy-two communitarian media outlets, and approximately 100 Internet portals, according to the director of the School of Communication at the Central University, Adolfo Herrera. After the RCTV shutdown, Venezuela has been left with only three private television stations: Venevisión, Televén, and Globovisión. The latter does not even have national coverage, and Venevisión hardly covers politics.

There is more. SENIAT, the government's tax agency, frequently harasses media companies. There have been 134 reports of acts of aggression against reporters (*Versión Final* 2008b). A social responsibility law bans media from issuing information that is contrary to national security or disrespectful of elected officials. Certain news programs cannot air outside of prime time, under the pretext that they are not suitable for children. The government coaxes the media by threatening not to spend on publicity or to provide dollars to buy paper. Private media is obligated to broadcast seventy weekly minutes of free government publicity. As of mid-2008, the president's personal TV program, *Aló Presidente*, had been aired 311 times, each with an average air time of four hours and twenty-one minutes. (In 2006, the average was six hours and twenty-two minutes; see *Versión Final* 2008b.)

In 2009, the government's assault on the remaining private media escalated, with repeated threats to shut down Globovisión, a twenty-four-hour news channel, accused of "contaminating" Venezuelans and inciting insurrection for its coverage of the government's response to national disasters. Furthermore, the National Assembly approved a reform to the National Law of Telecommunications that, in the spirit of "democratizing" the airwaves and protecting the mental health of Venezuelans, authorizes the state to "eliminate media *latifundios*" held by twenty-seven families that presumably control 32 percent of the country's radio waves. In August, thirty-four radio stations were shut down, part of a group of private radios accused of failing to comply with media laws.

In short, the Venezuelan administration has assaulted freedom of expression probably further than was the case under the Alberto Fujimori administration in Peru, known in Latin America as the elected government that went the furthest in efforts to control the media. Whereas Fujimori employed mostly bribes and harassment of reporters to control the media, Chávez has deployed a more diversified and powerful artillery – state nationalizations, discretionary shutdowns, draconian laws, and even Orwellian arguments – to reduce the size and operation of the private media.

Discretionary Spending

The most notable spending characteristic of Chavismo is not so much huge fiscal spending, which is unquestionably astounding in the history of Latin America (see the next section), but rather huge discretionary spending. The law in Venezuela stipulates that any government revenues that exceed the projected and congressionally approved amount must be deposited into a special stabilization fund. Chávez has taken advantage of this provision to expand discretionary spending by making use of two gimmicks.

The first gimmick was to undermine the autonomy of the stabilization fund. Essentially, Chávez draws from this fund as he sees fit, rather than only in moments of declining oil revenues, as the fund creators intended, and by 2008, had simply ceased putting money in it, as rules stipulate. In the second gimmick, between 2002–07, Chávez sent budget bills to Congress that deliberately underestimated the projected price of oil. For instance, for the 2008 budget the government made revenue projections based on a US$35 price per barrel of oil, a figure that was far below the actual figure even for the previous year. For three weeks in 2008, Venezuelan oil sold for at least US$116 per barrel, which was 233 percent higher than the budgeted amount. Then-Finance Minister Rodrigo Cabezas justified this underestimate by arguing that it was a way to "minimize the risk" of lack of fulfillment in the event of any external shock and promising to channel any surpluses to the service "of the people and only for the people" (*El Economista* 2007). But the actual result of this systematic underestimate was to generate an average of 20 percent surplus in revenues every year (see Figure 2.1) which Chávez was free to use without legislative oversight.

These gimmicks violate democratic principles on two counts. First, they violate the notion that the expenditure of public monies should be subjected to congressional scrutiny. Second, they enlarge the power of the presidency to control the economy – and thus politics – far beyond the already large formal and informal powers of the executive. These gimmicks give Chávez far more unaccountable powers than any other elected president of Venezuela, and arguably Latin America, ever had.

The 2007 Constitutional Reform Referendum

Chávez attempted to arrogate more presidential powers in 2007 through a constitutional reform. Although the effort failed electorally, it nonetheless revealed the extent of the government's intent to concentrate power. If approved, the forty-four-page reform proposal would have constituted the most radical blank check for any elected president in the democratic history of Latin America. It included the following provisions, among others: The president's term in office

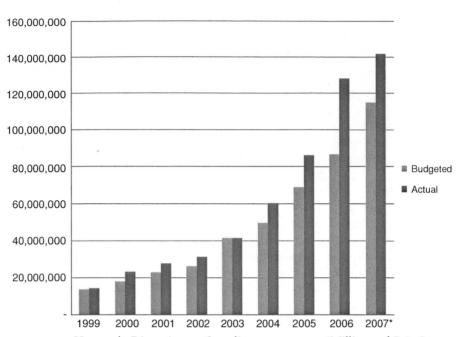

FIGURE 2.1. Venezuela-Discretionary Spending, 1999–2007 (Millions of Bs). *Source:* Pérez Martí 2008. 2007 is an estimate.

was to be extended from six to seven years. The president (but no other elected official) was to be eligible for indefinite reelection. Presidentially appointed *consejos comunales* were to receive constitutional ranking, thereby bypassing and possibly replacing local and regional elected offices. The "missions" – programs under the complete jurisdiction of the president – were to obtain constitutional ranking, undermining the authority of local and regional offices (all elected bodies). The state was to obtain the right to expropriate private property without prior judicial authorization. Article 115 of the constitution, which stipulates that all persons have the "right to...enjoy and use freely (*disponer*) their property (*bienes*)," was to be deleted, thereby abolishing the right to private property. External funding of political groups was to be banned (while simultaneously allowing the state to finance the ruling party). The number of vice presidents was to be expanded, all of whom would be designated without legislative approval. The armed forces were to be assigned a domestic enemy (the *oligarquías*), which is almost a declaration of civil war. The education sector was to be required to promote a socialist state, thereby undermining the notion of freedom of education. And finally, presidential powers during states of siege were to expand – due process would be eliminated and the right to the presumption of innocence would be abolished, with no limits set to the duration of states of siege – thereby violating key rights upheld by the United Nations Committee for Human Rights and the Inter-American

Court for Human Rights (Human Rights Watch 2007). This constitutional reform proposal, together with the RCTV affair, generated the same effects as previous power grabs: unification of the opposition, defections from the government, and a showdown in the streets. This time, the government lost at the polls (albeit not in every state).

The "Coup" against Elected Opposition Leaders

Some observers thought that the 2007 defeat would yield a new era in politics and policy. Many hoped that Chávez would read the signs of electoral disapproval and desist in his efforts to concentrate more power.

However, the 2007 referendum changed politics little, and policy even less. In terms of policy, the 2007 defeat hardly mattered, because the government responded – not by changing course – but by insisting on finding other means to enact the very same reforms that had failed. In early 2009, Chávez organized another referendum to change the constitution to allow for indefinite reelection, despite the fact that it was unconstitutional (Article 346 states that electorally defeated constitutional reforms cannot be reattempted during the same constitutional period) and carried out through illegal means (no funding was provided for the No vote). The government requested a third Enabling Law, which unlike the first two, was granted in economic good times and therefore could not be justified in terms of economic exigency. This law was even more extravagant than the previous two, as it allowed Chávez to legislate in almost every domain: state institutions, popular participation, public values, economic affairs, social affairs, financial institutions, the tax system, security issues, national defense, infrastructure, transport, service, and energy.

Furthermore, the government reverted to the practice of blacklisting citizens, this time, citizens interested in running for office. In 2008, the government created the *Lista Russián*, which included names of citizens disqualified from running for office for the 2008 midterm election. These citizens were blacklisted without having been charged by any tribunal. Although a majority were *Chavistas* (suggesting that Chávez was trying to purge less obsequious followers), the list included some of the most popular leaders of the opposition.

But in terms of politics, the 2007 referendum defeat may have unleashed a new era. A new electoral cleavage seems to have emerged, not so much between high-income and low-income sectors (in Caracas, for instance, the referendum lost in every jurisdiction, rich or destitute) but between high-population states (which overwhelmingly rejected the reform) and low-population states.

This cleavage was confirmed in the pivotal 2008 regional elections for state governors, mayors, and local legislatures. The opposition retained two governorships (Zulia, Nueva Esparta), added three more (Miranda, Táchira, Carabobo), and obtained the mayoralty of Caracas, Maracaibo, and several other cities. The opposition defeated the ruling party in the jurisdictions with the greatest concentration of both population and economic assets.

The 2007 and 2008 elections suggest a divide between the more modern/industrialized states and the more rural states (Alvarez 2008). Like Fujimorismo in Peru in the late 1990s, Chavismo may be becoming a disproportionately nonurban phenomenon. Furthermore, the 2007 and 2008 elections also boosted the morale of the opposition, because these constituted the opposition's first electoral victories in the Chávez era. The election ended the tendency of opposition voters to abstain from the electoral process – a tendency that had cost them dearly in previous elections. It was the governing party that experienced the highest abstention rates. If this political trend continues, it demonstrates a decline in the electoral competitiveness of the regime.

After these opposition victories, Chávez staged what amounted to an inside coup (a so-called *golpe 'desde' el estado*). The targets were the new elected opposition officials. The elected mayor of Maracaibo and former presidential candidate Manuel Rosales was forced to go into exile after Chávez issued an arrest warrant on questionable corruption charges. The elected mayor of Caracas, Antonio Ledezma, and the governor of the state of Miranda, Henrique Capriles, were stripped of their office (through mobs), the bulk of their budgets (through presidential decrees), and the bulk of their staff (through budget cuts). Ledezma also lost the bulk of his authority through the transfer of mayoral responsibilities to a newly created office, head of government, led by a presidential appointee. Capriles also lost control of ports, airports, a hospital, and an asphalt plant. His police force, one of the best performing in the country, had to surrender three thousand firearms to the central state. In July, Chávez described the governors as "enemies of the people" and threatened to prosecute them for allegedly raising paramilitary armies.

In sum, the Chávez administration has expanded presidential powers to the detriment of check-and-balance institutions, increased the costs and obstacles of being in the opposition, curtailed the operations and content of private media, granted far more power to the military than any other democratic administration in Latin America, and disregarded electoral victories for the opposition. After the 1999 constitutional reform, Chávez failed to expand presidential powers through electoral means and has employed alternative means to reach the same ends. Although the regime has encouraged participation by new actors (mostly in its early years) and has respected some autonomous political spaces and political liberties, it has nonetheless become considerably more restrictive for nonincumbent groups than any other regime in Venezuela since 1958. It may not qualify as a full-fledged autocracy, but it is a long way from the more open, more opposition-friendly political regime that existed between 1958–99. No doubt the previous regime was fraught with problems, and almost every scholar who studied it, regardless of ideology, obsessed about its shortcomings (e.g., Naím and Piñango 1984; Coppedge 1994; Crisp 2000; Buxton 2001; Márquez and Piñango 2004; Myers 2004). Nevertheless, the previous system allowed opposition forces to win in five of seven presidential elections, two of which were won by nontraditional parties (the 1993 election by MAS and Convergencia and the 1998 election by the Polo Patriótico). Under Chávez, presidentialism has expanded to the detriment of any other powerholding group in the country, and this expansion shows no sign of slowing down.

OLD ECONOMICS

Economically, as opposed to politically, the break with the past has been less palpable. Chávez's political economy seems instead to be a case of déjà vu: A return to the policies of import-substitution industrialization (ISI) and oil boom mismanagement that characterized Venezuela prior to the 1990s, especially in the 1970s. The irony of Chávez's ideology is that despite being so virulently antiparty and opposed to policies of the Punto Fijo era, the president advocates economic models that are similar to those of Venezuela's traditional parties, especially Acción Democrática under Carlos Andrés Pérez in the 1970s.

The Return of ISI

Venezuela under Chávez has returned to a modified form of ISI. ISI was the model of economic development that prevailed in most South American countries and Mexico between the 1930s and early 1980s. Table 2.2 lists all the policies that were typical of ISI in its heyday (the mid-1970s). Venezuela under Chávez fits into almost all of these ISI categories.

Essentially, Venezuela has experienced a dramatic expansion of the state in almost every domain of the economy through nationalizations, firm buyouts, expropriations, direct subsidies, special credits, heavy spending, and business-unfriendly regulations. The Heritage Foundation Index of Economic Freedoms, which ranks countries according to their levels of economic state intervention, shows Venezuela's descent into a more state-centric economy. Venezuela had one of the lowest starting scores (2002) and experienced one of the steepest drops by 2008 (Figure 2.2).

Public spending as a percentage of GDP increased from 18 to 34 percent between 1998 and 2008 (data in this section drawn from *Veneconomía* 2008). State-owned enterprises have expanded in all sectors through the introduction of new state-owned firms (e.g., the airline Conviasa), nationalizations (e.g., CANTV, Electricidad de Caracas, Sidor, cement companies), expropriations (seventy-four oil service providers, more than forty factories and firms), and conversion of private firms into joint ventures (e.g., foreign oil corporations). Also directly in line with ISI, Chavismo is relying heavily on price and exchange rate controls. The former have been imposed on a large list of items. The latter led to three exchange rates: the official, the preferential (for designated importers), and the parallel or informal rate. This exchange rate was abruptly replaced with the 2010 devaluation, which established two new official rates.

One way to grasp the expansion of the nonfinancial, nonoil state-owned sector is to look at the income generated by these firms. Between 2003 and

TABLE 2.2. *ISI Policy Toolbox during the 2003–2008 Period*

ISI Policy Tool	Examples
Industrial Policy	
State-owned enterprises or mixed-equity enterprises	Nationalization of CANTV, Electricidad de Caracas, Verinauto, SIDOR; purchase of Banco Santander (the third-largest private bank); expropriation of Mexican CEMEX (and acquisition of two other foreign-owned cement companies), 74 oil-related firms in Zulia, textile firm INVELEX in Cojedes, dairy factory in Los Andes, various rice producers, including U.S.-owned CARGILL and some firms owned by POLAR, approximately 50 factories, 1,500 hectares of Smurfi Kappa, paper-maker VENEPAL in Carabobo, iron-related factories through CGV, and 2.2 million hectares in land. The government is increasing its presence in tourism, including nationalization of hotels (e.g., Caracas Hilton). By early 2009, the government has identified 30 more firms as potential targets for nationalization.
"Buy National" laws	Misión Fábrica Adentro and other programs establish joint ventures designed to generate "endogenous development," the Chavista term for import substitution.
Require foreign firms to establish joint ventures	In 2006, 32 private contractors in the oil exploration sector were forced to "migrate" into joint ventures, with PDVSA becoming the majority shareholder. Only 21 joint firms survived. In the Orinoco Oil belt, three private firms were forced to become mixed enterprises; one became fully owned by the state.
Require foreign firms to increase local content	To obtain foreign exchange, firms have to show the government a "Certificate of No National Production," demonstrating that they need imports because there are no locally produced substitutes.
International Instruments	
Tariffs on consumer goods	Few
Quotas on imports	Few; mostly on cars, car parts, and some other products.
Exchange rate overvaluation	Exchange rate has been fixed since 2005; the 2010 devaluation has eased, but not eliminated overvaluation. The inflation rate was 16.2 percent in 2005, 13.6 percent in 2006, 20 percent in 2007, and 31 percent in 2008.
Exchange rationing	Comprehensive system of exchange rate control (CADIVI). Currently, three rates operate: the official rate, the special rate for importers (*Mercado permuta*), and the unofficial rate. Approximately 20 percent of foreign exchange transactions in the private sector relies on the nonofficial rates.

ISI Policy Tool	Examples
Import licenses	Few (but exchange rate controls, which limit access to dollars and thus to imports, are heavily restricted and offered on a select basis).
	Fiscal and Monetary Policies
Subsidies for cheap inputs (e.g., electricity)	Tax credits are offered to designated sectors, especially in agriculture. Price controls are in place on a variety of consumer goods. Periodic increases of gas prices were stopped in 1999. As of 2008, the government offered one of the cheapest prices of gasoline in the world (US$0.12 per gallon, or 1/15 the price of a liter of bottled water), a subsidy of almost US$11 billion in 2007.
Tax breaks on production	Tax revenues have increased but there is uneven application of tough tax laws.
Preferential interest rates and loans	Private banks are obligated to channel 47 percent of capital to designated sectors. Furthermore, new controls have been established

Source: Franko 2007; Veneconomía 2008; *Versión Final* (26 July 2009); *Business Week* (23 May 2008).

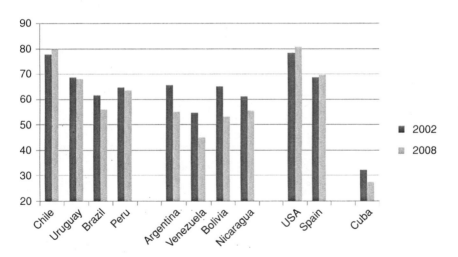

FIGURE 2.2. Index of Economic Liberties, Selected Countries, 2002–2008. *Source:* Heritage Foundation.

2007, income from these corporations almost doubled from 7.4 billion to 13.5 billion bolivars.

The growth of state-owned enterprises under Chávez is often justified discursively in terms of the need to regain control over sectors deemed by the state to be strategic. But as was true in previous episodes of ISI, state expansion under Chávez seems to fulfill political rather than strategic purposes. To pave the way for nationalization, the government tends to pursue two channels. One is for the state to actually encourage labor conflicts, thereby driving a firm to bankruptcy, which justifies the government taking over (e.g., Constructora Nacional de Válvulas and now Coca-Cola FEMSA; *Veneconomía* 3 October 2008). The other is for the government to take over the firm, promising workers that it will expand employment and relax productivity standards – all of which pleases labor and thus helps the government meet electoral challenges success-fully. Teodoro Petkoff makes this point in discussing the 2007 nationalization of Sidor:

Polls show dwindling support for Chávez in Bolívar state – home to the steel plant and other heavy industry facilities and thus of strategic importance to the government – and the nationalization decision was an effort to stop the electoral hemorrhaging in this region. Seen from the vantage point of the progressive weakening of the president's standing, the Sidor nationalization is a case of offense being the best defense. That labor unions and most company employees rejoiced at the announcement came as no surprise: the current statist drive has rekindled an old, conditioned reflex in the labor force. Before privatization in 1997, Sidor needed twenty thousand workers to produce less than 3 million tons of steel a year. As the employer, the state eagerly agreed to unrealistic collective agreement terms knowing the national purse would make up for any red ink. After privatization, the payroll was cut to six thousand and Sidor started producing 5 million tons of steel a year (Petkoff 2008: 11).

Either way, the result is the same: The state becomes the principal eco-nomic agent in a region or in a group of workers, which increases the state's cooptation capacity. Although Petkoff argues that this political bias makes Chávez's nationalizations "qualitatively different" from previous statism, his point may be overstated. Similar political intentions have been identified in previous episodes of ISI expansion (Kaufman and Stallings 1991).

One political motive behind these nationalizations is to increase the size of the workforce under state control. Between 2007 and mid-2008, when nationalizations picked up pace, nationalizations allowed the state to absorb almost 41,400 new workers into the public payroll, a 7.2 percent increase from the early 2007 level and a 53.5 percent increase from the start of the Chávez administration (from 1,348,181 to 2,064,027 workers). In contrast, the private sector has expanded its payroll by only 28 percent since 1999 (from 7,343,257 to 9,405,568 workers; see Tejero Puntes 2008). Because private-sector job creation is lagging seriously behind the state sector, the economy is being left with a phenomenally large shortfall in employment of approximately 8.7 percent (*Veneconomía* 30 April 2008).

Not only the motives, but also the outcomes of Venezuela's current ISI seem to be repeating a similar story. The public sector is getting bloated (with labor), while productivity is plummeting. PDVSA is the best illustration. In 2009, the minister of energy and president of PDVSA announced that PDVSA's payroll increased by 266.7 percent, going from thirty thousand to eighty thousand employees (*Infolatam* 19 July 2009). And yet – measured in terms of barrels per day produced – the company's production declined by 22.4 percent since prestrike levels, from 2.35 million in 2002 to 1.82 million at the end of 2008 (EIA 2009; Espinasa 2009). (Private firms in strategic association with PDVSA have not experienced productivity declines, suggesting that this is a company-specific, rather than an industrywide, outcome.) The company's operating costs have more than doubled, from US$6.7 per BBL in 1997 to US$15.1 in 2007 (Romero 2008). This productivity drop is all the more remarkable and unexpected given the large world demand for oil since 2003.

Modified ISI

Despite the similarities, there are at least two major differences between classic ISI and Chávez's ISI. First, Chávez has spent little effort on restricting imports. Tariffs and import quotas do exist (e.g., in auto parts), but they are not that salient, widespread, or rigid. In fact, the government is relying on an avalanche of imports to combat inflation (because foreign items exert downward pressure on prices) and to alleviate consumer goods shortages, which have increased in Venezuela since 2006. Insofar as import controls exist, they occur by way of exchange rate controls: Importers must obtain dollars from the government, and the government is restricting the number of dollars it sells. Consequently, Venezuela has experienced an import boom that is inconsistent with the goals of classic ISI. However, it is consistent with the import boom that took place during Venezuela's first oil boom under Carlos Andrés Pérez, in which imports registered an average 33.7 annual growth between 1973–78 (Echevarría 1995: 58). It is important to note that the market-reform period of the second Carlos Andrés Pérez administration (1989–93), often billed as a time of trade-induced deindustrialization, actually registered a decline in imports.

An even greater departure from ISI is the dearth of public and private investments in diversified industrial activities. This contrasts with the 1960–90 period, when investment levels in industrial activities actually expanded, in defiance of traditional resource-curse theories that predict export booms to yield deindustrialization (Di John 2009). The decline in public investment under Chávez is noticeable in both oil and nonoil activities. Public sector investment in oil declined from an already low 9 percent in 2003 to an even lower 8 percent of total sector revenues in 2007. In nonoil sectors, public-sector investments declined even more dramatically, from 7 percent in 2003 to 4 percent in 2007.

By neglecting investments in capital, the state is leaving only the domestic private sector to shoulder the burden of investing. And yet this private investment is not forthcoming, mostly because the government is doing very little – other than offering a fiscal stimulus – to help business thrive. The World Bank *Doing Business Index*, which ranks countries in terms of their favorable domestic investment climate, places Venezuela near the bottom of the list (World Bank 2008).

The consequence of these industrial policies – openness to imports and business-unfriendly regulations – is, of course, fewer private industries. The number of private manufacturing firms in Venezuela declined by 13 percent between 2001 and 2006; food- and beverage-related manufacturing industries declined by 8.4 percent (Pérez Martí 2008). Another consequence has been capital flight starting in 2006. This decline in firms and increase in capital flight are completely unexpected in a country undergoing the most impressive consumer boom in decades. But they are perfectly predictable in the context of a proimports/anti-investment economic model. Di John (2009) argues that the worst economic effects of the resource curse – oil booms leading to deindustrialization – never happened in Venezuela, at least until the 1980s. Under Chávez until 2009, these effects were in full swing.

One result of the Chavista political economy is that, like most heavy-handed statist models, it contains a mechanism for permanently generating its own demand. The state creates poor business conditions for many sectors, which yields unemployment or capacity underutilization or both. The government then uses this outcome as an excuse for taking over. In a famous critique of capitalism, Charles Lindblom (1982) argued that the private sector can hold the government hostage because it can always threaten politicians with unemployment and thus force them to adopt business-friendly policies. Chavismo has discovered that a petro-state can actually reverse this relationship. The state can afford to corner the private sector into underperformance and thus generate demand for more state interventions. In a nonresource-based economy this model would be unsustainable – at some point the state would run out of funds. In a petro-state enjoying an oil-price boom such as Venezuela in 2003–08, the model was impossible to break because both supply and demand were feeding on each other.

Figure 2.3 shows some of the economic results of Chávez's modified version of ISI, which, as argued, is similar to Venezuela's ISI in the 1970s. Imports

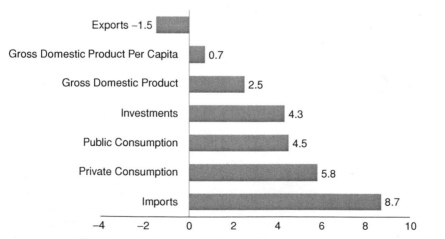

FIGURE 2.3. GDP Growth Rates by Different Components, 1998–2006 (annual percent). *Source:* Penfold 2008.

is the sector of the economy that has expanded most conspicuously, which is a departure from textbook ISI; whereas nontraditional exports have shrunk, which is compatible with both traditional ISI and typical resource-curse theories that predict nondiversification of exports in situations of oil dependence during boom times.

In short, Chavismo represents another ISI experience with some modifications. It differs from classic ISI (but not Venezuela's previous ISI) in that it welcomes imports. It also differs from both classic ISI and Venezuela's previous ISI in that it purposefully represses public and private capital investment.

Social Policies, Clientelism, and Cronyism

Weyland's chapter poses the question of how did leftist administrations in Latin America in the 2000s address issues of social equity? Chávez has become known worldwide for vigorous social policies, especially his "Missions to Save People." Regime supporters claim that Chávez's social policies are truly revolutionary (Gibbs 2006; Wilpert 2007; Buxton 2008; Ellner 2008; Weisbrot 2008). They argue that Chávez's policies of poverty alleviation and income redistribution – both in terms of ingenuity of program design and populations reached – represent true breaks with the past. The reality is far less rosy.

There is no question that some of Chávez's missions are innovative and accessible to previously neglected populations. Yet the claim that Chávez's overall social spending represents a break with the past is overstated. No doubt social spending levels measured in per capita terms have increased, with one estimate placing the increase at 314 percent between 1998 and 2006 (Weisbrot 2008). But spending levels measured in terms of proportion of overall spending are not that much greater than those of previous administrations. There is more spending simply because Chávez enjoyed the largest inflow of revenue in Venezuela since the 1930s. There are also press reports that many missions began contracting in terms of budget, people served, timely payment of salaries, and facilities running, from the peaks of 2006–07, even before the economic crisis hit in late 2008 (e.g., Conde 2009). For instance, Barrio Adentro's budget declined from US$1.3 million in 2007 to US$100,000 by September 2008 (e.g., *El Universal*, 10 February 2009).

Although social spending is a crucial tool to alleviate poverty, it is not the only factor that matters. Inflation and unemployment rates are also decisive. They affect purchasing power directly, especially among low income groups. Measured in terms of these two indicators, the Chávez government's performance has been quite unimpressive. Venezuela's inflation rate under Chávez has far surpassed the region's average and is one of the world's highest. The unemployment rate was also above Latin America's average every year except for 2007 and 2008. Figure 2.4 provides a picture of Venezuela's poor performance with these indicators. It combines the unemployment and inflation rates to create what some analysts have labeled as the misery index. Unless Venezuela is a major exception to standard economic forces, the prevalence of

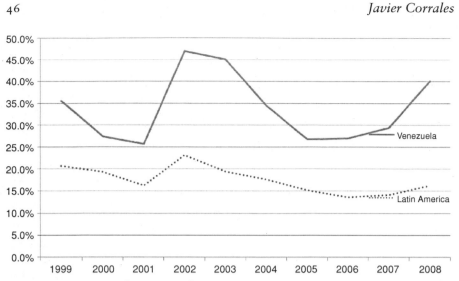

FIGURE 2.4. Misery Index: Venezuela v. Latin America, 1999–2007. *Note:* Misery Index is the sum of the annual consumer price inflation rate and the open urban unemployment rate. *Source:* World Development Indicators and CEPAL.

high unemployment and very high inflation suggests that poverty alleviation must be less impressive than official figures suggest.

Furthermore, when examined in terms of the relationship between investment and return, it is not clear that Chávez's policies are all that impressive. The most serious studies of these missions' impact reveal that poverty reduction is considerably less than what might have been expected from an economy exhibiting such a spectacular growth performance and fiscal stimulus. In fact, education and health achievements are not more impressive than Venezuela's historical trend since the 1960s, and income inequality has actually expanded, as confirmed by both unsympathetic (Rodríguez 2008) and sympathetic (Pérez Martí 2008) analysts. Income among the poor has risen, but the income share of the upper echelons of society has expanded at a faster rate. Furthermore, there is plenty of corruption (Coronel 2006) and politically minded spending (Penfold-Becerra 2007), which indicates that Chávez's social spending is actually exacerbating, rather than correcting, old pre-Chávez-era political vices.

One final domain in which Chávez's political economy is exacerbating pre-Chávez-era political vices is cronyism, or state economic favors for the privileged. Most state contracts to the domestic private sector are awarded without any form of bidding. In addition, a wave of mergers and acquisitions flourished in the half-decade boom of 2004–08, in which many of the buyers were individuals and firms politically linked to the government. Many of these mergers and acquisitions took place in the financial sector. For instance, the fourth-largest insurance company in Venezuela, La Previsora, was acquired in mid-2009 by Bainvest, an investment firm run by Arné Chacón, brother of the minister of science, technology and intermediate industries, Jesse Chacón (*El Universal*,

19 June 2009). The transfer of state and private assets into private hands that are closely linked to the government – locally known as *boliburgueses* – has led many actors to talk about Chávez's *robolución*. The former term is a play on the Spanish words for "Bolivarian" and "bourgeoisie"; the latter, a play on the words for theft and revolution.

The Ax-Relax-Collapse Cycle All Over Again

Thus far, I have provided a snapshot picture of economics under Chávez by 2009 to argue that the prevailing model looked not unlike a slightly modified version of ISI. If one instead examines how the regime's policies evolved since its inception, it is possible to identify yet another economic similarity with the past: a repetition of Venezuela's famous boom-bust cycles.

In a 2000 essay, I argued that Venezuela's economic management between the late 1970s and 1999 repeated a consistent cycle: An oil boom is misman-aged and overspent (which fuels deficits and corruption), leading to a macro-economic crisis (which aggravates poverty) and underinvestment in the oil sector (which leads to oil production decline), followed by a period of austerity (which further aggravates poverty and ignites political discontent), ultimately forcing governments to abandon reforms, which then brings the country back to economic crisis until a new oil boom appears (see also Villasmil, Monaldi et al. 2004). I have called this the "ax-relax-collapse" pattern. The Chávez administration replicated this path (see Table 2.3).

The ax stage: Chávez inherited a country experiencing both a short-term and a long-term economic crisis. The short-term crisis was a massive recession and exchange rate crisis in 1998, which was an aftershock of the 1997–98 Asian crisis. The long-term crisis was the chronic decline of oil revenues on a per capita basis, which had been generating fiscal deficits, inflation, and debt since the early 1980s (Hausmann and Rodríguez in press). When Chávez took office, he found the economic situation, in his words, "unimaginable... There was no money even to pay salaries" and "No one wanted to lend us a penny" (Chávez, Harnecker, and Boudin 2005: 66–7). Economic conditions deteriorated further in 2002–03, with the government blaming opposition strikes for the recession,

TABLE 2.3. *Venezuela: Stuck in "Ax-Relax-Collapse" Cycles*

Administration	Ax	Relax	Collapse
Luis Herrera Campíns	1979	1980–1	1983
Jaime Lusinchi	1983–5	1986–8	1988
Carlos Andrés Pérez, Ramón J. Velásquez, Rafael Caldera	1989–91	1991–2	1993–5
Rafael Caldera	1996	1997	1998
Hugo Chávez	1999–2003	2003–08	2008-present

Source: Adapted from Corrales 2000.

and the opposition blaming Chávez for the strikes. Regardless of the cause, there is no question that the first four years of the Chávez administration were characterized by economic hard times. Chávez's approach to these hard times was not that different from that of previous presidents confronting economic crises: He turned to austerity measures (this section draws from Kelly and Palma 2004). He began by retaining the finance minister from the Caldera administration, Christian Democrat Maritza Izaguirre; freezing PDVSA's investment plans; using decree powers in 1999 to establish a series of new taxes; cutting the budget across the board by 7 percent; and focusing on controlling inflation through exchange rate overvaluation and import promotion. Social spending – in fact, government spending in general – was limited (Penfold-Becerra 2007). Chávez also showed openness to foreign direct investment, especially in the telecommunications sector. This was a period in which some observers even called Chávez a neoliberal.

The Relax Phase

The austerity phase ended with two developments in mid-2003, first, the sudden and rapid rise in the price of oil, and second, the sudden emergence of a serious electoral challenge to Chávez, namely, the opposition's campaign to hold a recall referendum. Chávez's popularity had declined precipitously between 2001–03. The opposition became majoritarian (according to most polls), took to the streets, and pressured the government to enact a recall referendum. In response to this political crisis, the government launched one of the most expansive fiscal stimulus programs in the history of Latin America. It was during this phase (2003–08) that Chávez implemented most of the ISI and social policies just described. Figure 2.5 shows this dramatic change in policy. Between 1999 and 2003 (the ax phase), the budget had expanded modestly or actually shrank overall. In contrast, between 2004–07, it expanded by double digits annually. In fact, expenditures grew at a faster rate than the already phenomenally high rates of revenue growth, a bold procyclical policy

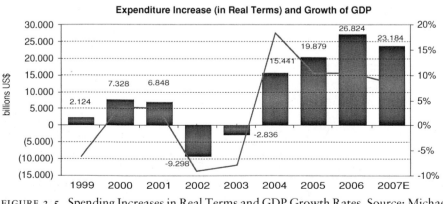

FIGURE 2.5. Spending Increases in Real Terms and GDP Growth Rates. Source: Michael Penfold-Becerra based on Ministerio de Finanzas and Ecoanalítica.

that has generated unjustifiable deficits (Pérez Martí 2008). As in the past, a key component of this relax cycle was inattention to investments in oil – social spending was privileged over capital spending. Consequently, Venezuela's oil production declined.

The Collapse Phase

As in previous boom-bust episodes, the relax phase soon gave way to macro-economic and microeconomic problems: rising debt, inflation, exchange rate distortions, declining oil production, consumer goods shortages, and capital flight. By 2007, the state had lost control of the expenditure side, and soon liabilities began to surpass state revenues, which created fiscal pressure. The government responded by tightening price, exchange rate, and interest rate controls and curtailing bank liquidity, all in a futile effort to avoid more serious austerity measures, such as severe spending cuts, massive devaluation, and profound tax increases. Tightening these controls led, in turn, to consumer goods shortages, economic slowdown, and more capital flight. This combination of rising inflation and consumer goods shortages is particularly taxing on low-income groups in almost every country, even when there is economic growth. This is one reason that poverty alleviation in Venezuela stopped in 2008.

By early 2009, the Chávez government was in a typical collapse-phase mode: withdrawing foreign reserves from special funds, repurchasing foreign reserves from the Central Bank, cutting the amount of foreign currency offered to private actors by more than 60 percent compared to 2008, reducing the budget by 6 percent, increasing the value-added tax by 3 percentage points, defaulting on debts held by PDVSA with local companies, and expropriating many of these firms. In 2010, Chávez had to resort to a massive devaluation. Except for privatizations, Chávez was repeating some of the same policies that dominated the late 1980s and 1990s.

However, it may very well be that – barring a profound drop in the price of oil – the current collapse phase in Venezuela will be less severe in macro-economic terms than pre-Chávez-era collapse phases. One reason that previous collapses were more severe is that Venezuela between 1981 and 2003 found itself in a situation of chronic oil revenue shortage, which deprived the state of mechanisms for responding to economic contraction countercyclically. The collapse phase under Chávez is not yielding equally severe macroeconomic strains because the external side remains unusually healthy. Oil prices continued to rise until 2008 to levels never before seen in Venezuela's oil history, and as of this writing, they remain historically high.

And yet despite this difference, the strains on the Venezuelan economy in 2008–09 were significant. In 2008, Venezuela registered one of the highest inflation rates in the world (25.8 percent annually), despite its imposition of the broadest system of price control in decades; consumer goods shortages in a broad variety of products, despite massive imports; stagnation in the agricultural sector leading to food shortages, despite heavy agricultural subsidies; and credit shrinking, despite negative interest rates. In early 2009, the

administration continued to have sufficient revenues to sustain fiscal spending and thus avoid a procyclical response to economic contraction. But the
microeconomic distortions this time around seemed severe enough to generate
poverty and political discontent, as in previous collapse periods. Venezuela
is also overexposed internationally. In the past few years, Venezuela bought
Argentine bonds and guaranteed part of Ecuador's foreign debt. If these countries default, Venezuela faces onerous foreign obligations.

WHY ECONOMIC MISMANAGEMENT TODAY IS LESS THREATENING
TO REGIME SURVIVAL

What are the implications of economic collapse for the sustainability of
Chávez's regime? Any discussion of regime survival in Venezuela must address
the issue of economic sustainability, which in turn entails discussing oil flows.
Chávez has been able to build his economic model because of oil. Nobody
disputes this point. The key question is whether the regime will collapse in the
event of a severe oil downturn. My answer is "Not necessarily."

There is no question that the Venezuelan state remains dependent on oil
revenues, more so now than at any other time since the 1970s. This dependence
introduces volatility, since the international price of oil, and thus, income from
oil exports, fluctuate dramatically. For that reason, Venezuela had periods of
a steep rise in oil revenues in the 1970s, rapid decline in the 1980s, volatility
and decline in the 1990s, and another steep rise since 2003. It is worth asking
what would happen – economically and politically – in the event of another
sustained downturn in oil revenues.

Indeed, in 2008, world oil prices took a dramatic downturn. Between July
and December 2008, prices of Venezuelan crude declined by 68.5 percent
from a high point of US$129.54 per barrel. The full impact of this decline
may dissipate as oil prices have since then recovered to some extent, but the
experience of late 2008 shows that a severe exogenous drop is possible.

I would suggest that an oil bust will not necessarily bring about the demise
of Venezuela's new political model. This is because oil flows impact economic
and political sustainability differently, depending on the regime type in place.
Massive oil booms, I argue, risk weakening democracies but have a high chance
of strengthening authoritarianism, whereas massive oil busts jeopardize democracy more than authoritarian regimes. (Smith 2006 reaches a similar conclusion
but his causal argument is different.) To understand these different impacts,
it helps to review the effects of both oil booms and busts along three regime
dimensions: economic policy, checks on executive power, and societal response
(see Table 2.4).

Oil Booms

Economic Policy. Under both democracies and autocracies, as Karl (1997) and
Coronil (1997) made abundantly clear, oil booms have an inebriating effect on

TABLE 2.4. *Effects of Oil Flows on Political Regimes*

Key variable	Effects of Oil Booms On:		Effects of Oil Busts On:	
	Democracy	Authoritarianism	Democracy	Authoritarianism
Economic policy	Heavy fiscal expansion; party-mediated clientelism	Ditto, except that cronyism and clientelism are not mediated by opposition parties. Opposition finds it hard to capture oil rents.	Structural adjustment; high chance of policy paralysis or state-society conflict	Clientelism declines, cronyism can persist.
Presidential powers	Spending capacity increases the incumbent's capacity to co-opt; limits on presidential power will depend on the vitality of political party competition.	Increase with few limits	Executive becomes tempted to rule by decree and/or circumvent parties and congress. Traditional parties suffer dealignment and fragmentation, which can exacerbate policy paralysis.	Fewer resources available to stay electorally competitive; will avoid elections or create obstacles for the opposition
Societal Response	Rising rent seeking; possible increase in party competition, at least initially	Bandwagoning	Growing resentment against politicians	Beneficiaries of clientelism will protest the decline in clientelism, but cronies can reaffirm support.
Net effect	Regime declines (Venezuela 1973-9)	Regime strengthens; incumbent turns electorally competitive (Venezuela 2003-07)	High probability of instability and regime collapse (Venezuela 1989-2001)	Two scenarios: regime turns more authoritarian and survives; regime collapses if regime is unwilling or able to repress

state leaders. Oil booms drive presidents to overspend, typically on megain-frastructure projects, often in utter disregard of macroeconomic and financial viability. One key difference is that in a democracy, exaggerated statism is channeled through (or occurs under the scrutiny of) political parties, whereas under authoritarianism there is no mediating institution between the state and economic agents receiving state funds. Oil booms can therefore promote party competition in democracies (see Levine 1978; Karl 1987), at least initially, because large opposition parties, not just the ruling party, can benefit from state largesse. In an authoritarian regime, on the other hand, because the incumbent has a virtual monopoly over state largesse and its accompanying policies of clientelism and cronyism, the chances of rival forces capturing state resources to challenge the state are more limited.

However, oil booms in a democracy may eventually result in party collusion (see Norden 1998), as traditional parties begin to collude with one another in sharing the spoils of office. To compete, parties overemphasize patronage to the detriment of sound capital investments, which is especially unfortu-nate for development (Collier 2007: 44–5), may impede economic adjustment (Naím 1993; Di John 2009), and can lead to antiparty/anti-status quo senti-ment (Myers 2007; Di Tella, Donna et al. in press).

Checks on the Executive Branch. Higher spending expands the capacity of incumbents to co-opt political actors (especially in the context of weak institu-tions). Consequently, incumbents become very hard to defeat or restrain during oil booms. Their enhanced power to spend inadvertently leads to declines in key democratic features, such as notions of limited government, transparency in fiscal affairs, equal treatment of the opposition, and reduced asymmetry of power between incumbents and the opposition, as Karl (1997) argues took place in Venezuela under the first Pérez administration. The key point is that these trends are detrimental for democratic governance but not necessarily for nondemocratic regimes, because they obviously do not base their legitimacy on these democratic features.

Societal Response. In many petro-states, a consistent economic response by societal actors to oil booms is to become addicted to oil-based rents (see Romero 1997 for Venezuela). Economic agents devote their energies to finding ways to extract oil-based rents. Because the state controls the oil sector, this societal response translates into demand for statism. In democracies, the rising demand for oil-derived rents does not necessarily erase political competition. Political parties will compete for votes in their quest for state power, with each party advocating its own view of what constitutes the fairer or better way to distribute rents. But ideological competition among parties does decline: All parties end up defending one version or another of heavy statism. A free-market economist, Hugo J. Faría, thus complains that in Venezuela there is no one (no party, media group, or politician) openly defending any economic ideology other than statism (Faría 2007; Faría 2008). In a democracy, wherein both incumbents and opposition forces share rent revenues, rent seekers across societies can satisfy their appetite for rents by capturing both incumbent forces and opposition forces. In an authoritarian setting, by contrast, there is only one way to satisfy the appetite for rents – by bandwagoning with the incumbents. Because the opposition, if it is active at all, has almost zero chance of winning, there are weak incentives for rent seekers to side with the opposition. It is a hopeless and possibly dangerous gamble. Economic agents thus side instead with the state in the hope of getting a government contract, a government job, or a government subsidy.

In short, oil booms risk weakening democracies, if not right away, then in the medium term. Booms lower checks on the executive branch and increase society's demand for rents. Party competition for electoral office may still survive, but collusion expands, and ideological competition wanes. Consequently, over time, oil booms also risk weakening party competition and provoking voter dealignment, as citizens turn increasingly against party life. In authoritarian settings, all these same effects only serve to strengthen the regime, because autocracies – by definition – thrive in contexts of declining institutional checks, societal demand for statism, bandwagoning, and declining respect for civilian politicians. Furthermore, oil booms allow authoritarian regimes to embrace larger degrees of clientelism and cronyism, which expands the number of their supporters, and greater hegemony over the distribution of these benefits, which expands the degree of bandwagoning and the extent to which the autocrat can turn into a competitive autocrat.

Oil Busts

By the same token, oil busts can jeopardize democracies far more than authoritarian regimes.

Economic Policy. Because petro-states have few sources of income other than oil, they are particularly susceptible to oil busts. Oil busts tend to produce severe fiscal crises and recessions, which force presidents in both democratic and autocratic petro-states to implement spending cutbacks, with serious costs for incumbents' popularity. For democracies, economic adjustment is particularly difficult because most necessary reforms (e.g., reducing spending, raising taxes, privatizing, and deregulating) require adherence to the law (Haggard and Kaufman 1995; IDB 2005). Presidents must seek legislative approval for reforms, which in turn requires support from political parties and their constituents, all of whom are highly addicted to oil rents and are thus reform adverse. An autocracy, on the other hand, can more easily get away with ruling by decree – or at least with writing off certain constituencies. This gives authoritarian regimes a greater probability of surviving oil busts and may be one reason that Przeworski, Alvarez, Cheibub, and Limongi (2000) find that autocracies survive economic crises more often than do democracies.

Checks on the Executive Branch. Facing the urgency of addressing a severe
fiscal crisis together with a congress/society that is unwilling to accept the cost
of adjustment, presidents in democratic petro-states will feel tempted to carry
out profound reforms by fiat, often circumventing existing democratic channels
(e.g., by governing through decrees, bypassing consultations with parties; see
O'Donnell 1994). Insofar as they push executives to concentrate more power
and consult less, oil shocks have the potential of eroding levels of democracy.
Many times in democracies, societal demand for more concentration of power
in the hands of the executive can increase during economic bad times. For
instance, a public opinion survey of Venezuelans between 1995–98 – a period
of poor economic performance (Corrales 2000) – shows that the proportion
who supported "government intervention in the economy" skyrocketed across
all income groups (from 29 percent to 80 percent of upper-income Venezuelans
and from 68 percent to 86 percent among lower strata). The proportion supporting "radical political changes" expanded as well, most remarkably among
the upper classes, from 8 percent to 17 percent (Canache 2004). In dictator-
ships, oil busts hinder the capacity of presidents to be generous (i.e., to spend
heavily on clientelism) but do not technically cause an erosion of democracy,
because the starting point was not democracy. Demand for radical change
across the population may very well increase, especially among cost bearers,
but the disaffected groups will lack institutional avenues to channel their discontent or will fear the costs of protesting.

Societal Response. In democracies, the politics of adjustment engender two
spheres of political conflict. One axis of conflict occurs between the state and
cost bearers, those societal actors who bear the brunt of economic adjustment
(Nelson 1989; Przeworski 1991; Haggard and Webb 1994; Eckstein 2001).
The second axis of conflict is between the president and the political organizations that resist the executive's efforts to concentrate more power (Geddes
1995). The rise of either delegative powers or party-neglecting policies produces a severe clash between the democratic forces of society and the state. In
autocracies, adjustment will engender mostly the former type of conflict. The
latter type of conflict is less significant, or, rather, would have either predated
the oil shock or would have been resolved already (if the dictatorship had
consolidated power).

Overall Outcome. For democracies, especially fragile ones, the most likely
overall outcome of an oil bust is an increased risk of regime decay or collapse.
All institutions come under strain. This explains Venezuelan politics between
the 1980s and the early 2000s. Economic adjustment generated policy paralysis and muddling through. State-society conflict centered on citizen protests
against economic adjustments, especially among the urban poor, and top-down
efforts to reform the economy. Traditional parties suffered voter defection and
dealignment, driven by rising voter discontent with professional politicians.
Because the economic crisis lasted long (from 1979 to 2001), resentment about

the status quo and politicians became especially acute. Nobody likes austerity or politicians who appear immobile before crises. From almost every angle, the politics of adjustment in democratic petro-states risks jeopardizing the quality and institutional foundations of democracy.

For autocracies, the outcomes of an oil bust can go in one of two ways. One route is for the executive branch to survive in office, maybe even become stronger. This can occur if the executive branch intensifies the authoritarian features of the regime, repressing protesting cost bearers and preventing the defection of cronies. The other possible outcome is for the executive not to survive in office. This occurs if cost bearers become too hard to repress or cronies abandon the regime.

Which of these two outcomes is more likely in the case of a prolonged oil bust under Chávez, whose regime currently sits somewhere between democracy and autocracy? Many analysts contend that an oil bust will automatically terminate populist spending, thereby disarming Chávez. However, I suggest a different answer. First, even if austerity provokes protests by cost bearers, it could very well be that Chávez will find himself with a stronger capacity to repress than in 2002, given the regime's enormous spending on weapons, the rise of military training (for domestic insurrection), the creation of urban militias, and the increase in loyalism within the armed forces. Second, the regime controls important institutions that will side with the incumbent and not the opposition (the Congress, the courts, the regulatory agencies, and the expanding state-controlled media). Third, and more important, I have argued that the support for the regime does not rest entirely on clientelism. The regime also relies on cronies, who receive tangible benefits, and on other supporters, who receive intangible rewards (impunity, radical ideology). It is not clear that an oil bust will jeopardize the regime's capacity to provide these two other forms of rewards. Populist spending might need to be curtailed, but corruption spending (to maintain the cronies) can remain affordable, and intangible resources such as impunity from corruption and radical ideologies to seduce activists can endure even in austerity periods. And now that the opposition has won in five states, Caracas, and Maracaibo, the government can apply austerity measures to those jurisdictions, thereby saving resources to be channeled to true allies elsewhere.

CONCLUSION

"Revolution" can mean two things: radical changes or repeating cycles. Chávez's Bolivarian Revolution encompasses both meanings, but in different realms. In politics, Chávez has introduced radical changes (e.g., greater restrictions on and obstacles for the opposition, less transparency in government, heightened power concentration). In economics, on the other hand, he has repeated old vices (dependence on oil for state revenues, politically minded statism verging on classic ISI, and ax-relax-collapse economic policy cycles).

Economic mismanagement has different impacts on different regimes. In a democratic setting – when the political regime is less restrictive – economic management has a detrimental effect on the political regime, leading to corruption, party collusion, voter distress, and ultimately regime unraveling. By the 1990s, few citizens found their democracy to be credible, responsive, or worth defending. Under the new political regime – characterized by political restrictions on the opposition and excessive presidential discretionalism – the impact of this economic approach may be less damaging to the regime: Oil dependence, statism, and ax-relax-collapse may not be that lethal for an authoritarian political system. During an oil boom, economic agents in an authoritarian system are tempted to bandwagon with the state, because siding with the opposition offers no payoffs. During a collapse phase, the president can repress the cost bearers (if they protest), blame exogenous actors for the economic misfortune, and simultaneously offer cronies and ideologues much of what they like – impunity and radical ideology. These steps can yield regime survival rather than regime demise. A competitive autocracy like Chávez's, facing the need to implement economic adjustment, will surely spend less on clientelism, but he might still be able to invest in the other pillars that keep him in power. An oil bust may force a competitive autocracy such as Venezuela's to lose its "competitive" label but not its "autocracy" designation. The paradox of the Chávez regime is that its rise and consolidation was very dependent on oil flows, but its sustainability in office may not depend as much on oil.

3

The Challenge of Progressive Change under Evo Morales

George Gray Molina

Evo Morales's presidency has caught the attention of scholars and activists in Latin America.[1] Alain Touraine (2007) has remarked that the Bolivian left charts a "third way" with respect to both Chile under Michelle Bachelet and Venezuela under Hugo Chávez. Typologies of governance in Latin America place Bolivia on the radical wing of existing political projects (Arnson 2007; Roberts 2007). Morales's own personal trajectory and his government's strong link to social and indigenous movements have been scrutinized and contrasted with other Latin American left-wing political projects (see Stefanoni and do Alto 2006; Molina 2007). Despite the sharp political focus on Bolivia, less attention has been paid to policy outcomes and outputs or to the achievements of the administration's first term in office. This essay looks at this less-examined side of the Bolivian experiment in postneoliberal politics.

Many contentious and unresolved issues frame the Bolivian policy agenda in the present, including the nationalization of natural resources, fiscal and political decentralization, and indigenous peoples' rights, among others (Crabtree and Whitehead 2008). I argue that the Morales policy agenda, although clearly postneoliberal in the chronological sense, may not be sufficiently postneoliberal in raising labor and welfare standards at home and transforming Bolivia's role in the global economy. This is a predicament shared with most Bolivian governments of the democratic era. If the past is any guide, however, there are unlikely to be any technical fixes to Bolivia's intractable problems in the future (Gray Molina 2009). Progressive change is sought and resisted on contested terrain. This dimension of the debate is often misunderstood in the Bolivian context. Opponents of Morales tend to characterize the regime as being too political, often missing the point over how social and economic change actually happens. On the other hand, proponents of Morales tend to minimize the importance of shared standards of

[1] The author would like to thank Milenka Ocampo and Rodrigo Arce for their assistance.

legitimacy and legality, and sometimes question the very existence of a democratic opposition. Both sides malign the other side's politics. Contrary to these views, the historical record shows that both contestation and pacted politics have been significant drivers of social and economic change over the past three decades – before and after Evo Morales – as is evidenced by improvements in long-run standards of well-being (see Gray Molina and Purser in press).

What has been accomplished policywise in the first Morales administration? To what extent is the Bolivian policy experiment new, and to what extent does it build upon past policy initiatives? Does progressive social and economic change emerge slowly and cumulatively or unevenly and rapidly? How do contested politics fit into the story? To answer these questions, the chapter addresses four dimensions of the postneoliberal challenge in Bolivia. First, I describe the political tensions that have framed the Morales administration's first term in office. This includes a look at the debate over autonomy, the new constitution, and disputes over the democratic rules of the game. Second, I focus on key economic and social policy decisions in Evo Morales's four years in government. Third, I analyze some of the policy challenges and opportunities that have not been taken up by Morales and could be regarded as the core of an alternative progressive policy agenda. Finally, I conclude with some thoughts on the politics of change for the future.

POLARIZED POLITICS

Procedural Differences: Disagreeing on the Rules

Evo Morales's landslide electoral victory in December 2005 was based on a broad coalition of peasant, indigenous, and urban middle-class voters. With 54 percent of the popular vote, the Movimiento al Socialismo (MAS) transformed the social and political landscape in Bolivia. The traditional political parties of the 1980s and 1990s – Movimiento Nacionalista Revolucionario (MNR), Movimiento de Izquierda Revolucionaria (MIR), and Acción Democrática Nacionalista (ADN) – and offshoots of the traditional parties, Unidad Nacional (UN) and Poder Democrático y Social (Podemos), earned less than a third of all votes. With more than 100 parliamentarians of a total of 157 and the support of some of the most vocal social movements in the country, the Morales administration initiated its term with the highest level of public support of any government in Bolivia's democratic era.

Despite the electoral landslide, Bolivia was engulfed between 2006 and 2009 in a relatively protracted social and political impasse over the rules of the game that should guide political change. The discrediting of traditional political parties after the 2005 elections left the political system with a new modus operandi, less reliant on pacted democracy and more reliant on a zero-sum game of political positioning. The new modus operandi has, as suggested by many observers, depended upon a homegrown mix of democratic procedures and institutions and the strength of social and regional movements on the streets.[2] A typical political negotiation is a three-act drama involving, first, a show of strength from social and regional movements on the streets; second, forced negotiation; and third, a continued postponement of substantive agreements on the issues of the day (land, autonomies, constitution, and intergovernmental relations, among others). The consequences of this are both a devaluation of democratic procedures and a weakening of public debate on substantive policy issues.

Four procedural impasses have defined the current political period. The first impasse concerned the rules for constitutional approval. A two-thirds majority rule was included in the compromise law that convoked the Constituent Assembly in 2006. It was meant as a safeguard that would induce negotiations between all parties in the assembly and deliver a majority report that could be submitted for referendum approval at the end of the process. As deadlines expired in June 2007, opposition parties denounced their exclusion from both majority and minority reports in many commissions. A crisis over the procedural rules ensued.

The two-thirds rule was interpreted by the MAS as being relevant only for the final constitutional text and not the commission reports. Most legal analysts agreed that the MAS interpretation was politically biased (see Knaudt 2006; Ordenes 2006). As the 6 August deadline approached, both sides decided to draft a new law extending the assembly's mandate another 90 days until December. The new law explicitly included the two-thirds majority rule, but it also included a two-step referendum rule that implicitly made the majority rule moot. The entry referendum would consider dissensus questions on the final text, but that meant possibly submitting an entire constitutional text (minority or majority) for approval. The exit referendum would ratify the whole text.

As the extension expired in December, conflict erupted in Sucre over the issue of the capital city. The question over whether to locate the country's capital in Sucre or in La Paz drove a wedge within the MAS but did not ultimately become a national issue. As police clashed with university students, leaving two dead on 3 November 2007, the assembly approved a general version of the constitutional text, postponing detailed treatment until February 2008 in the city of Oruro. Both approvals were done in the absence of the political opposition, despite overtures by the UN and MNR to sign a compromise text. The Oruro session approved not only the draft text but also a dissensus question for the entry referendum. This unilateral approval process set the stage for future confrontations during the constitutional approval referendum in 2009.

The second impasse involved the referenda for the approval of autonomous statutes of Santa Cruz, Tarija, Beni, and Pando, departments that voted in favor of autonomy in July 2006. The autonomy question was initially part of

[2] See Calderón and Gamarra 2004 for a discussion of hybrid mechanisms in the 2000–03 crisis period.

the Constituent Assembly debate. The Commission on Autonomies delivered majority and minority reports that recognized departmental autonomies as well as municipal, regional, and indigenous autonomies. The watering down of the Santa Cruz proposal was perceived as threatening the road map laid down in the assemblies (*cabildos*) of 2006 and 2007. Various rounds of negotiations led by President Morales (in January) and by Vice President García Linera (in February) failed both to bridge the gap between the draft constitution and statutes and to provide a legal framework that might deal with both issues.

The regions called for departmental referenda that would reposition their demands on a national level. The first referendum vote in Santa Cruz ratified the "yes" agenda with 85.4 percent of valid votes and a 37.9 percent abstention rate, some fifteen points above the average rates in past elections (Corte Departmental Electoral de Santa Cruz 2008).[3] The referendum found resistance in rural areas of Santa Cruz and popular neighborhoods in the city, with episodes of violence and burning of ballot boxes. On balance, however, the Santa Cruz referendum moved political momentum decisively toward the regional agenda. Regional referenda in Beni, Pando, and Tarija all approved departmental statutes between May and July 2008.

Most analysts agree that the Santa Cruz statutes are illegal under both the old and new constitution (see Alarcón 2008; Barrios 2008; and Böhrt, Chavez, and Torres 2008). The National Electoral Court refused to recognize the results in the regions in what has become a political battlefield for electoral legitimacy. The Santa Cruz Electoral Court presided over the referendum, causing a schism in the court. The courts of Beni, Pando, and Tarija followed Santa Cruz in defying the national court. Questions about the legality of both the regional referenda and the approval of the new constitutional text point to a weakness in the institutions that preside over constitutional judgments and the electoral process.

The third impasse involved a lack of agreement over appointments to the Constitutional Tribunal and the National Electoral Court. The Constitutional Tribunal, which plays a key role in a highly contested political atmosphere, was paralyzed for more than a year for lack of judges. Congress was summoned to appoint four new judges to complete a five-judge court. The tribunal suspended work in 2007 and stopped 2,313 cases involving 15,438 people. The key decisions, of course, relate to the Constituent Assembly and referenda. The interruption of the tribunal's work is only part of a larger paralysis in judicial reform that also requires political compromise (Tribunal Constitucional 2008; Rodríguez Veltzé 2008).

Something similar happened with the National Electoral Court. The court has worked with three officials out of five for more than a year, one of whom is a presidential appointee. The impasse over court appointments and accusations of partiality toward the government have affected the constitutional referendum results as well as the buildup toward the 2009 general elections. The decisive

---

[3] See Romero 2003 for an analysis of abstention rates in past Bolivian elections.

MAS victory in December 2009 is likely to lead to regional accusations against the national court, whereas a decisive regional victory will provoke accusations from the government against the regional courts. This is all the more sensitive as the electoral schedule is one of the few processes currently agreed upon by the government and the opposition.

The fourth disagreement involved the approval of the new constitution. In August 2008, President Morales called for a referendum on the draft constitution and an election of departmental councilors, subprefects, and prefects. The January 2009 referendum and election delivered a strong victory to President Morales, with 61 percent of voters approving the new constitution. It again placed the resolution of potential conflict in the hands of electors and bypassed the Congress, political parties, and regional opposition. Most analysts agree that an unfortunate effect of multiple referenda is that they corner the opposition and devalue the role of political and popular representation.

The approval of the constitution gave new impetus to President Morales, who called for general elections in December 2009. The new constitution provides for one successive reelection. Because Morales won the presidential contest with 62.5 percent of the vote, this means at least a nine-year period of government, transforming what used to be regarded as a fickle and highly unstable political environment. The procedural impasse is thus about the rules that sustain political power in Bolivia, including the duration of a long-term political project. Even on these balance-of-power criteria, however, the key question is political survival. Is a hegemonic political project sustainable? The approval of the MAS draft constitution is likely to be the last electoral battle played out by the old rules of the game.

Substantive Differences: New Constitution and Draft Statutes

Beyond the procedural standoff, the political process in Bolivia also mirrors substantive disagreements over policymaking. Perhaps the starkest substantive differences are between the new constitution approved by national referendum in 2009 and the departmental autonomy statutes approved by regional referenda in four departments. From a political point of view, these are confrontational texts meant to annul each other in the political arena rather than to coexist. From a technical point of view, however, there are some similarities and some common ground that point to potential compromise in the future. They both address the critical issues of any viable political project in Bolivia. What are the key differences between these political projects?

First, they reveal a substantive disagreement over the plurinational nature of the Bolivian state, its laws, institutions, and policies. The new constitution defines – in the very first article – that the Bolivian state is "unitarian social, plurinational and communitarian, free, independent, sovereign, democratic, intercultural, and decentralized with autonomies." Articles two and three add that "the people" include all social classes, nations, and indigenous peoples in Bolivia and that "nations and indigenous peoples" have the right to self-determination and self-government, including the legal recognition of territorial rights. These three articles represent a substantial reform of the 1967 and 1938 constitutions, which framed both the national revolution of the 1950s and the democratic transition of the 1980s.

The key disagreement, however, is related to political power rather than conceptual hairsplitting. The departmental statutes conceive of the Bolivian state as a composite of peoples within "regions"; under the new constitution, they are nations under "peoples." In the first case, the regions are the political subjects that make democratic self-government possible. In the second case, the people – organized in nations, indigenous communities, and social movements – are the subjects that make democratic self-government viable. The nation imagined by the National Revolution in the 1950s has been replaced by regions and peoples in the current debate. As social and political conflict increases over procedural and substantive issues, the question of who the people are has become critical for both government and opposition. In addition, Article 11 of the new constitution defines three systems of political participation or representation to articulate the demands and aspirations of the people: direct democracy via Constituent Assembly, referenda, and *cabildos*; representative democracy through free and open elections; and communitarian democracy through indigenous and customary forms of selection of social and political leaders. The choice of three systems – rather than one with three forms of representation – is likely to strain the current debate over the nature of Bolivian democracy.

Second, the new constitution and departmental statutes display a strong disagreement over natural resources rights, property, and uses, including land rights and uses. Articles 348–58 of the new constitution define natural resource policy based on two conditions: First, that all natural resources are "indivisible and direct property" of the Bolivian state and, second, that the state will define the conditions under which natural resources are used or jointly exploited with private or communitarian partners, subject to social control defined by the constitution in previous articles. Articles 393–403 describe the scope of land rights and uses. The most obvious issue of dispute is the definition of land rights, which is restricted in terms of land size and uses the "social and economic function" caveat of previous constitutions. The key distinction with respect to past constitutions, however, is that the "social function" is defined in terms of "laboring the land," and the economic function is defined in terms of "the sustainable use of land in productive activities . . . benefiting society, collective interests, and private owners." Previous legislation defined social and economic functions based on taxation and land use. Articles 6 and 103 of the autonomy statute of Santa Cruz also include a "social and economic function" proviso, defined regionally by departmental legislation. In the end, the land and natural resource dispute is also a political one, likely to shape future conflicts over legislation and administration of land in Bolivia.

The politics of land use and rights drive conflict at the local and regional level in Santa Cruz, Tarija, and Chuquisaca. After more than a decade of land titling, the dispute over fiscal land, colonization, and indigenous peoples and communities has increased. A long-running extractivist land and forest policy has tended to exacerbate conflict over the first link of the natural resource chain (UNDP 2008). Most analysts agree that the current fight over natural resources and land rights is both about rights (landowners vs. other social actors) and about uses (extractivist uses vs. environmentally sustainable uses). The Bolivian economy, based on natural gas, minerals, and soybeans, is caught in a primary natural resource trap that feeds more political polarization. This is an issue that cuts across politics and economics and defines the new pattern of development and conflict in Bolivia.

Third, the two political projects demonstrate a radical disagreement over autonomies and decentralization of the state. The new constitution describes a four-tier state based on departmental, regional, municipal, and indigenous autonomies. The autonomy model devised in the constitution is designed to create checks and balances above and beyond the departmental level. Again, as this is precisely the key wedge issue between government and opposition, the draft constitution and statutes mirror antagonistic political projects. Articles 270–306 describe the organization of the Bolivian state under the four tiers. The plurinational state has exclusive competency over forty-two responsibilities, including natural resource policy, land policy, forestry policy, taxation, police and armed forces, as well as more obvious areas, such as foreign policy. The new constitution shares thirteen responsibilities with decentralized governments and delegates twelve responsibilities to departmental and regional levels and twenty to indigenous territorial entities. Most subnational responsibilities have to do with planning and administration of central government competencies.

The autonomy statute of Santa Cruz reverses the areas of national and departmental responsibility in almost mirror fashion. Articles 6–8 of the draft statutes define forty-three exclusive responsibilities for the departmental level, including natural resource policy, land policy, and taxation in the region. The statutes add another dozen joint responsibilities, including international treaties that involve the department and police and public security responsibilities. The statutes include a "preferential application" clause (Article 10) that regulates how national legislation is applied at the departmental level and a "constitutional control" clause (Article 13) that elevates disagreements between national and subnational responsibilities to constitutional disputes. Perhaps the most controversial aspect of the statutes is the quasi-federal figure of a departmental legislature that drafts laws and decrees for departmental application. The legislative quality of subnational governments in Bolivia was hotly disputed in the Constituent Assembly and is likely to challenge the legal hierarchy implicit in the draft constitution.

The three substantive disagreements described previously – on the plurinational nature of the Bolivian state, on natural resource and land policy, and on autonomies and decentralization – bridge political and economic domains.

The following sections focus more explicitly on the economic challenge of changing the neoliberal model in Bolivia and setting the stage for an alternative development pattern.

CHANGING THE NEOLIBERAL MODEL

An Eclectic Policy Agenda

Evo Morales inaugurated his term with a broad mandate for change. The democratic revolution promised in the electoral campaign made way for a new policy agenda, described in a National Development Plan (NDP) in June 2006. The NDP was the first official document to dissect policy design and implementation issues and propose a road map for social, economic, and political change. The Ministry of Development Planning drafted the document and coordinated discussions within government and with civil society groups throughout 2006. Reactions to the document were mixed. Opposition analysts from the right described it as a "nostalgic return to the past" (Fundación Milenio 2006) and "ready for the garbage can of good intentions" (Oporto 2007). Sympathetic analysts from the left saw it as a "watered-down development program," tainted by "continuation of failed neo-liberal policies of the past" (CEDLA 2006; Orellana 2006).

Two aspects of the NDP are worth underlining, as they relate to decisions that were eventually taken in the economic and social policy arena. First, the NDP is a relatively eclectic development plan that borrows freely from economic structuralism, dependency theory, indigenous multiculturalism, social-democratic protection policies, and neoliberal monetary and exchange rate policy. The plan underscores the need to "change the primary-export pattern of development" inherited from a neocolonial and neoliberal past (Government of Bolivia 2006). The policy record is described in terms of a relatively coherent succession of development stages, cushioned by the whims of international donors and academic fashion: Social protection initiatives in the 1980s followed by human development policies in the mid-1980s extended to poverty reduction targets in the 1990s and complemented by Millennium Development Goals (MDGs) at the dawn of the new century.

Second, the NDP focuses specifically on hydrocarbons and anticipates the nationalization policies of 2006. The role of natural gas is strategic and is perhaps the cornerstone of the new development agenda. The focus on gas and hydrocarbons runs, paradoxically, against the grain of changing the primary-export pattern of development. The key imperative, it would seem, is to diversify the sources of exports and improve labor and environmental standards to compete not on the basis of cheap labor and plentiful natural resources but on the basis of high value added, increased productivity, and fair livelihood conditions. In the course of two years, one strategic objective (increasing state participation in hydrocarbons) has tended to overshadow the other, admittedly more important, objective (changing the primary-export pattern of development). The implementation of the plan has revealed tensions between "changing the model" and "changing the pattern" of development.

Beyond the ins and outs of the NDP, what seems most important is to evaluate the sequence of policy decisions and actions adopted in the first four years of the Morales government. Between 2006 and 2009, the Morales administration achieved a number of the objectives described in the government plan in a three-part sequence: First, by increasing government takeover of hydrocarbons revenues (nationalization of gas) in 2006; second, by increasing public investment, both centralized and decentralized, in 2007; and third, by upscaling existing social transfer mechanisms for children and the elderly (via the Bono Juancito Pinto and Renta Dignidad) in late 2007 and early 2008. The policy actions that were taken, however, draw attention to the limitations faced by the Morales administration, which struggles with weak administrative capacity and the need to show tangible results.

Nationalization and Increased Government Take

The Morales administration's National Development Plan reads: "The proposal for change consists of: recovering state sovereignty over hydrocarbon resources, strengthening the state-owned hydrocarbons company as the key agent in the chain of production, granting the state the power to make decisions about production quantities and sale prices, defining new rules of the game through new contracts, and attracting new revenues for the Bolivian state" (Government of Bolivia 2006: 100).

The nationalization of Bolivian natural gas was achieved under two different administrations, with a law approved during the Mesa administration in July 2005 (Law 3058) and a decree passed by the Morales administration in May 2006 (Decree 28701). Neither legal instrument nationalizes in the conventional or historical sense – via expropriation or changes in property rights. Both measures increased the government's take by an order of magnitude: Law 3058 increased government participation from 18 to 50 percent of production value, whereas Decree 28701 increased this figure to up to 82 percent and included a renegotiation of contracts with close to a dozen multinational companies. Taken together, however, the two measures represent a pendulum swing with respect to the past. This is the third time that the Bolivian state has nationalized hydrocarbons in the past century. The two previous occasions involved Standard Oil (1937) and Gulf Oil (1969).

Two aspects of the nationalization process are worth considering in closer detail. The first is the new structure of the government's take. Government participation in hydrocarbons has four sources: the first is an 18 percent royalty over the value of production; the second is a 32 percent Direct Hydrocarbons Tax; the third is a payment to the state-owned Bolivian gas company, Yacimientos Petrolíferos Fiscales Bolivianos (YPFB), of recoverable costs, negotiated on a contract-by-contract basis; and the fourth is the distribution of the remainder as shared utilities between YPFB and the operator based on a formula that accounts for new and depreciated capital investments, the price of natural gas, and volumes of production (Medinacelli 2007a). Under the new contracts, the government's take fluctuates between 67 percent of gross production value (at US$1 dollar per million BTUs) and 75 percent of gross production value (if prices reach US$4.5 dollars per million BTUs) (Medinacelli 2007b). Under the new contractual terms, hydrocarbons operators pay a little more than the 50 percent negotiated in Law 3058 and a little less than the 82 percent included in Decree 28701.

It is also worth considering the content of the new contracts signed by multinational corporations in April 2007 on a contract-by-contract basis. The new contracts are hybrid instruments that combine elements of shared production and operational contracts with YPFB (Zaratti 2007). Government participation in benefits is similar to the level for contracts signed in Peru, whereby government participation starts once private companies recover their operational costs and capital investments. This provision has been seen as a loophole in the nationalization process because it removes risk from multinational companies in their calculations of future investment decisions (Medinacelli 2007b).

The increase in government take and the new contracts have had at least two positive and three negative impacts over time. The first positive effect is that, due to extraordinary increases in prices and better bilateral negotiation with Argentina and Brazil, Bolivian GDP topped US$10 billion in 2006, more than US$2 billion of which was due to the hydrocarbons sector. The second positive effect is a significant increase in government revenues accruing from the hydrocarbons sector, reaching US$967 million in 2007, about twice as much as Bolivia received in total foreign aid (donations plus credit). On the downside, the price effect of exports weighs heavily over the production effect in explaining additional export revenues. In 2006, average prices were 5.4 times greater than prices eight years earlier and three times greater than three years earlier. Second, the gas sector in Bolivia has become increasingly uncertain with respect to new investments in exploration and higher export volumes. This has been evident in the 2008 negotiations with Brazil and Argentina, in which Bolivia has not been able to fulfill existing contracts. Third, to the extent that the global gas market is expanding, Bolivia needs to look beyond the regional market, including the Pacific basin, to improve its leverage position over regional competitors and regional demand.

Expanded Social Transfers and Increased Public Investment

Additional revenues from the hydrocarbons sector finance social transfer programs to school-age children (Bono Juancito Pinto) and the elderly (Renta Dignidad) and account for more than US$240 million, or approximately 2 percent of Bolivian GDP in 2007. The transfers reach close to 2 million children and approximately 730,000 men and women over the age of sixty-five. The Bono Juancito Pinto is modeled on the Bono Escuela program of the city of El Alto and similar programs in Brazil (Bolsa Família) and Mexico (Progresa), and the Renta Dignidad is an expansion of the Bonosol payment implemented with the capitalization of public companies in the 1990s. The difference from the Bonosol is in how the transfer is funded. For nine years, funding for the payment came from utilities from capitalized companies and internal debt, whereas it is now paid with hydrocarbons taxes and royalty payments to the regions.

The Juancito Pinto payment was designed to increase school attendance and reduce desertion, and it has been in place since November 2006. In 2007, more than 1.32 million children enrolled in public schools from first to sixth grade, in alternative and technical education schools, and in special education programs. The program expanded to 2 million children in grades first to eight, by the end of 2009. Each child receives an annual payment of 200 Bolivianos (about US$26), subject to an annual evaluation confirming that the child is attending school. The sources of the payment are YPFB (53 percent), the Treasury (33 percent), and COMIBOL (13 percent). In 2009, the annual cost of the Juancito Pinto payment was expected to be about US$40 million.

The Renta Dignidad is an annual payment to 600,000 Bolivians over the age of sixty-five who have no retirement income and an additional 130,000 Bolivians who do receive a retirement payment. The amount paid to those without retirement income is 2,400 Bolivianos (about US$320), and the amount paid to salaried retirees is 1,800 Bolivianos (about US$240). The source of the payment is highly controversial. In 2008, it amounted to about US$55.6 million paid by the prefectures and US$134.4 million paid by the Treasury, municipalities, universities, and capitalized enterprises. The deduction of prefectural funds has been contested by civic committees and prefects, who argue it amounts to a 38 percent reduction in their IDH transfers, or about 8 percent of their total funds. In 2009, the total annual cost of the Renta Dignidad was about US$200 million.

Beyond transfers, public investment has increased significantly over the past two years. Total public investment has increased from US$629 million in 2005 to US$1.1 billion in 2007 and nearly US$1.9 billion in 2009. Most of the new investments have been channeled into roads and infrastructure, which made up to close to 60 percent of total investments in 2007. Social investment has decreased over this period to less than 30 percent of total investments in 2007. Although the public investment boom has had a multiplier effect in construction, services, and transportation, there is still a healthy debate over whether and how public investment projects increase long-run competitiveness and human development capabilities, as well as create the conditions for better jobs. Much of the decentralization agenda focuses on this issue at the local and departmental level.

A recent simulation by Paz Arauco (2008) estimates the long-term impact of the current distribution of hydrocarbons taxes and royalties over time. Given the uneven distribution of current revenues (departments like Pando receive on average seven times the per capita rate of Oruro), the human development gap between the richest and poorest departments will increase rather than decrease until 2015, putting off the achievement of the poverty, health, water, and sanitation MDGs by close to a decade. The inertia of past policies and rent redistribution has not been overturned in the current debate over decentralization and fiscal revenues.

CHALLENGES BEYOND THE NEOLIBERAL MODEL

The Morales administration's National Development Plan proposes changing not just the model of development, but also the pattern of development. It states: "The key objective of the Plan is, therefore, to suppress the factors that cause inequality and social exclusion in the country, which means changing the primary resource export-driven pattern of development and the foundations of colonialism and neoliberalism that sustain it" (Government of Bolivia 2006: 7).

Beyond changes to the model, has Bolivia been able to change its pattern of development? Has the Bolivian economy gained global markets and created employment at home in ways that are *not* based on cheap labor and abundant natural resources? This is a difficult question to answer, because the global evidence would seem to favor a tendency for natural resource-based economies to diverge over the past three decades (Pritchett 1997; Milanovic 2005). And although a look at average Bolivian growth, investment, and productivity figures for the last thirty years paints a bleak picture, there are some pockets of growth that are not based on lowering labor and environmental standards (Gray Molina and Wanderley 2007). It is important, however, to evaluate whether pockets of growth can be replicated and whether all pockets are good for long-term sustainable and fair growth. This effort, I believe, is at the core of an alternative left-wing policy for Bolivia and other Latin American economies in need of diversification policies.

The Bolivian economy can be described as a three-gear economy. The first gear is the traditional mining and hydrocarbons economy that has attracted foreign investment over the century, explained approximately half of observed per capita growth since the 1950s, and provided a modest fiscal cushion over the long run. The shortcomings of this gear, however, are well known. The extractive sectors have functioned as enclaves for long spells, isolated from domestic markets and short on job creation. The second gear is an incipient nontraditional export sector, emergent since the mid-1980s. This sector is mostly based on natural resources but has added value with light manufacturing products (leather, jewelry, wood furniture, textiles, and agro-industrial goods). It is the core of a diversified, export-oriented, and broad-based economy. The third gear is a massive nontradable service sector that includes an urban informal sector and a growing transportation sector. This has traditionally been a low-productivity sector of the economy but is closely tied to the competitiveness of the emerging nontraditional export economy. This final gear, the peasant, nontradable, agricultural, and rural economy, is the lowest-productivity sector of the Bolivian economy. Despite accelerated urbanization, the peasant, rural economy continues to account for almost a third of the Bolivian labor force.

Bolivia's Position in the Global Economy

The Bolivian economy is a low-growth, low-investment, and low-productivity economy located in the heart of a relatively low-growth region. Despite the overall gloomy picture, there are pockets of growth that are exceptions to the rule. A few investment opportunities linked to natural resources paid off well in the 1980s and late 1990s and averaged growth rates even higher than the Latin American averages. Some gained market share in a context of expanding markets, thus improving regional and global competitiveness in market niches. Which commodities are these? How did they fare on a regional and global level? Did they fizzle out, or do they constitute a pocket of export success within a rather dismal national economy? Figure 3.1 presents information on overall exports from 1980 to 2005 and tracks episodes of nontraditional commodity booms in Bolivia.

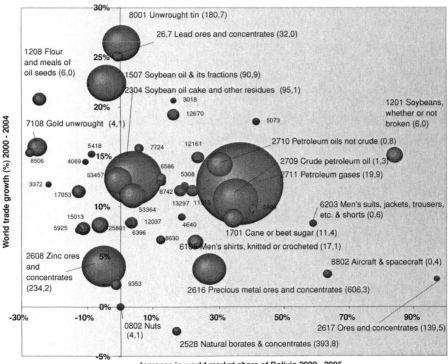

FIGURE 3.1. Pockets of Growth in the Bolivian Economy, 2000–2005. *Source:* Gray Molina and Wanderley 2007.

Three filters are used to identify high-return products in the tradable sector for the period 2000–05. The first and broadest excludes export products for which Bolivia has preferential market access but does not export any goods. Bolivia exports only 503 of 1,223 products for which it has preferential trade access. The intuition behind this filter is that there are hundreds of products for which the high structural costs of the Bolivian economy are a nonstarter. The second filter excludes export products that are not in expanding regional or world markets. Of 503 products, 193 are in expanding markets. The third filter estimates Balassa indices for exports in expanding markets, thus revealing Bolivian comparative advantage in world markets. Of 193 Bolivian products in expanding markets, there are only 76 products that show Balassa indices higher than one.

Two findings of this descriptive exercise are worth mentioning. First, the core of successful export products is highly concentrated in natural resource exports. This includes both traditional exports, such as natural gas, tin, zinc, and other metals and ores, as well as nontraditional products, such as soybean, wood, and jewelry products. Second, the core of successful Bolivian products is highly correlated with successful episodes of worldwide economic expansion. Many of the pockets of growth in the Bolivian economy are not based on in-country increases in productivity but on across-country increases in prices and quantity demand.

Bolivia is, on both counts, stuck in a narrow-based economic development pattern that depends on primary natural resource exports and is highly vulnerable to changes in world commodity prices. Gray Molina and Araníbar (2006) have quantified some of the costs of such an economy in terms of growth, employment, and poverty reduction. The UNDP (2005) elaborates on a number of additional effects of a narrow-based economy, including high levels of inequality and low levels of domestic market linkages, which make poverty reduction barely responsive to increased economic growth. Over the twenty-five-year period between 1980 and 2005, no Bolivian products gained market share in expanding markets. In other words, no Bolivian products remained continuous champions over a twenty-five-year period. Over a fifteen-year period, however, there were fifteen champion export products, including the wood, jewelry, and soybean sectors analyzed in the following section.

MISSED OPPORTUNITIES: FAIR, ORGANIC, AND BIOTRADE,
AND ALLIANCES BETWEEN PRODUCERS

If Bolivian growth pockets are mostly in the wrong kind of trade niches – in price-sensitive, low-skilled labor pockets – what are the prospects for moving into better pockets? A recent study by the UNDP (2008) suggests that prospects are rather good for a small economy with enormous advantages in the fair, organic, and biotrade niche markets. Many of the advantages, including high rates of species endemism, high biodiversity, low rates of pesticide and insecticide use, high volumes of uncontaminated natural water sources, and low rates of primary forest deforestation, among others, are related to underdevelopment over the past century.

The discounted rates of return for products such as organic cacao, quinoa, coffee, ecotourism, environmental services, and some tropical forestry products are higher than rates of return for traditional commodities, including most mining, soybean production, cattle ranching, and even coca leaf production. The move from traditional export products to nontraditional ecofriendly and fair-trade market niches is not an easy one, but it already accounts for more than US$300 million in exports, another US$100 million in services, and more than fifty thousand sources of better-paid and more sustainable jobs. The dilemma of the alternative natural resource markets often relates to scale and opportunity, where leaders often enjoy market and price advantages over latecomers. Bolivia needs to take a leadership position in developing these trade markets to avoid fallacy of composition effects in saturated markets.

Most economists agree that for a small and relatively open economy with little industrial development like the Bolivian economy, the move from traditional to organic, bio-, and fair-trade labor and environmental standards will on balance attract rather than dissuade investors with a long-term and ecofriendly investment profile. The important impact, however, is not so much in expanding and diversifying exports but in improving labor opportunities at the bottom of the value-added chain, where most workers and peasant, indigenous, and community producers are under the poverty line.

If the first missed opportunity under the Morales administration has been concentrating too much on gas and too little on alternative natural resources, the second missed opportunity has been not moving aggressively enough in incorporating large and small producers in policy initiatives, access to credit, technical assistance, and access to international markets. The Bolivian tradable sector suffers from a critical mass problem. There are only about one thousand exporters in Bolivia, employing close to 30,000 workers and close to 300,000 indirect sources of labor (see UDAPE et al. 2006). This means only one in ten working-age Bolivians is linked to the tradable sector, either substituting imports, exporting goods and services, or running contraband back and forth between the formal and informal economies. The lack of a critical mass of job creation means that Bolivia follows a dismal path of impoverishing growth. At 4 percent growth, absolute poverty increases by about 130,000 every year, reaching about 170,000 per year when the economy slows down to 2 percent growth. At the average growth rate of the past 20 years, the inertial exit rate of poverty in Bolivia is 178 years (UNDP 2005).

THE POLITICS OF CHANGE

Politics, Part of the Solution

Can radical politics deliver progressive social and economic change? Although it might be too early to answer based on a study of the Morales administration alone, a longer-term view poses a different question altogether. One of the interesting stylized facts of development in Bolivia is that it has largely proceeded in disjointed and uneven bursts of policy activism. This has typically involved short periods of political polarization followed by longer, less confrontational periods of cumulative social and economic change. First, the national revolution of the 1950s, which delivered agrarian reform, nationalization, and universal suffrage; then, the neoliberal reforms of the 1990s, which despite current disfavor, delivered significant improvements in education, maternal and infant health, and municipal decentralization; and now, a postneoliberal period, which is channeling rents from hydrocarbons to some of the poorest groups of the Bolivian population. Each of these periods of cumulative social and economic change was preceded by rapid political change, contestation, polarization, and defiance. Are, perhaps, such waves of contested and pacted politics a *driver of* rather than a hindrance to progressive social and economic change? The answer to this question requires both examining past social and economic indicators, and describing some of the political coalitions that made progressive change possible.

Figure 3.2 displays changes in human development in Bolivia between 1980 and 2007. The figure shows the three components of the human development index: indices of gross domestic product, education, and life expectancy. Three things stand out from this longer-term picture. First, Bolivia is one of the top twenty countries (of eighty-seven countries with comparable data) in its rate of human development achievement in this period (see Gray Molina and Purser in press). It has achieved an overall rate of social change, comparable to Vietnam and China in the same period, despite having a much lower level of GDP per capita growth over time. This means achievements in reducing infant mortality,

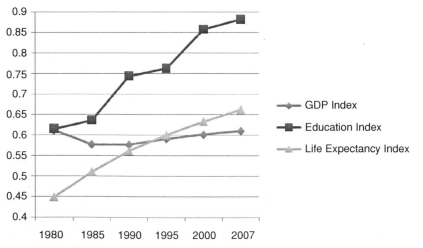

FIGURE 3.2. Human Development over the Long Run, 1980–2007. *Source:* Gray Molina and Purser in press.

extending life expectancy, reducing absenteeism in school, and increasing adult literacy were somewhat faster than even the top achievers in the world. This is no small feat. Second, the distributional breakdown of change suggests that, despite this overall success story, much of the increase in well-being can be explained by rapid improvements in the top 40 percent of the population, which reaches European levels of "high human development," whereas the bottom 40 percent is still comparable to much of sub-Saharan Africa in the "low human development category" (see Grimm et al. 2009). In other words, despite considerable improvements, there is still a significant pending equity agenda for the middle and bottom of the income pyramid.

Third, a long-run reading of human development trends suggests that a complex combination of factors lay behind this cumulative story. A starting point is rapid demographic change, which together with the early 1982–3 droughts and the collapse of tin mining in 1985, explain much of domestic internal migration and rapid urbanization. A middle point is reached with the neoliberal reforms of the 1990s, particularly the health care and education reforms, which rapidly increased social service coverage in urban areas and began to extend coverage in remote rural areas. A final point is reached with current policy reform efforts, aimed at many of those who are still at the bottom of the distribution pyramid today: rural communities, impoverished households in urban areas, children, and the elderly. Although not sufficient to overturn decades of inertia in the poorest deciles of the population, they are likely to succeed in making inroads in welfare for these groups in the future (see Gray Molina and Yáñez 2009).

The political coalition that made change possible in the 1990s unraveled in the 2000s. It was mostly sustained by the political clienteles of the MNR, MIR, and ADN, with the important contribution of the so-called "populist" parties of the 1990s: CONDEPA and UCS (see Mayorga 2002). The politics of pacted democracy relied on demobilizing the grassroots opposition, Bolivia's main labor federation, the powerful Central Obrera Boliviana. It also moved the sphere of politics out of the streets, where it had taken place since the National Revolution, to a more institutionalized setting in the legislative and executive branches of government (Gamarra 1997). Both steps were resisted by the opposition. The new political coalition of the MAS has proceeded in similar fashion. It has demobilized grassroots civic movements and aims to open the sphere of politics to arenas where it has a strong majority: the streets, the Chamber of Deputies (not the Senate), and the Supreme Court (not the constitutional tribunal). The MAS has gained most of the rural vote and has made inroads into the political clienteles of the traditional parties in some of the eastern departments, particularly Chuquisaca, Cochabamba, and Pando.

Although strong enough to deliver Morales a second term in office, the new coalition is likely to be insufficient to accelerate further change in missing dimensions of human development, namely, as discussed previously, income and employment. A proemployment coalition will need to include productive

actors of the lowlands, urban middle classes, and many actors linked to manufacturing, fair and organic trade, who are mostly outside of the MAS political
coalition today. Based on the best available data for long-term development
progress, periods of contested politics followed by periods of pacted politics did
not harm Bolivia's prospects for long-term change. The long-run picture does
not look like a smooth progression of technocratic progress. Rather, it looks
disjointed and uneven, much like Bolivian politics itself. I would argue that the
long-run view should temper the short-run inclination to attribute social and
economic stalemate to contested politics today. There are, however, limits, to
how contested and polarized politics might drive change or hinder progress in
the future. I believe that limit is, paraphrasing Vice President García Linera,
at the point where the catastrophic stalemate (which stifles change) becomes
the catastrophic breakthrough, which undermines the democratic framework
for legitimate democratic dissensus. This is the key issue for future political
development.

Politics, the Tipping Point

In 2005, Vice President García Linera coined the term "catastrophic stalemate"
(*empate catastrófico*) to describe the political impasse that divides the country along regional and class lines (Stefanoni 2007). Most political observers
agree that, despite the electoral majority and mobilized social movements, Evo
Morales has presided over a highly polarized political landscape. On the one
hand, politics within the MAS coalition tend to unravel from time to time and
exert an enormous amount of pressure upon both the executive and Congress.
MAS political actors include hard-line radical left and ethno-nationalist movements as well as more moderate popular, *indigenista*, and urban middle-class
sectors. The dynamics of intra-MAS politics revolve around the conciliatory figure of Evo Morales himself and around the challenge of a more radicalized and
mobilized opposition. On the other hand, the opposition is also fragmented
and divided between relatively radical civic committees and more moderate
prefects, congressional deputies, and senators. The opposition in the run-up to
the 2009 elections has never been weaker at both the national and regional
levels.

The political and policy process has also revolved around a split agenda.
From the government's perspective, the Constituent Assembly, led by a MAS
majority, spearheaded a process of change by pulling together disparate social
and political coalitions around a common theme: a new plurinational social
pact to inaugurate a new cycle of popular and indigenous politics. From the
opposition's perspective, the agenda of regional autonomies, and fiscal and
political decentralization led by the civic committees and prefects of four
departments set the stage for a drawn-out process of political confrontation.
With veto power in the regions and a growing coalition of regional and opposition constituencies, the autonomy agenda has become perhaps the most visible
and effective political opposition to an otherwise overwhelming MAS majority.

Within this polarized context, the dynamics of policy initiative, contestation, and conflict took a more radical turn after the referendum of August 2008, and the violence in Pando in September 2008. The Pando events, which resulted in the death of at least eleven peasants and two civic committee members, in particular, discredited the regional opposition, which found itself mired in paramilitary violence. For much of 2009, the regional opposition tried to save face, and the congressional opposition fragmented into multiple political fronts for the end-of-year elections.

In early 2009, the approval of a new constitution delivered President Morales a way to break the stalemate. Although the legality of the constitutional referendum was itself disputed, it is likely to be remembered as the point in the road where Evo Morales consolidated a national political victory. In the past, the search for a way to break the stalemate has simply postponed a number of unresolved tensions, which returned to the political stage with new balances of power and, in some instances, new actors. In this case, procedural and substantive disagreements over politics are tied to an alternative economic model. The stakes are high. President Morales wagered all of his political capital in the 2009 elections, which he won decisively.

CONCLUSIONS

This chapter has examined the policy outputs and outcomes of Evo Morales's first term in office and discussed some of the administration's future challenges beyond natural gas. A distinct policy sequence frames this period. First came the nationalization of hydrocarbons, which effectively increased the government's take to between 67 percent and 75 percent of the value of gas exports. Second were increased government revenues, which allowed a steady expansion of public investment – particularly roads programs – and gradually increased independence from the international donor community, which had played a key role in previous administrations. Third came an expansion of conditional and nonconditional transfer programs for the elderly and children of school age. All of these initiatives represent policy changes or amendments that were achieved in a context of significant political conflict and negotiation.

For a government with little previous experience in national-level governance, an environment of fairly extreme political polarization, and relatively elevated expectations from urban and rural voters, the political stakes continue to be high. In one sense, the Morales administration is truly *sui generis* in terms of the breadth and scope of social and political change experienced in the country. The strong popularity of the president has helped boost support for democracy as the best system of government as well as support for many of the legal and political institutions in Bolivia today. In another sense, however, the Morales administration follows in the footsteps of previous governments in that the political arena is highly fragmented and polarized. There is also evidence to suggest that Bolivians have never felt closer to violent conflict than they have during these four years. How to account for this politically?

The Challenge of Progressive Change

I have argued that the consolidation of a progressive social and economic policy agenda in Bolivia is still pending. In order for such an agenda to advance, the country needs to sustain, first, a consistent focus on the welfare of the poorest citizens, who still face significant challenges in educational attainment, infant and maternal mortality rates, and income generation; second, foster productive and environmental alliances that bridge the political divide between large and small producers, middle classes and peasant and indigenous communities and peoples; and third, seek, an alternative place for Bolivia in the global economy, moving from being a provider of primary natural resources to a leader in organic, bio-, and fair trade. All of these aims require bolder action on the policy front and perhaps a more long-run horizon on the political front.

Bolivian history suggests there are no technical fixes to long-run development challenges. Politics, including contestatory politics, play a role in driving and securing progressive social and economic change. However, what is often missed in the current pendulum swing in Bolivia is a more open discussion about the content of long-run change. Policy activism over the past thirty years has delivered significant improvements in Bolivian human development. To the extent that most improvements occurred at the top of the income pyramid, there is a pending distributional challenge in the middle and bottom. It should not be surprising that distributional issues continue to drive much of current Bolivian politics. However, there is a point where political polarization no longer adds to a progressive development agenda. Short-term political struggles over procedural rules (two-thirds or simple majority voting rules?), legislative hierarchy (Can the Constituent Assembly overrule Congress?), and constitutional interpretation (Does a Constituent Assembly take precedence over a referendum?) have taken up most of the past four years. Meanwhile, more than 200,000 new children and adults have been added to the ranks of the poor (UNDP 2008), natural disasters have affected more than a third of the national territory (ABI 2006), and nearly 300,000 people have left the country looking for better life opportunities elsewhere (World Bank 2008).

A progressive policy agenda implies taking both a closer look at the social and economic conditions of Bolivian citizens and applying closer scrutiny to how all of this relates to changes in development conditions at the global level. Bolivia is only one of dozens of countries that are poor, dependent on natural resources, and open to the global economy. Changing labor and environmental conditions in one country requires both policy change at the national level and changes in governance at the global level. This is not likely to happen on its own, and it will not occur by speaking only to the converted. To advance an effective alternative agenda, the country – comprising both government and opposition – must face up to both its own political challenges and those of millions of Bolivians who hope for a better future. A progressive policy agenda will thus require dialogue, compromise, and a long-run view of democratic politics.

4

The Chilean Left in Power

Achievements, Failures, and Omissions

Evelyne Huber, Jennifer Pribble, and John D. Stephens

In his introduction to this volume, Weyland locates the administrations of Socialist Presidents Ricardo Lagos (2000–06) and Michelle Bachelet (2006–2010) closest to the moderate pole among current leftist governments in Latin America. We concur and hope to contribute to the discussion by elucidating the sources of this moderation and examining the performance of these governments in the areas of political management, economic policies, and social policies and labor market reforms. The Lagos and Bachelet governments have pursued similar market-friendly economic policies to their predecessors. Although both presidents have made important progress in overcoming the political institutional legacies of Augusto Pinochet's dictatorship, moderate progress in labor market policies, and impressive progress in two social policy areas, very little improvement has been seen in the realm of fostering citizen participation and empowering labor and social movements through organization and linkages to political parties. We compare the Lagos and Bachelet governments to those of their Christian Democratic predecessors as well as to each other with the goal of identifying policy successes, failures, and omissions. We argue that the administrations' moderation stems from the political experiences of the leadership and their resulting approach to building relationships to the party rank-and-file and to civil society, the fact that these are coalition governments, and the constraints of the Pinochet political and economic legacies.

POLITICAL CONSTRAINTS AND MANAGEMENT

Political constraints in contemporary Chile originate from institutional design (the Pinochet-era constitution), political learning among left-party elites, the organizational weakness of left-leaning parties, and the fact that these are coalition governments. All four forms of political constraint have contributed to the moderation that characterized the left governments of Lagos and Bachelet. In this section we discuss the evolution of these constraints, paying particular attention to the extent to which the two governments were able to manage and ease the political restrictions.

Lagos assumed office in 2000 as the first Socialist president since Salvador Allende. Just like his predecessor *Concertación* presidents, he found his political space constrained by the authoritarian enclaves institutionalized by means of the Pinochet-era constitution. One of the key constraints imposed by the constitution was the provision of appointed senators. These senators kept the *Concertación* parties from obtaining control of the Senate, thus forcing the left government to negotiate with the opposition on all important legislation. Other constraints imposed by the military-era constitution were the lack of civilian control over the chief commander of the armed forces and an electoral system that favors the minority right-wing parties.

Arguably one of the most important achievements of the Lagos presidency was the package of constitutional reforms adopted in August 2005 that – among other measures – eliminated the appointed senators, gave the president the power to remove the chiefs of the branches of the armed forces, and curtailed the powers of the National Security Council. The publication of findings of a commission to study torture appointed in 2004 indirectly helped prepare the ground for these constitutional changes by highlighting the horrors that had been committed by a military institution devoid of any external accountability. These reforms, then, essentially completed the transition to democracy by eliminating the last clearly antidemocratic legacies of the dictatorship.[1] Importantly, however, this package of reforms did not constitute a sweeping change to the overall institutional configuration of the Chilean state. The institutional continuity in Chile stands in stark contrast to the efforts made by Hugo Chávez in Venezuela and Evo Morales in Bolivia to fundamentally restructure the national constitution, which Javier Corrales and George Gray Molina examine in their chapters in this volume. In part, this difference is a result of the very long and strong tradition of constitutional rule in Chile and of the strength of the military dictatorship. The military regarded itself as successful at the end of its rule and still enjoyed significant support among parts of the population, which made renewed intervention in case of radical departures in the 1990s a real possibility.

A second important political constraint that has influenced the moderation of the Bachelet and Lagos administrations is the fact that these are coalition governments. The coalition is decidedly center-left, and maintaining the political partnership and negotiating candidacies have been key tasks for the top leadership. Various authors have emphasized the strong incentives for coalition formation built into the binomial electoral system (Carey 1999, Fuentes 1999),

[1] See Agüero (2006) and Funk (2006) for a discussion of these reforms and their significance. The electoral system is another Pinochet legacy that has not been changed yet, but the reforms made it easier to change, and there are many electoral systems (including the American and British systems) that discriminate against smaller parties and/or overrepresent certain political forces, such as conservatives from rural areas.

but others have pointed to the incentives for the member parties to distance themselves from a potentially unpopular president and to the possibility of a collapse of the coalition (Siavelis 2005). So far, the coalition has held at the electoral level, but at the parliamentary level, the government lost a crucial vote for funding Trans-Santiago in November 2007 because of the defection of Christian Democratic deputies led by Senator Adolfo Zaldívar.[2] Clearly, this was a major setback for President Bachelet, and it highlighted the imperative of seeking compromise internally in the *Concertación* and, where possible, with the *Alianza* as well.[3]

Indeed, a major challenge to both Lagos and Bachelet relates to political management, the task of maintaining the coalition, and achieving agreement on policy initiatives. This challenge has been all the more difficult because of serious internal splits within the member parties of the coalition. The main ideological divide at the mass and the elite levels since the beginning of the transition has been between the prodemocracy and the pro-Pinochet or authoritarian camp rather than between the market-friendly and the state interventionist camp (Fuentes 1999, Luna 2006, Ruiz 2006). Yet, there are also consistent differences at the level of political elites between the *Concertación* and the *Alianza*, and within the *Concertación* parties between those embracing the market and those preferring a stronger role of the state. Data from three waves of interviews with members of parliament show that these political elites place parties and themselves on a left-right scale. The Christian Democratic Party (PDC) is located in a centrist position and the Socialist Party (PS) and the Party for Democracy (PPD) to the left of it. Both party placement and self-placement correlate with preferences regarding the relative weights of state and market (Luna 2006, Ruiz 2006). The differences between the *Concertación* and the *Alianza* are not large but very consistent over the three periods (1993–7; 1997–2001; 2001–05). There are no differences on preferences for state interventionism between the PDC and the other two *Concertación* parties in the first period. But in the second and third periods, the PDC members of parliament have a lower preference for state intervention than the PS and PPD members (Ruiz 2006: 91). There are additional factors that divide the *Concertación* parties: religiosity and moral conservatism. The PDC members of parliament indicate a higher degree of religiosity than even their counterparts in the RN; only the UDI members are more religious and morally conservative (Ruiz 2006: 93).[4]

---

[2] Zaldívar was expelled from the party in December 2007. In January 2008, Zaldívar and three other independent senators reached an agreement with the right-wing *Alianza por Chile* to share the presidency of the Senate for the following two years. According to the agreement, the group of independent senators would hold the presidency for the first year and the *Alianza* would hold the spot for the second year.

[3] This imperative is responsible for the failure of a redistributive provision to be included in the final version of the AUGE health plan, for instance.

[4] Certainly this division explains why it took until 2004 to legalize divorce and why abortion legislation remains the most conservative in Latin America (Blofield 2006).

Added to these programmatic divisions between *Concertación* member parties have been internal divisions within these parties. On the one hand, several authors have highlighted the existence of a *partido transversal*, that is, a set of political leaders from all the *Concertación* parties who share a commitment to the preservation of a market-friendly economic model and to a technocratic style of policymaking (Boeninger 1997; Fuentes 1999). This group of leaders has dominated the political process and held the coalition together. On the other side are politicians within each of the *Concertación* parties who would prefer more state intervention to address the problems of poverty and inequality more aggressively. They also would prefer a more open style of policymaking, more input from the base, and closer relations to civil society. So far, their influence has been weakened by historical legacies and structural factors.

Another constraint is generated by the fact that a large sector of the *Concertación* tends to exhibit an aversion toward popular mobilization. Indeed, the two main Chilean left parties, the PS and PPD, were formed during (in the case of the PPD) or reconstituted after (in the case of the PS) the dictatorship as elite-directed parties without strong base organizations or ties to civil society. The hegemonic elite groups in both parties, who had gone through the Allende years and the experience of persecution and exile, had concluded that uncontrolled popular pressures had been a major factor in the fall of Allende. Therefore, they deliberately kept their distance from party bases and popular organizations.[5] The parties' resistance to open discussions and democratic procedures for the formulation of party programs and candidate selection stands in contrast to classic left parties in Europe, as well as to the Broad Front (FA) in Uruguay and the Workers' Party (PT) in Brazil. It weakens the organizational capacity of Chile's left. And, of course, this practice stands in stark contrast to the mobilization efforts of the contestatory left in Venezuela and Bolivia.

Chile's left parties do have statutes that regulate internal policymaking and candidate selection in principle, but in practice, party business is mostly done through negotiations among the leadership.[6] As Pepe Auth, the secretary

---

[5] See Roberts (1998) for an analysis of the experiences of these leaders during the Allende period and the dictatorship. See Pribble (2008) for an analysis of the structure of these parties since the transition.

[6] The closed and elite-centered nature of the parties bears a significant part of the responsibility for the fact that the *Concertación* lost the Presidency in January 2010, when its PDC candidate and former President Eduardo Frei was defeated by Sebastián Piñera of RN. The victory was narrow, with Piñera obtaining 51.6 percent of the vote in the second round of elections. Despite the Right's electoral victory, Bachelet maintained record-high levels of approval and *Concertación* policies such as AUGE and the pension reform continued to enjoy strong support. Indeed, Piñera had promised not to roll back the *Concertación*'s social programs. Thus, rather than a rejection of the *Concertación*'s political program, the 2010 electoral defeat seems to be tied to the coalition parties' exclusive character and to a lack of renovation among the party elites (Siavelis 2009). The impressive performance of independent left candidate, Marco Enríquez-Ominami, who won just over 20 percent of the vote in the first round of the elections after campaigning against the lack of new leadership inside the *Concertación* coalition, provides clear evidence of public frustration with the nature of the center-left parties.

general of the PPD, put it: "The PPD went through a period that could be characterized as one of anomie, that is, of absence of norms that would explain, justify, and legitimize the decisions taken by the leadership bodies" (Auth 2007). In an effort to improve democratic procedures in a party originating in the fight for democracy, the PPD became the only party that finally made its membership list public. In 2007, it undertook a major renovation of its statutes to strengthen transparency and adherence to formal procedures.

The fact remains that neither left party provides for much input from the base and for transparent and democratic ways to resolve internal disagreements. The weakness of input from the base reinforces the tendency of officeholders to avoid radical departures from the status quo and instead seek compromise by moving toward the center. This has certainly increased the maneuvering room that left politicians enjoy in Chile, but it has also deprived them of the opportunity to mobilize popular support for reform policies that they favored but the right opposed. Labor law reform is perhaps the area where this became clearest. There is another potential danger inherent in this distancing. Leaders of social organizations have no trusted partners in the government with whom to negotiate and instead have to rely on mobilization in the streets if they want to achieve something. This puts the government on the spot – forced to choose between appearing weak in the face of pressure if it makes concessions and having to use repression if it makes none. The student demonstrations in 2006 and 2007 are a case in point. They did not bring much in terms of desired reforms for the students but damaged the image of the government. Certainly, this distance has prevented the formation of a strong proreform group of politicians within the *Concertación* able to build coordinated pressure from within and without to make progress in areas where reform has stalled.

One factor that keeps party organization weak is lack of resources. The parties do not have an income from dues that would allow them to work with a significant full-time staff in charge of building the party and directing internal party life toward greater institutionalized participation.[7] The lack of a large dues-paying base and of close ties to popular organizations that could be mobilized at election time empowers the moderate sectors of the leadership in still another way. It renders the left parties dependent on large private donors for financing elections. This is a particularly serious problem in light of the very high cost of Chilean elections. Estimates show that the cost of a campaign for the Senate in 1997 and 2001 in districts with more than 500,000 voters, ranged from US$850,000 to US$5 million. For an average-sized district, the cost ranged from US$250,000 to US$3 million. The average cost of a campaign for the Chamber of Deputies ranged from US$100,000 to US$340,000 (Fuentes 2004). After years of failed efforts to provide public financing to parties and regulate campaign expenditures – efforts for the most part blocked by the right – in 2003 the Congress finally passed a law (complemented in 2004 with a law that established sanctions for violations) that regulated the financing

---

[7] Garretón (2005) discusses party finances, campaign costs, and legislation.

of campaigns. The law was part of the "Agenda for the Modernization of the State," which began to command support in the midst of a number of corruption scandals (Garretón 2005). The law established caps on expenditures for each candidate, as well as limits on private donations from each individual, and it provided for state reimbursement of campaign expenditures. However, the law did not provide public funding to political parties for their ongoing activities – only for election campaigns – and it did not provide public funding for presidential elections. Moreover, the ceilings on expenditures and donations were set very high, thus perpetuating the advantage of the right, which greatly outspends the left, and the enforcement capacity of the electoral administration has been limited. As a result, dependence on private donations – including from corporations – remains a factor favoring a proprivate sector policy orientation.

Indeed, the Chilean case is characterized by a high level of political constraints, including institutional design, political learning, organizationally weak left parties, and the need to govern in coalition. In the remainder of this analysis we provide an overview of the accomplishments, shortcomings, and omissions of the Lagos and Bachelet governments in the area of economic, social, and labor policy. We pay close attention to how political constraints moderated the speed and breadth of transformation.

ECONOMIC MANAGEMENT

The main goals of the *Concertación* governments have been to protect macroeconomic stability, generate economic growth and employment, invest in human capital, and alleviate poverty. In the pursuit of these goals they adopted conservative fiscal policies, strengthened the independence of the Central Bank, deepened Chilean integration into world markets, increased expenditures for education and health care, increased the minimum wage, and provided targeted programs for those in extreme poverty. The Lagos and Bachelet governments followed this set of commitments just as their Christian Democratic predecessors had, intensifying efforts in health, education, and poverty relief. However, they did originate two major departures away from targeting on extreme poverty and toward universalistic, rights-based social policy, with the Regime of Explicit Health Guarantees (AUGE) under Lagos and the pension reform under Bachelet, both of which will be examined later in this chapter. Put simply, Chile's left governments have maintained the orthodox economic policies of their predecessors, but they have pursued a distinct form of social policy that moves toward a more universal system of social protection, inspired by left commitments to social equity, justice, and solidarity (see Weyland's introduction).

In fiscal policy, the *Concertación* governments of the 1990s adhered to the unwritten rule of fiscal responsibility, stipulating that all new expenditures required new revenue. Under Lagos, the government established a rule that the primary balance should yield a surplus of 1 percent under conditions of expected growth and "normal" copper prices (Muñoz Gomá 2007). In September 2006, the government promulgated the fiscal responsibility law (Ley 20128) that established (1) the requirement that each president at the beginning of her/his term establish the bases of fiscal policy for her/his administration and spell out the implications of this policy for the structural balance; (2) a contingency program to combat unemployment; (3) a pension reserve fund; (4) a fund for economic and social stabilization; and (5) capital transfers to the Central Bank. The structural surplus was to be channeled into these funds and the Central Bank. The Fund for Economic and Social Stabilization incorporated the existing stabilization fund based on copper revenue.

All *Concertación* governments justified fiscal austerity with the constraints imposed by international financial markets and the argument that macroeconomic stability is crucial to protect the poor and invest in human capital on a consistent basis. Of course, in the early years of the transition the government did have to prove to domestic and foreign investors that the *Concertación* would provide a stable economic environment. It is also true that high inflation and wild economic fluctuations hurt those without assets and stable employment the most, and that social expenditures are particularly vulnerable to recessions and budget deficits. On the one hand, one might question whether maintenance of macroeconomic stability and investor confidence requires a 1 percent structural surplus more than a decade after the transition. On the other hand, one might see the provisions of the financial responsibility law as a smart move to earmark revenue for pensions and counter-cyclical spending. One might even portray it as the opposite of Reaganomics – U.S. President Reagan created structural deficits and thus pressures to cut expenditures. Lagos invested the structural surplus and thus created resources to sustain expenditures during economic downturns.

To explain the fiscal conservatism of the *Concertación*, one certainly has to come back again to the political experiences and ideology of policymakers.[8] There is clearly a visceral aversion among the hegemonic leadership group against any kind of populism, defined as expansionary economic policies in response to popular pressures. This aversion stems from their analysis of the failure of the Allende government. As one high official in the Ministry of Finance who was politically active during the Allende years explained it: "It is not about 'levels' of orthodoxy; once you cross the threshold you don't know where you will end up. You cannot be half pregnant; either you are or you are not. I guess we probably have the feeling . . . that eventually the market will catch you" (Pribble 2006a).

The leadership group also firmly believes in the benefits of international markets and in the need to accept their constraints. During the early 1990s, Chile put in place controls on international capital flows in the form of a deposit requirement designed to discourage short-term flows (Ffrench-Davis 2002: 224). Arguably, these controls protected Chile from suffering even worse effects from the Asian crisis in 1998. Nevertheless, these controls were lifted

---

[8] We use the concept of ideology here to include the following three components: an analysis of the deficiencies of the existing social order, a vision of a desirable social order, and a strategy to get there from here.

in 2001, along with the requirement of advance notification of the entry and exit of capital, as a signal to international markets that Chile was trying to attract foreign capital (Muñoz Gomá 2007: 122). Another policy that signaled a commitment to conservative monetary policy was the strengthening of the independence of the Central Bank by the Lagos government. Finally, in regards to international commodity markets, tariffs have continued to be lowered since 1990 and the *Concertación* governments signed a number of free trade agreements, most importantly with the United States, the EU, and Japan. The agreements with the EU and the United States were signed under Lagos. In short, it is clear that there was no deviation from the commitment to free markets and conservative fiscal and monetary policies under the Lagos government at all. If anything, liberalization of markets was deepened and the commitment to a structural surplus was strengthened.

However, the real significance of the fiscal responsibility law with its provisions for stabilization funds will only emerge over the medium and long run. In the short run, it has already facilitated the adoption of the pension reform, because part of the future funding is to come from the Pension Reserve Fund. This fund receives up to 0.5 percent of GDP from the fiscal surplus every year, and no less than 0.2 percent of GDP, to be invested and to grow for ten years, at which point it can be used as a complementary source to pay for basic solidarity pensions and for supplementary solidarity pensions. The program to combat unemployment does require budgetary funding each year, so it is not protected against declines in revenue. However, the Economic and Social Stabilization Fund, to be financed by the copper stabilization fund and what remains of the fiscal surplus after contributions to the Pension Reserve Fund and possible transfers to the Central Bank, could be used for counter-cyclical spending. In the wake of a public debate about the merits of the 1 percent surplus rule, in which prominent economists and members of the *Concertación* parties participated, the Bachelet government decided to lower the structural surplus rule to 0.5 percent in 2007 (Muñoz Gomá 2007: 112). However, due to the copper boom, the current surplus reached a high of 8.7 percent of GDP in 2007, up from the previous historic high of 7.7 percent of GDP in 2006. The Pension Reserve Fund received US$1.5 billion and the Economic and Social Stabilization Fund US$14 billion (figures from Government Budget Director, reported in Infolatam 2008). In 2008, following a significant decline in the price of copper, Chile's budget surplus was smaller, equaling about 5.2 percent of GDP (EFE 2009).

The importance of the *Concertación*'s fiscal surplus policy was made acutely clear in January 2009, when the Bachelet administration drew on national savings to fund an economic stimulus package worth 2.8 percent of GDP (Moffett 2009).[9] The stimulus seeks to minimize the negative consequences of the global economic crisis and economists project that as a result, Chile's GDP

---

[9] As a point of comparison, the stimulus package passed by U.S. President Barack Obama was equivalent to about 2 percent of GDP (Moffett 2009).

should decline by less than 1 percent during 2009 (Moffett 2009). The ability of the government to respond quickly and decisively to the economic crisis appears to have had positive political consequences, with President Bachelet's approval reaching a record level of 67 percent in May 2009, making her the most popular president since Chile's return to democracy (CEP 2009: 20). Moreover, the same poll revealed that Finance Minister Andrés Velasco is currently the second most popular politician in Chile, with 50 percent of the population expressing positive sentiment about his work (CEP 2009: 37). This is a notable turnaround from 2007, when many citizens, politicians, and members of the media called for Velasco's resignation because of his refusal to spend the windfall copper profits. These numbers suggest that the *Concertación*'s commitment to prudent fiscal policy may have provided long-term political returns.

In order to shed some light on the relative role of international economic forces, the coalition with the Christian Democrats, and the market-friendly orientation of the *Concertación*'s top economic advisors, we can compare the macroeconomic policies of the Lagos and Bachelet governments with those of European social democracy in general – and those of Nordic and Austrian social democracy in particular – where social democracy has been very strong and thus least constrained by other political forces (e.g., coalition partners). During the golden age of postwar European capitalism, before the end of the Bretton Woods system and the first oil shock in the early 1970s, these countries were faced with an open trading system, both low tariffs and high dependence on manufactured exports, and closed international capital markets. Contrary to commonplace assumptions, social democratic governments carried out austere fiscal policy during this period, running budget surpluses in most years (Huber and Stephens 1998). They did this in large part to counterbalance the stimulation they were applying on the monetary side. With government control of central banks and a range of capital controls in place, they were able to set interest rates below international rates in order to stimulate investment and economic activity.

All advanced industrial countries moved to reduce the controls on international capital flows after the end of the Bretton Woods system. In this environment, it was impossible to control exchange rates and interest rates at the same time. Eventually, all European countries opted to pursue stable exchange rates, thus tying their hands in monetary policy. It was only a small additional step to make central banks independent of government as the governments had little monetary latitude anyway. Thus, the experience of European social democracy suggests that the Lagos and Bachelet governments could not have followed very different macroeconomic policies had they been freed from the constraints of their coalition partners and/or had they had economic advisors of a more neo-Keynesian bent. The most that would have been possible would have been to set somewhat lower interest rates and thus accept a lower value of the peso.

In the area of infrastructure investment, much has been done, primarily via concessions to private enterprises; the financing has come from a combination of state and private investment and user fees. This seems to have worked very well in the case of toll roads. For instance, the connection from the airport to downtown (and uptown) Santiago is much faster than it used to be. Similarly, the expansion of the Santiago Metro to poorer areas further from the center is an area of important success. On the other hand, Metro prices are high for low-income people who have to take it to work. Even worse, the attempt to reduce congestion, noise, and exhaust fumes from minibuses by substituting large modern buses connecting to the Metro, known as Trans-Santiago, was a spectacular failure. The new system lacked the capacity to transport all the passengers, and public frustration reached boiling levels. In order for Trans-Santiago to work, massive additional investments in buses would have been required. The government asked for additional financing but suffered a major defeat in the Senate when Christian Democratic senators defected in late 2007.

The overall economic performance seems to vindicate the *Concertación*'s policy commitments. Inflation was brought down from the two-digit range in the early 1990s to below 5 percent in the period 1998–2006.[10] Economic growth has been high, with only 1999 being a year of negative growth. Growth rates of GDP per capita from 2003–06 were in the range of 3–5 percent. This remains a high rate of growth, even though observers have pointed out that average growth rates declined from 7.3 percent of GDP under Aylwin to 5.3 percent under Frei, 4.3 percent under Lagos, and 4.2 percent under Bachelet (Muñoz Gomá 2007: 20). Investment rates (gross fixed capital formation) have been high – between 20 and 25 percent – among the highest in Latin America. Of course, copper prices helped greatly in the past few years. Chile's terms of trade jumped from 103 (index 2000 = 100) in 2003 to 184 in 2006, an increase only rivaled by Venezuela's terms of trade among all the Latin American countries. Some of the benefits of this growth clearly trickled down. Real average wages had increased by 11 points (index 2000 = 100) by 2006. The minimum wage increased in nominal terms by 640 percent from 1990 to 2003, while the consumer price index increased by 280 percent (Marinakis 2007; BADEINSO/ECLAC). It kept increasing, from 127,500 pesos to 135,000 pesos in 2006 and 144,000 pesos in 2007. Poverty decreased from 39 percent in 1990 to 19 percent in 2003 and 14 percent in 2006 (CASEN 2006).

Still, weaknesses in the economic model remain that do not augur well for a future when the present commodity boom will be over. Most importantly, the export-led growth is heavily based on copper, wood products, and agricultural goods. Very little technological upgrading has taken place. Investment in research and development (R&D) is low by international comparison, and in particular, private participation in it is low (Muñoz Gomá 2007: 165). In an effort to boost funds available for research and development, the Lagos administration passed a royalty tax on private copper mining companies operating in Chile. Although Chile was one of few countries not taxing the profits of private firms, the 5 percent tax on companies with output of more than fifty

---

[10] The data in this paragraph are all from ECLAC 2007, unless otherwise noted.

thousand tons faced fierce opposition from the right. Therefore, its approval is an important achievement.

Essentially, the *Concertación* governments have stayed away from an activist industrial policy, preferring a horizontal (not sectorally focused) and demand-driven approach, following the lead of the private sector (Peres 2006). This of course has been the approach preferred by neoliberals (if they conceded the need for any kind of industrial policy at all), but it is not the approach that successful developmental states or successful parts thereof have used (Evans 1995). Without strong incentives provided by the state, one should not expect major Chilean investors to develop new industries. The Chilean economy is highly concentrated, with ten large and highly diversified corporations controlling 89 percent of all corporate assets in 1999 (Agosín y Pastén 2003; cited in Muñoz Gomá 2007: 31). As long as the current economic model produces growth and lets them profit handsomely, they have little reason to take major risks by breaking into uncharted territory and investing in high-technology manufacturing. A strong indicator of the lack of interest among Chilean employers in upgrading is the fact that more than 60 percent of the resources made available by the state to enterprises for labor training are not used (Muñoz Gomá 2007: 172). This is particularly remarkable given the comparatively low average quality of the human capital base in Chile (OECD/Statistics Canada 2000: 136–7).

In the political discussion about the best ways to make use of the copper windfall, the proposal for an innovations fund has attracted considerable attention. There is wide agreement on the need to prevent "Dutch disease,"[11] and the Ministry of Finance under Bachelet proposed to use the Social and Economic Stabilization Fund in part for investment in education and technological innovation. Other proposals abound, such as proposals from the political right to lower taxes and finance social expenditures with copper revenue, which of course would make them highly vulnerable to copper price fluctuations.

A further weakness in the Chilean model that is rarely mentioned is the low labor force participation rate, fluctuating around 55 percent since 1999. This is one of the very lowest participation rates in Latin America (ECLAC 2007: A-16). It is heavily due to the very low female labor force participation rate – the lowest in Latin America – with only 42 percent of women in the labor force in 2000. The female economic activity rate as a percentage of the male rate was 57, tied with Mexico for the lowest (Abramo and Valenzuela 2006: 375). The reasons for this state of affairs are complex, stemming from both the demand (job creation) and the supply side (making it possible for women to combine work and family obligations, and changing attitudes about gender roles), but

---

[11] Dutch disease is the decline of the manufacturing sector caused by large inflows of foreign exchange and thus an overvaluation of the exchange rate. Generally, this inflow of foreign exchange is due to the discovery and export of natural resources, but it could also happen because of a large inflow of foreign direct investment. The term was coined to describe the experience of the Netherlands after the discovery of a large natural gas field in 1959.

the first change on the supply side came with Bachelet's plan to greatly expand public child care.

Certainly a persistent and fundamental weakness of the Chilean model – if we take the commitment to growth with equity or simply to investment in human capital seriously – is the low tax burden. In 2005, the tax burden was 19 percent of GDP, clearly lower than countries in other regions with comparable levels of development. In 1990, the Aylwin government succeeded in negotiating with the right a tax increase of 2 percent of GDP to finance social expenditures. Thereafter, however, business and the right strenuously opposed an increase in direct taxation, forcing the *Concertación* to rely on more regressive indirect taxes. Despite a 2001 law that managed to reduce tax evasion to some extent (Muñoz Gomá 2007: 113), legal tax avoidance remains a major problem. The major vehicle is the formation of corporations and the channeling of personal income and expenditures through these corporations, with a tax rate of 17 percent compared to a top marginal income tax rate of 40 percent.

Tax policy is one area where constraints resulting from an overrepresented right and a powerful business lobby become very clear. In the negotiations in 1990, the *Concertación* wanted to increase the corporate income tax from 10 percent to 20 percent but had to settle for 15 percent. President Lagos emphasized that total taxes had to increase, but he was only able to raise the corporate income tax rate to 17 percent. This compares to a Latin American average of 30 percent (Fairfield 2007, based on data from Price Waterhouse Coopers).

SOCIAL POLICY AND LABOR LEGISLATION

Whereas economic policy was characterized by continuity between left presidents Lagos and Bachelet and their Christian Democratic predecessors, social policy was propelled forward in innovative ways, albeit under the constraints of the coalition and a powerful right. The key reforms introduced under Lagos were Plan AUGE in health care, Chile Solidario in the fight against poverty, unemployment insurance, legalization of divorce, and an attempt at changes in labor legislation. Bachelet continued to expand Plan AUGE and to seek better protection for workers through regulation of subcontracting. She implemented a far-reaching reform of the pension system and proposed an ambitious expansion of child care and preschool education.

When the *Concertación* came to power, they inherited a two-class health care system established by Pinochet. Employees could choose to direct their mandatory contributions to the public health care system FONASA, or to a private health insurance company, an ISAPRE. ISAPREs are free to require additional contributions, decide on different contributions for different categories of subscribers, and determine coverage of services. As a result, they attract particularly upper income, younger, and healthier subscribers. In 2003, 72 percent of users used the public system and 16.3 percent relied on an

ISAPRE (Lenz 2005: 288). Despite significant increases in public health care expenditures during the 1990s, the differences between the public and the private health care sectors remained large. In 1999 ISAPREs spent an estimated 177,633 pesos per person compared to 99,308 pesos per capita by FONASA (Titelman 2000: 17). Moreover, when ISAPRE subscribers got seriously ill, they would often seek treatment in the public sector because of coverage limits in the private sector. AUGE was conceived as universal coverage for the most common illnesses for users of both public and private sector health care, to be financed in part by directing a part of everybody's health care contributions to a national solidarity fund.

The plan was launched in 2002, but negotiations delayed adoption until 2004 and resulted in several curtailments. Originally, fifty-six illnesses were to be covered immediately, but finally they were phased in, beginning with twenty-five illnesses in 2005 and reaching the full fifty-six in 2007. Importantly from a point of view of equity, the solidarity fund was eliminated and replaced with an inter-ISAPRE risk-pooling fund. There was internal opposition in the coalition against this fund, coming from sectors of the Christian Democrats, as well as strenuous opposition from the ISAPREs and the parties of the right (Dávila 2005). The proposed financing through a tax on alcohol and cigarettes was replaced with a 1 percentage point increase in the value-added tax and by new copayments (Espinosa, Tokman, and Rodríguez 2005). However, income-related caps were put on the total copayments for AUGE illnesses from families (Pribble 2008). The law also created a new regulatory agency (*Superintendencia de Salud*) in charge of enforcing the guarantees of timely treatment of these illnesses. The Bachelet administration extended the illnesses covered under AUGE to sixty-two by 2008 and committed to a goal of eighty illnesses by 2010.[12] AUGE clearly was and remains a big step toward guaranteeing universal affordable health care to all Chileans, but it failed to correct the highly inequitable allocation of mandatory contributions to the health care system and thus do away with the two-class health care system. Moreover, it left a hole in coverage insofar as the poor enjoy free access to public health care, but informal sector workers above the poverty line – who mostly do not contribute to FONASA – are left out of the system.

As in the rest of Latin America, noncontributory social transfers, or social assistance programs, have been poorly funded in Chile. In the fight against poverty, the *Concertación* relied primarily on economic growth and adjustments in the minimum wage for the short and medium run, and investment in human capital for the long run. Despite the impressive achievements in lowering poverty rates overall, there remained a sector of indigents outside the reach of the support mechanisms and human capital investments offered by the state. Chile Solidario was established in 2004 as a program that would bring some income support along with counseling from social workers to families

---

[12] As of May 2009 the presidency and the finance ministry were finalizing details of the bill that will expand the illnesses covered by AUGE to eighty.

in extreme poverty. It gives access to a small cash benefit, paid to the female head of household, for participating in the program that consists of psychological and social counseling, visits to a health center, and school attendance of children. It also offers access to the family-assistance subsidy, social-assistance pensions, and water subsidy, along with entrance into public preschool, drug and alcohol rehabilitation, and public employment programs (Serrano and Raczynski 2004). Preliminary evaluations indicate a high degree of support for the program among the participants (Perticará 2004) as well as an increased uptake of social assistance benefits, improved school attendance, and an expansion in the use of primary health care services among Chile's most vulnerable citizens (Galasso 2006). This program was set up in an extremely targeted manner, and to magnify its impact, President Bachelet proposed its extension to the homeless. The cost of the program is difficult to calculate. It depends on whether the preexisting state subsidies like the family-assistance subsidy, social-assistance pensions, and water subsidy are included in the calculations. Even if they are, the total costs of noncontributory social transfers in Chile remain low, with spending totaling 0.7 percent of GDP in 2003 (Lindert et al. 2006: 95).

A third innovation that started on a very small scale but could potentially become important if extended is unemployment insurance. It was introduced in 2002 and now covers about half of the Chilean labor force (Muñoz Gomá 2007: 223). However, coverage will not grow under current labor market conditions because it is restricted to formal sector employment. Moreover, half of the labor force is an overestimate, because even in the formal sector job instability is high, so workers do not easily accumulate the necessary length of service to qualify for meaningful benefits. It is funded by contributions from employers, employees, and the state. As of now, the dominant protection in case of job loss in Chile remains lump sum compensation for the years of work in a job. That system has two major problems: First, it is inadequate for an economy with high levels of employment instability. Most workers do not have a chance to accumulate years of work with rights to compensation. Second, we know from comparative research that high levels of job protection or high costs of layoffs have a negative effect on employment (Bradley and Stephens 2007). Thus, it would be preferable to replace the present system with a universal unemployment insurance scheme.

Labor law reform has been on the agenda of every *Concertación* president, but progress has remained highly limited. Pinochet's labor legislation was designed to keep unions weak by restricting bargaining to plant-level unions, encouraging multiple unions in an enterprise, and making it possible for employers to replace striking workers and fire workers without cause by claiming "business reasons" (Winn 2004). One of the key demands of unions since the transition has been legalization of bargaining above the plant level in order to strengthen worker solidarity and leverage. Another key demand has been the elimination of the right of employers to replace striking workers. Aylwin's labor law reforms of 1991–2 did not meet either one of these demands.

Frei proposed a reform package that included elimination of the right to replace striking workers, but militant opposition from business and the right led to a rejection of the reform by the Senate. Despite years of negotiations, major concessions by the government, and passage of a reform package by the Chamber, the right remained intransigent and used its overrepresentation in the Senate to reject reforms a second and a third time (Frank 2004). President Lagos launched another attempt at labor law reform, and again the attempt ran into very stiff opposition from business and the right. Initially, the government announced that the prohibition on replacing striking workers was nonnegotiable, but under intense pressure from business, internal tensions in the *Concertación*, and in a situation of lingering high unemployment, this change was dropped (Frank 2004). As long as employers offer wage increases to keep up with inflation, they can replace striking workers and pay a small amount of money to each replaced worker. The 2001 reforms introduced additional protection for unionization and a reduction of the work week from forty-eight to forty-five hours as of 2005. The official figures indicate an increase in the unionization rate from 16 percent in 2001 to 19 percent of the employed labor force in 2005, but unions have remained weak as economic and political actors.[13]

The struggle over legalization of divorce deserves some comment as it exemplifies most clearly the constraints on the left stemming from its Christian Democratic coalition partners and from the overrepresentation of the right in the Senate, even on an issue for which there is overwhelming public support. As noted previously, in the three surveys of members of parliament carried out since 1990, Christian Democrats self-classified as markedly more religious than PS and PPD parliamentarians, and they were even more religious than members of the RN (Ruiz 2006: 93). The Catholic Church has consistently opposed legalization of divorce. Public opinion, in contrast, has long favored legalization, with various surveys showing two-thirds of the public being in favor of legal divorce even before 1990, and in 2002, 85 percent favored legal divorce on the basis of mutual consent (Blofield 2006: 97). Despite this overwhelming public support, it took until 2004 to pass legislation. The law allows couples to file for divorce after a one-year separation, but the judge takes up to three years to process the filing, a process that includes mandatory mediation (Blofield 2006: 101–3).

The most important achievement of President Bachelet as of early 2009 was the pension reform. For some two decades, the Chilean pension reform, rammed through under the dictatorship, was the poster child of neoliberal social policy reform. Its architects, sometimes with the support of the World

---

[13] These figures have to be discounted. They are based on official membership figures from unions, which tend to be inflated. Data from the World Values Survey of 2000 paint a different picture. They show that only 4.8 percent of "employed workers" reported being a member of a union in Chile, the same level as neighboring Peru, clearly lower than Mexico with 9.8 percent, and Uruguay in 1995 with 16.7 percent and Brazil in 1995 with 25.2 percent (Martin and Brady 2007: 569).

Bank, traveled the world with missionary zeal to convince governments confronting pension systems under stress that privatization would be the solution to all their problems. The reality looks quite different. Despite the initially high returns on the investments in the pension funds, which were broadcast by the neoliberal reformers, the results in the longer run have failed to meet promises of reformers in virtually every respect. Effective coverage, that is, the proportion of the workforce making contributions to the pension system, did not increase. Administrative costs are very high, mainly because of marketing expenses. The system of commissions and fees weighs particularly heavily on lower-income earners and significantly lowers the real rate of return compared to the one claimed by the private Pension Fund Administrators (AFPs) (Mesa-Lago and Arenas de Mesa 1998: 69). And there is no evidence that the new system caused an increase in the national savings rate (Uthoff 1995).

Given the instability in the labor market, the low wages, and the size of the informal sector, a large percentage of the workforce at their age of retirement will not have contributed for the required twenty years and thus be dependent on social assistance pensions. Another large percentage will not have accumulated sufficient funds in their accounts to get beyond a subsidized minimum pension. In other words, the state will have to subsidize the pensions of low-income earners without having the benefit of the contributions from middle- and high-income earners.

The new system will offer two kinds of solidaristic pensions for old-age, disability, and survivor benefits to individuals who have lived at least twenty years in Chile, including four of the five years immediately preceding their request for the pension. Old-age pensions can be requested by those sixty-five years and older. One kind is a basic universalistic pension for all those who have not contributed to a private pension fund and who are in the bottom 60 percent of income earners. The other one is a solidaristic supplementary pension for all those whose accumulated pension funds yield a pension below a defined limit. All benefits will be phased in between 2008 and 2012. The basic universalistic pension in 2008 was set at 60,000 pesos per month, the equivalent of $120, the total supported by a solidaristic supplementary pension at 70,000 pesos. In 2009, the basic pension will increase to 75,000 pesos and the supplementary pension will be paid to people with pensions lower than 120,000 pesos. Pensions supported by a supplementary pension will reach 255,000 in 2012. There remains, therefore, a strong incentive for people to contribute to the pension system.

The basic and supplementary solidaristic pensions will be financed by general revenue and by the Pension Reserve Fund set up under the Financial Responsibility Law. The reform also contains some gender egalitarian elements, such as a bonus for time lost in the labor market by women due to the birth of a child. It further abolishes fixed commissions charged by AFPs, which weigh particularly heavy on low incomes, and it requires more transparency from the AFPs. It also contains some tax incentives for the middle classes whose pensions are above the limits that would entitle them to a supplementary pension. The reform also allows AFPs to invest more abroad. The original bill approved by the Chamber included the establishment of a state-run AFP, but that provision was eliminated by the Senate. In sum, this is a major innovative reform because it establishes the right of every Chilean to a basic minimum income in old age and because it reintroduces the principle of solidarity into the individualistic Chilean pension system. It was one of Bachelet's priorities in her campaign, and she was able to get it passed.

A second major theme in President Bachelet's campaign and her reform efforts was gender equity. In her program of government, she promised to increase women's labor force participation by creating a universal net of child care and preschool education, and to seek a national accord to get enterprises to offer more part-time work.

Chilean policy toward working mothers is actually among the most generous in Latin America when it comes to maternity leave. Women have the right to eighteen weeks of paid leave from their job, six weeks before and twelve weeks after the birth of a child (U.S. Social Security Administration 1999). The leave is paid for by the state. They also enjoy protection from firing from the time when they inform their employer of their pregnancy until twelve months after the end of the maternity leave. Moreover, all employers who employ twenty or more women are required to offer day care for children of up to two years of age, either on the premises or by contracting with a child care provider elsewhere. Whereas women are well informed about their maternity leave rights and demand enforcement, the picture with day care is murkier (Stephens 2008). Some employers try to stay below the limit of twenty women, others pay some money directly to mothers instead of offering day care. And of course the huge proportion of women who work in the informal sector or in the formal sector without contracts have no access to any of these benefits.[14] And it is among low-income women where labor force participation is particularly low. Therefore, President Bachelet focused on expanding provision of public day care places and as of May 2009 the administration had created 3,500 new public facilities (*El Mercurio* 2009). In January 2008, the minister in charge of SERNAM declared that women's labor force participation had increased significantly, from 38 percent to 40.3 percent, and she attributed this increase to a combination of increases in day care places, increasing levels of education among women, and the high economic growth environment (SERNAM 2008).

The most obvious difference between President Bachelet and her predecessors was her emphasis on gender issues, in particular her initial insistence on gender parity in all cabinet appointments. The women's movement (or movements, that is, there was not one united movement but different groups) played a visible role in the push for democracy, and initial expectations for progress

---

[14] Low-income women in Chile are much less likely to have access to contracted work than middle- and upper-income women. In 2000, about 86.5 percent of females in the formal sector with earnings in the top-income quintile were contracted, while only 29.7 percent of women in the bottom income quintile had contracts (Pribble 2006c: 90).

toward gender equity under democracy were high. President Aylwin created SERNAM, a ministry in charge of women's issues. Under Christian Democratic leadership, SERNAM concentrated on protection for women in their roles as mothers and spouses or partners, staying clear of controversial issues related to sexuality or women's equality in the labor market. As noted previously, Bachelet's campaign emphasized the issue of public day care and preschool education to enable women to join the labor force. In a demonstrative gesture to underline the availability of highly qualified women and her administration's commitment to bringing them into leadership positions, she appointed women to half the cabinet and undersecretary positions.

The evaluations of the success of this attempt are complex. In subsequent cabinet reshuffles, some prominent women leaders were replaced with male politicians with longer political experience. However, so were some of the initial male appointees. As insiders see it, Bachelet attempted a rejuvenation of the political elite and brought in not only women but also men with limited prior experience in top governmental positions.[15] She herself is not a member of the inner circle of the renovated Socialist leadership. There is a generational difference and a difference in social networks. Given the importance of personal connections in getting things done in Chile, this put her and her new appointees at a disadvantage, particularly when dealing with difficult political projects where concessions and compromises had to be obtained. Still, despite the difficulties encountered, there is no doubt that her presidency and her appointment strategy constitute a major symbolic advance for women. That symbolic advance is complemented by substantive advances in women-friendly policies such as in the pension reform and the expansion of public day care and preschool education.

The Pinochet legacy in education has been a three-tiered system with extreme quality differences. The *Concertación* governments have greatly increased expenditure on education but have not made much progress in reducing quality differentials. Schools are administered by municipalities and receive a per pupil subsidy from the national government. The subsidy from the national government is not sufficient to provide a high-quality education. Poorer municipalities are not in a position to supplement education expenditures. As a result, the quality of public schools in poor municipalities is very low. The chances for students who attended all public schools to make it into university are close to zero. In the 2008 PSU, Chile's university entrance exam, about 57.6 percent of students from public (municipal) schools scored above 450 points, while 92.6 percent of students from private schools did (*El Mercurio* 2008). Publicly subsidized private schools may select students and they may levy additional fees, which of course excludes the poor. It was the *Concertación* government under Christian Democrat Aylwin that introduced the additional payments in

---

[15] This information is based on interviews done by Huber in November 2007 with a former high-level official and with outside experts who work closely with the government.

these schools (Cox 2006: 13), a practice that clearly contributes to increased inequality. Socialist Bachelet attempted to reverse this practice but failed.

Presidents Frei and Lagos did not enact major changes to the administration of education, but they did increase funding significantly. Additionally, the Frei administration passed an education reform that created a full school day. Lagos oversaw the implementation of this reform and extended mandatory education to twelve years. President Bachelet initiated a major discussion on educational reform, in part in response to large and partly violent student protests in 2006. The attempt to draft a reform law brought severe tensions to the surface, and the result was an interparty/intercoalition agreement that omitted the key issues of municipal control of schools and of extra payments in publicly subsidized private schools.[16] This agreement formed the basis for the new education law, which was passed in April 2009. In a separate piece of legislation, the public subsidy for vulnerable students was increased.

Another major campaign theme of Bachelet's was citizen participation, or open and participatory government. Rhetorically, the commitment to political inclusion has been a theme for all *Concertación* governments, and under Lagos, a law on citizen participation was passed. However, as noted previously, all these governments have kept organized groups at arm's length. Rather than attempting to strengthen civil society and build organizational ties to various groups, the *Concertación* parties have kept their distance and have discouraged mobilization. The following quote from interviews conducted by Pribble illustrates this well:

"In the 1980s Chile was full of strong and organized social groups... Beginning in 1990, however, all of that changed because the *Concertación* worked to de-mobilize and disarticulate these groups. This process of demobilization was achieved by bringing people into the bureaucratic apparatus, but also by ensuring the political parties cut off all relations with social groups and didn't help such organizations extend their power... The political parties in this country aren't concerned with strengthening organization and mobilization" (Pribble 2006b).

CONCLUSION

In sum, the Socialist-led coalition governments under Presidents Lagos and Bachelet have notable achievements to point to. Certainly the completion of the democratic transition, with the abolition of the designated senators and the reestablishment of civilian control over military appointments, was fundamental symbolically and in practice for making progress in other crucial reforms. Plan AUGE and the pension reform constituted major departures from the neoliberal model of narrowly targeted and market-driven social policy.

---

[16] The agreement makes only a vague commitment to eliminating admissions standards. It states: "norms will be established to ensure that admissions processes in each educational establishment are transparent, objective, and do not discriminate arbitrarily" (Government of Chile 2007, translation by authors).

The key here is that the left presidents implemented programs that benefit large majorities of the population and thus leave a policy legacy with a strong political support base that will make it difficult for successor governments to curtail the programs. We know from the comparative literature on welfare state retrenchment that the programs with the largest reach are the most difficult to cut. Moreover, the Pension Reserve Fund constitutes a major step toward putting the financing of the solidaristic pensions on a firm basis.

Prominent among partial achievements in crucial areas, where improvement is still needed, is campaign financing. Reducing the influence of large donors on campaigns is critical for curtailing the advantage of the right and the powerful influence of business on the political process. Critical areas from the point of view of a successful left project where business and the right have been intransigent and able to block progress are labor law reform and tax reform. Reform of the electoral system could be a further step toward reducing the advantage of the right, depending on the type of reform introduced. Electoral reform is being put on the agenda, but it will be exceedingly difficult to reach consensus within the *Concertación*, not to speak of an intercoalition agreement.

The clearest general failure of the left governments, at least up to 2007, has been a reduction of inequality in income and wealth. The figures for 2007 show a very slight decrease in income inequality, but it remains to be seen whether this is a solid trend. The governments tried in several ways to reduce inequality, such as through the AUGE solidarity fund, efforts to reduce the quality differences in education by making it impossible for publicly subsidized private schools to select students and charge additional fees, and the tax reform. However, they could not generate sufficient support to overcome opposition to these redistributive reforms. Another case of failure is labor law reform, which would have indirectly contributed to lowering inequality by giving workers more leverage to demand wage increases. Together with labor law reform, arguably the most critical area of failure is tax reform, because a significant increase in tax collection would allow for an equally significant increase in social expenditures that could be directed at the lower three quintiles of the income distribution.

We would argue that these critical failures are related to omissions, that is, areas where the governments did not develop any initiatives, specifically in strengthening unions and other social movements and in establishing links between parties and civil society. Leaving these movements weak and disconnected from left parties means that the governments failed to shift the balance of power in society by establishing a counterweight to the powerful business sector. The top political leadership circles also have not strengthened their parties as organizations with an internally participatory and democratic life, and a strong ongoing recruitment effort. On the one hand, these omissions have protected the maneuvering room of the top leadership, but on the other hand they have deprived the leadership of a larger organized base and of institutionalized channels for internal conflict resolution that would produce decisions accepted as legitimate by the members. They have also deprived the leadership of relationships to social movements and unions characterized by mutual trust. Accordingly, if these social actors want to exert pressures for change, they need to resort to mass mobilization and confrontational tactics, and confrontation carries the potential of escaping the control of the leaders. As a result, both the government and the social actors may get locked into postures that obstruct progress on reforms and hurt both sides in terms of support among the population at large. Comparative evidence shows that the most successful social democratic projects were carried by alliances between left parties and social movements.

5

From Cardoso to Lula

The Triumph of Pragmatism in Brazil

Peter R. Kingstone and Aldo F. Ponce

The election of Luiz Inácio Lula da Silva of the Brazilian Workers' Party (Partido dos Trabalhadores – PT) in November 2002 triggered both trepidation and exultation.[1] For observers on Wall Street, the election of a one-time Socialist and seemingly dedicated leftist president raised concerns about Lula da Silva's commitment to the market-oriented reforms and financial stability achieved by his predecessor, Fernando Henrique Cardoso (Party of Brazilian Social Democracy – PSDB). For the left in Brazil – and Latin America generally – the triumph of the PT represented a crucial victory for the forces of social justice, for participatory decision making, for honest and transparent governance, and most notably for a rejection of the neoliberal paradigm. As it turned out, there was little cause for either reaction. Lula da Silva has not been a firebrand leftist, promoting populist, redistributive policies regardless of the economic consequences. Nor has he introduced new modes of decision making that open the doors to social movements and other previously excluded – and presumably largely antineoliberal – voices. In fact, Lula's government has offered little to suggest the emergence of a clear leftist alternative to the Washington Consensus or a new political style as an alternative to Brazil's traditional pattern of coalition building and bargaining.

Instead, the Lula da Silva administration, like the Cardoso administration before it, has embraced a generally market-oriented economic orientation and the traditional clientelistic rules of operating within Brazil's legislature (*fisiologismo*). To many on the left, Lula's administration has been an outright betrayal of the most cherished principles and causes of the PT and the left. Social justice, honest and transparent policymaking, and a reversal of the "cursed legacy" of neoliberalism have not featured prominently. Nevertheless, as Barros Silva et al. point out in this volume, Lula secured reelection to a second mandate

---

[1] The authors would like to thank the editors for their helpful comments on earlier drafts of this paper. IBOPE opinion surveys were obtained through the Roper Center for Public Opinion Research at the University of Connecticut.

in 2006 and continues to enjoy consistently positive performance evaluations in public opinion surveys (IBOPE 2007). The reason is that Brazil's overall performance on a host of economic indicators has been solid to good, both in relation to the past and in relation to the rest of Latin America. Lula's success is not a reflection of a sharp break with the past and an inversion of priorities. Instead, he benefited from an unusually positive international economy until 2008, and by maintaining continuity with the policies and policy orientations of his predecessor, Cardoso. Likewise, Lula has managed to minimize the effects of the 2009 international crisis on the Brazilian economy. In fact, the International Monetary Fund (IMF) has predicted a contraction of only 1.3 percent in the size of its economy, considerably superior to the Latin American mean of −2.6 percent. Moreover, Brazil – along with Peru – is expected to lead the economic recovery of the region with growth rates of 3 percent and 3.6 percent respectively in 2010.[2]

The policies that emerged under Cardoso and have been maintained by Lula da Silva reflect the triumph of a pragmatic market orientation that has come to occupy a kind of consensus centrist position in the Brazilian polity. This pragmatism places Brazil, along with Chile, squarely in the moderate left category described by the editors of this volume. Brazil's pragmatic market orientation is marked by three crucial elements: first and foremost, a steadfast commitment to monetary stability; second, a relatively flexible approach to the rest of the market reform agenda (i.e., incomplete adherence to the Washington Consensus policy program); and finally, a commitment to address some of the country's fundamental issues of poverty and inequality.[3] In fact, Brazil's policies bear a strong resemblance to the Chilean policy set discussed by Huber, Pribble, and Stephens in this volume. Together, these policies have helped Brazil achieve stability, modest growth, and a steady, gradualist commitment to addressing historic injustices. Some might argue that this is not a spectacular achievement, and there is no question that it leaves many important issues unresolved. But it is a considerable achievement given Brazil's turbulent history, and it lays the groundwork for continued gradual improvement.

This essay makes the case in three sections. The first and second articulate a standard against which to consider the PT's performance, first through a brief review of what it means to be a leftist party in the Latin American context and second through an overview of the nation's economic and political performance under Lula's predecessors in the New Republic. The third section reviews the performance data under Lula and considers some of the underlying explanations for it. The most important factor is that Lula's basic orientation

---

[2] IMF 2009.

[3] Sola (2008) notes that a commitment to addressing poverty and inequality was actually a present and important element of policy in the New Republic well before the implementation of the highly touted Bolsa Família. Some of the elements of the neoliberal policy platform, notably the commitment to macroeconomic orthodoxy, have been more controversial and harder to settle on as a consensus centrist position.

has been pragmatic and moderate. This has entailed compromises on policies and principles regarding both social policy and political style. These compromises have disappointed the left (at the very least), but they have made possible the economic policies – and performance – that have been the basis of Lula's economic success and political strength.

LULA AND THE PT IN BRAZIL: WHAT IS A LEFTIST PARTY?

This essay focuses on Brazil's performance under Lula da Silva, regardless of whether he is a leftist or not or what kind of leftist he might be. But any assessment of Lula's administration needs to specify the standard by which the government is measured. Is it relative to the region or Brazil's past? Is it relative to some external, unchanging ideal standard or to the promises and expectations created by the government? Thus, it is worthwhile to consider briefly whether Lula is (or was) a leftist president as a way of understanding the expectations and the context in which he operates. Lula was voted into office in 2002 in a context of significant dissatisfaction with the status quo in Brazil (IBOPE 2001; Meneguello 2005). The PT and Lula's campaign tapped into widespread frustrations with Cardoso and his neoliberal policies and explicitly created expectations that the country would shift leftward under Lula. What exactly did that mean, however, and to what extent has Lula lived up to the expectations he helped create?

Unfortunately, the question of what it means to be a leftist in the Latin American and Brazilian context is not an easy one and has been subject to disagreement for much of the twentieth century. For example, the question of whether to link Communist and/or Socialist parties with labor-based, nationalist, and/or populist parties has been a central conceptual challenge for scholars of the left. The volume *The Macroeconomics of Populism* (Dornbusch and Edwards 1991) provides a clear illustration of this, as successive chapters offer differing – and at times conflicting – conceptions of what constitutes populism and which presidents and episodes can be considered populist, including disagreements about whether Socialists like Salvador Allende count or do not count. Ideology, support base, orientation (international or nationalist), and policies are among the various factors that affect how parties and movements get classified. These are some of the variables the editors to this volume identify as central to the growing literature on the current shift to the left in Latin America.

In *Utopia Unarmed*, Jorge Castañeda addressed this variability and offered an overview that helps link all leftist movements and parties. For Castañeda, leftists are characterized by a preference for change over continuity, democracy and human rights over domestic security, national sovereignty over international economic integration, social justice over economic performance, national control over resources and income distribution/redistribution over free markets, and social spending over controlling inflation and maintaining fiscal health (Castañeda 1993: 18). This list certainly captures much of the PT's program over the course of the 1980s and 1990s and was rhetorically present in the 2002 presidential campaign.

Yet Castañeda's majestic work is not so much a classification of the left but a call for the revival of the left and a political and economic program for doing so. Thus, Castañeda, like some other leftist critics (e.g., Green 2003), ends up accepting many of the neoliberal diagnoses of Latin America's economic ills and ultimately many of their prescriptions as well. In fact, Castañeda's program for the left can be summed up as "neo-liberalism with a human face," or "democratizing neo-liberalism." What this amounts to is essential acceptance of the market reform program, but with a social safety net and a more open, democratic, and participatory decision-making style.[4] For Castañeda, democratizing decision making is a corrective both for neoliberalism as well as for the Latin American left's uneasy historic relationship with democracy. At the time of his writing in 1993, the role model he envisioned for this new form of the left was none other than Brazil's PT, based on its record of participatory municipal budgeting and strong grassroots participation in party decision making.

This is a very modest claim for leftist politics – and some might object that it is something of a surrender to arguments about the globalized economy, with its attendant constraints on policy.[5] Certainly, it is a position that runs counter to both the rhetorical and actual policy positions of the more radical left discussed by Gray Molina and Corrales in this volume. Nevertheless, it provides a useful metric for evaluating the left and the promises that leftist politicians may make in such a context. It certainly captures the shift in the PT under Lula over the 1990s, especially with his publication of the "Letter to the Brazilian People" shortly before his electoral victory in October 2002. Lula published the letter as it became clear that global markets were reacting poorly to his likely electoral victory. In it, he echoed the traditional leftist sentiments about social justice and antipathy to neoliberalism that had been present in the party since its inception. But the letter also indicated that the country's precarious financial situation meant that he would have to maintain his predecessor's central economic orientation (Lula da Silva 2002).

Thus, Castañeda's work provides two meaningful alternative standards for evaluating Lula da Silva's administration in relation to what to expect from a leftist government: A traditional conception that privileges social justice and government intervention over the market, and a more modest one that accepts neoliberalism and the constraints of a globalized economy but emphasizes a social safety net and open, democratic decision making. There is no question that Lula and the PT have not lived up to the expectations of the traditional conception of the left, and by that standard their administration has been a disappointment. Their performance vis-à-vis the globalized conception, however,

---

[4] Castañeda also endorsed the use of industrial policy and private sector–state partnerships along European or Japanese models. The extent of his acceptance of the market, however, is a significant step away from traditional leftist approaches.

[5] For example, see Petras (2000).

presents a more uneven pattern. To fully understand it, it is worth reviewing some of the background conditions leading to Lula's inauguration as president in 2003. In brief, Lula has been a successful steward of the macroeconomy, primarily by following the orthodox path carved out by Cardoso. That orthodoxy has limited his efforts in the realm of social policy, where he has made some genuine gains largely by continuing and expanding the conditional cash transfer programs initiated at both the state and national levels during the Cardoso administration. Finally, his conversion to a pragmatic market orientation has entailed (and arguably caused) a wholesale abandonment of any pretense of a new style of governing. Instead, the Lula administration has been characterized by patronage, closed-door decision making, and an unexpected level of corruption.[6]

FROM COLLOR TO LULA: LESSONS ABOUT STABILITY

Brazil was able to maintain its nationalist developmentalist, import-substitution industrialization (ISI) orientation longer and more successfully than any other nation in Latin America. Nevertheless, the restoration of democracy in 1985 occurred under woeful economic conditions, made significantly worse by a host of factors, including economic mismanagement under the new civilian government of President José Sarney. The most notable aspect of the crisis was the dramatic increase in inflation from roughly 600 percent in 1985 to roughly 2,000 percent by the 1989 election. In general, Brazil's fiscal house was in serious disarray (Baer 1995).

The 1989 election featured Lula da Silva in his first presidential run against Fernando Collor (National Reconstruction Party, or PRN), a conservative son of an oligarchic family from a rural state. Collor, relying on populist language and theatrics and promising to kill inflation with a single bullet, defeated Lula with the votes of the country's poorest and least educated. He promptly initiated a series of neoliberal reforms and implemented the country's most draconian stabilization plan ever. Collor's presidency ended in failure in 1992, mired in corruption and with inflation resurgent. But Collor's aborted term in office set the country on a new economic path against considerable resistance, and it established a base for future reforms, including successful stabilization (Weyland 1998). It also played an important role in breaking the public's tolerance for invasive and drastic anti-inflation measures (Bresser Pereira 1993).

Collor's presidency set the stage for Fernando Henrique Cardoso, who first served as finance minister in 1993 and then won the 1994 presidential elections. Cardoso was responsible for a set of crucial reforms for Brazil that have come

---

[6] In fact, Lourdes Sola (2008) goes on to argue that the PT in power has not only been no better than previous administrations but arguably has done considerable damage to Brazil's political institutions.

to define the country's economic policy path. Cardoso's government deepened several elements of the neoliberal program initiated by Collor, most notably privatization (including many of the country's utilities and state-owned banks). In other areas, the Cardoso administration was less explicitly neoliberal – most notably in partially reversing the trade liberalization process in favor of moderate protectionism and continued reliance on industrial policy (Averbug 1999). Cardoso also initiated innovative social policy reforms in health and education. Some of these ideas originated with the PT, but their popularity triggered a competitive process of credit claiming between the PT and the Party of Brazilian Social Democracy, or PSDB (Melo 2008).

Perhaps Cardoso's most important achievements came in the area of monetary stability and moving the federal government back toward fiscal health (as well as the financial sector generally, as discussed in Chapter 6 by Barros Silva et al.). These measures included financial liberalization, increased control over state government debt, tax reforms (most notably the creation of a new tax on financial transactions), and public administration reforms. The centerpiece of Cardoso's achievement, however, was his stabilization plan, the Real Plan, initiated while he was finance minister in 1993 (Oliveira 1995).

The plan resulted in dramatic and almost immediate reductions in the rate of inflation, with positive effects on poverty, consumption, and foreign investment as well. Although the Real Plan was ultimately abandoned in 1999 in the face of a run on the Brazilian currency, the country has continued to enjoy low rates of inflation. One important reason is that perhaps the plan's greatest benefit was to teach all politicians the importance to voters of maintaining low inflation. Lula campaigned openly against the plan in 1994, decrying its orthodox, neoliberal elements and predicting a sharp drop in the purchasing power of the poor. Yet as the plan began to take effect in August 1994, it was clear that inflation was falling quickly and Cardoso was going to win the presidential election. Lula's criticism of the most successful stabilization plan in Brazilian history had been a serious mistake, from which the PT learned that voters like low inflation (Hunter 2007).[7]

But maintaining low inflation in the long term depended on passing difficult structural reforms to address the fiscal imbalances of the Brazilian state, notably of the tax and pension systems. Cardoso spent most of his two terms tackling them, with mixed success. In the absence of deep, comprehensive reforms, Cardoso was forced to rely on a series of measures designed to attract and maintain strong capital inflows, especially very high real interest rates. The cost of those high interest rates was rising public sector debt, limited domestic

---

[7] David Samuels (2004) provides an additional excellent account of the PT's shift to the center. Samuels focuses on characteristics of the party organization, while Hunter (2007) examines both external and internal factors to help account for the shift. In any event, Lula's pragmatism in office was not a sudden or extreme shift. Instead, it was part of a process of the PT's becoming a party capable of winning elections by expanding beyond its base.

investment, and economic sluggishness (especially with respect to employment rates). Furthermore, Brazil was buffeted by recurrent currency crises around the world. Together, these internal and external factors inflicted considerable pain on the Brazilian economy, most notably unemployment, which voters listed as their biggest concern in 2001 (IBOPE 2001).

This was the context in which Lula da Silva ran for the presidency again in 2002. Dissatisfaction with Cardoso and his neoliberal model was widespread enough that both Lula and José Serra – Cardoso's intended successor from the PSDB – ran against Cardoso's approach.[8] Despite Cardoso's many accomplishments, Brazil in 2002 faced a host of challenges, including high (and intractable) unemployment, sluggish growth, stagnant real wages, high levels of debt, and renewed fears of inflation (in addition to a series of corruption scandals and an unprecedented energy crisis that many blamed on Cardoso's privatization policies). Lula actively campaigned on the promise of social justice and the reversal of the "cursed inheritance" of Cardoso's neoliberalism. He promised change, but he also faced a Brazil buffeted by repeated financial shocks and an adverse reaction on Wall Street to his candidacy. Furthermore, his mistaken criticism of the Real Plan and his underestimation of the importance of inflation to voters in 1994 made clear the importance of protecting against a new cycle of inflation. Thus, Lula's election in 2002 placed him in a bind, caught between promises of social justice and the need to preserve currency stability.

So how should we assess Lula da Silva? First, we can assess Lula with respect to Castañeda's modest leftist standard of market-oriented reforms with a social safety net and democratic decision making. Second, we can assess Lula with reference to the context in which he was elected and the promises/expectations that context created. Specifically, Lula was elected with expectations of improving economic growth, employment, and wages, but he was constrained by the need to maintain price stability.

We argue that Lula da Silva has performed well on the economic measures. Brazil has done modestly well on growth and employment while maintaining low inflation. By contrast, Lula has performed only tolerably on social policy measures and poorly on political ones. These are not unrelated outcomes. Lula's economic performance reflects a combination of good international circumstances with a commitment to continuing the pragmatic market policies of his predecessor, especially with respect to macroeconomic policy. Lula's pragmatism, however, has limited his room to promote a more expansive social program and in fact led to one of his most significant policy betrayals of the left on social security reform. Maintaining his pragmatic market orientation has also shaped a political strategy that closed the door on the progressive elements of the PT and its base while seeking support from traditional political

---

[8] Although voters endorsed some aspects of the Cardoso administration policies, large numbers expressed a preference for policy changes on key neoliberal items such as trade policy and privatization, see IBOPE (2001).

players. In short, good economic performance has required him to maintain the policy orientation of a president he vilified while turning his back on the base that carried him to victory in the 2002 elections. We review the evidence for this claim later.

THE PT'S PERFORMANCE IN NUMBERS, 2003–08

Macroeconomic Data and Policy

The 2008 reports on the performance of the Brazilian economy are marked by optimism and good expectations for future performance. According to the Brazilian Central Bank (Folha de São Paulo 2007a), the Brazilian economy grew 5.2 percent in 2007. This was slightly lower than the Latin American average, which reached 5.6 percent in the same year. Thus, Brazilian economic performance was behind the achievements of Panama (9.5 percent), Argentina (8.6 percent), Venezuela (8.5 percent), Peru (8.2 percent), Uruguay (7.5 percent), Colombia (7 percent), Paraguay (5.5 percent), and Chile (5.3 percent). However, the Brazilian rate of growth exceeded those of Bolivia (3.8 percent), Mexico (3.3 percent), Nicaragua (3.0 percent), and Ecuador (2.7 percent). Likewise, the Brazilian Central Bank expected the country to achieve a similar rate of growth for 2008 – and again to be close to the Latin American mean.

In the same vein, in 2007 other key indicators, such as the level of unemployment and the purchasing power of Brazilians, experienced improvements. Between January and November 2007, 1.9 million jobs were created within the Brazilian formal sector. This substantial increase reduced the level of unemployment to 8.2 percent (Folha de São Paulo 2007b). Moreover, in 97 percent of labor contracts, Brazilian workers were able to adjust their salaries by amounts equal to or higher than the 2007 inflation rate of approximately 4.3 percent (Forbes 2007; for 2008, the Brazilian Central Bank estimated a GDP expansion of 4.5 percent).

Finally, between 2003–07, the Brazilian government reported that 20 million Brazilians belonging to the social classes D and E migrated to the class type C (on a scale measuring distribution of income from E to A) – a category that represents the middle class. Similarly, between August 2006 and December 2007, 17 million Brazilians joined this growing Brazilian middle class (Folha de São Paulo 2007b).

The Brazilian economy's positive performance from 2003–08 was only partially a result of Lula da Silva's policy choices. The results stemmed primarily from two reasons: First, the favorable international conditions in the world economy fostered mainly by economies of the developing world, such as China and India, encompassing an accelerated growth in the world economy of 5 percent in 2006, 4.9 percent in 2005, and 5.3 percent in 2004, as well as growth of global trade at 16.6 percent in 2003, 21.3 percent in 2004, and 13 percent in 2005 (Carneiro 2006; Macedo e Silva 2006; Martins Biancarelli 2006);

and second the relatively high degree of macroeconomic stability achieved by Lula's government since the beginning of his rule, based on a tight, orthodox management of the economy – in short, the maintenance of policy continuity between his and Cardoso's administrations.[9] Lula's commitment to macroeconomic stability and continuity with the Cardoso administrations' policies also have facilitated some degree of structural change in the Brazilian economy, and this has positioned the country well for the future, despite the global economic crisis. These other structural changes, as in agribusiness and the strength of Brazilian companies, are discussed at greater length by Barros Silva et al. in this volume.

Lula da Silva's overt shift to orthodoxy began with the "Letter to the Brazilian People" prior to his election in 2002 but deepened immediately upon his taking office as a way to reassure elite economic actors in Brazil and in particular on Wall Street (Hunter and Power 2007; Diniz, Kingstone, and Krieckhaus 2008). Once Lula took office, he strongly signaled his commitment to economic orthodoxy and low inflation by choosing Henrique Meirelles, a prominent market-oriented economist, as head of the Brazilian Central Bank (Martínez and Santiso 2003). His commitment to price stability is a critical piece to the successful economic story. Yet establishing inflation targeting as the central policy plank of his government was also a powerful signal of Lula's abandonment of a leftist program.

Lula da Silva's continued commitment to stability paid off in terms of economic growth, and his government showed better results than its predecessor, as shown in Table 5.1. The Brazilian economy grew at an average annual rate of 4.1 percent between 2003–08, compared to the modest rate of 2.3 percent under Cardoso's rule. As a consequence, Brazilians increased their per capita income at an average annual rate of 2.7 percent between 2003–08 – a rate considerably superior to the reduced rate of 0.7 percent registered under Cardoso (see Table 5.1).

In terms of inflation, the other critical macroeconomic variable, Lula's government also showed better results than its predecessor. The average rate of inflation under Lula (6.9 percent from 2003–08) has been lower than that achieved by Cardoso's government (14.9 percent). Although this rate still surpasses the inflationary standards of the OECD countries, which equaled 1.86 percent between 1995 and 2001 (Ihrig and Márquez 2003), inflation has been consistently declining during Lula's administration (see Table 5.1). Lula's commitment to low inflation rates remains credible, with projected rates for 2009

---

[9] Macroeconomic policy did experience an important shift in 1999 after the collapse of the Real Plan as the government shifted from a controlled exchange rate as the principal tool of macroeconomic control to explicit inflation targeting with a floating exchange rate. Although the shift in macroeconomic tools was important, the central goal of policy, currency, and price stability did not change. Further, Lula's new administration in 2003 continued inflation targeting as the central tool of macroeconomic policy, see Barbosa Filho (2008).

TABLE 5.1. *Comparing Cardoso's and Lula's Performances: Economic Indicators*

Economic Indicators	1995	1996	1997	1998	1999	2000	2001	2002	Average Cardoso	2003	2004	2005	2006	2007	2008	2009e	Average Lula
GDP growth (annual %)[a]	4.2	2.2	3.4	0.0	0.3	4.3	1.3	2.7	2.3	1.1	5.7	3.2	4.0	5.7	5.1	-1.3	3.4
GDP per capita growth (annual %)[b]	2.6	0.6	1.8	-1.5	-1.2	2.8	-0.2	1.2	0.7	-0.3	4.2	1.8	2.6	4.3	3.7		2.7
GDP per capita (US$ of 2000)[b]	3600	3622	3687	3633	3588	3688	3682	3726		3715	3872	3941	4043	4216	4374		
Trade (% of GDP)[c]	16.0	14.9	15.8	15.9	20.2	21.7	25.7	26.7	19.6	27.1	29.0	26.6	26.3	26.2			27.0
Inflation[a]	66.0	16.0	6.9	3.2	4.9	7.1	6.8	8.4	14.9	14.8	6.6	6.9	4.2	3.6	5.7	4.8	6.6
Investment rate (as % of GDP)[d]	21.3	18.2	17.7	17.3	15.5	15.7	16.6	15.7	17.2	15.4	15.7	16.1	16.8				16.0
International reserves (in US$ millions)[e]	51,840	60,110	52,173	44,556	36,342	33,011	35,866	37,823		49,296	52,935	53,799	85,839	180,334	206,806	208,969[f]	

Sources: (a) IMF, World Economic Outlook Database, April 2009 (e = estimated by the staff of the IMF); (b) Economic Commission for Latin America and the Caribbean; (c) World Bank, World Development Indicators; (d) Instituto de Pesquisa Econômica Aplicada (IPEA); (e) Banco Central do Brasil; (f) This amount corresponds to 6 July 2009. All data were retrieved in July 2009.

even lower (IMF 2009).[10] In summary, Lula's administration has remained committed to macroeconomic stability and predictability.

Lula da Silva's administration succeeded in reducing inflation for three main reasons: It has made substantial efforts to balance the Brazilian fiscal accounts, with a fiscal surplus of 4.25 percent in 2003, 4.59 percent in 2004, 4.83 percent in 2005, and 4.37 percent in 2006 (Mantega 2007); it has pursued restrictive monetary policies; and it has created greater openness toward international capital.

Regarding its efforts to balance the Brazilian fiscal accounts, Lula's administration was able to reduce the nominal public deficit to an average annual rate of 3.35 percent between 2003–05, considerably lower than the 6.23 percent of Cardoso's administration (Mercadante 2006); to consistently decrease the levels of public debt from approximately 51.3 percent of GDP to levels of 38.8 percent of GDP between 2002–08;[11] and to increase the primary (budgetary) surplus to the level of 4.32 percent in 2003, which exceeds by more than 0.5 percent the amount required by the IMF (Paiva 2006). In addition, higher rates of economic growth, an increasing tax burden as a percentage of GDP (31.9 percent in 2003, 32.7 percent in 2004, 33.7 percent in 2005, and 34.1 percent in 2006),[12] and the appreciation of the dollar (a change of 39.7 percent between 2003–07)[13] contributed to a better balance in Brazil's fiscal accounts during the Lula administration.

The reduction in both the public nominal deficit and the levels of public debt dampened expectations of greater future rates of inflation in the Brazilian economy, which were probably inflated at the beginning of Lula's administration due to investors' fears about Lula's past Socialist leanings and concerns about his intentions and commitment to fiscal stability.

Lula da Silva's administration set its inflation targeting through the Conselho Monetário Nacional (National Monetary Council, formed by the president of the Central Bank and the Ministry of Public Finance), which determined the planned rates of inflation and adjusted monetary policy accordingly. The council consistently established relatively low inflation rates as the target, which in turn demanded the implementation of restrictive monetary policies by the Central Bank (Prata 2006). For example, the Conselho Monetário Nacional fixed an inflation rate of 4.5 percent as the goal for 2005 (Fahri 2006; Prata 2006). To achieve this goal, the Central Bank decided to raise interest rates from the annual average of 16.24 percent in 2004 to 19.23 percent in 2005,

---

[10] In 2007, the exchange rate appreciated from R$2.20 against the dollar to R$1.80. This period of real appreciation against the dollar seems to have helped to keep inflation down, see Latin American Regional Report (2007).

[11] At the end of 2002, the last year of Cardoso's administration, the Brazilian public debt was approximately 51.3 percent of GDP. Lula's administration was able to reduce this amount to levels of 38.8 percent of GDP in 2008 (IPEADATA statistics). Consult http://www.ipeadata .gov.br/ipeaweb.dll/MenuCtrl?SessionID=1863122960&Mod=MACRO&Lang=Portuguese.

[12] IPEADATA statistics. Consult http://www.ipeadata.gov.br/.

[13] IPEADATA statistics. Consult http://www.ipeadata.gov.br/ipeaweb.dll/.

which reduced inflation but also cooled the growth of the Brazilian economy (Farhi 2006; data taken from Banco Central in Prata 2006).

Lula da Silva's administration also expanded the degree of openness for international capital, which contributed to the appreciation of the real exchange rate (Carneiro 2006; Fahri 2006).[14] Thus, the real exchange rate appreciated 14 percent in 2003, 2.2 percent in 2004, 16 percent in 2005, 0.8 percent in 2006, and 4.3 percent in 2007 (data taken from IPEADATA). This continuous appreciation also helped reduce inflationary pressures (Carneiro 2006; Fahri 2006). Despite their benefits for reducing inflation, these appreciations weakened the global export competitiveness of the Brazilian economy, though it has recently been partially offset by the devaluation of the Brazilian currency as a result of the international crisis. Thus, the loss of competitiveness from currency appreciation could pose a threat to the sustainability of the nation's economic growth in the long term.

Therefore, in general, Lula da Silva's administration has preferred maintaining macroeconomic stability with low inflation rates to stimulating more economic growth and employment in the economy. This conservative solution to the trade-off between inflation and unemployment is not commonly associated with leftist administrations. On the contrary, a leftist administration, in theory, would more likely emphasize greater levels of employment, lower interest rates, and greater fiscal spending instead of avoiding the costs of inflation in the economy. But the approach is consistent with the priorities established by Lula with the "Letter to the Brazilian People" and is understandable given Brazil's experience with inflation.

Despite the appreciation of the real, the greater economic dynamism in this period and the commitment to low inflation rates have allowed Lula's administration to maintain relative stability (and even increasing rates) in three key economic indicators: rates of investment, the amount of international reserves (in US$ millions), and trade openness (measured by exports plus imports divided by the gross domestic product). For more details on these statistics, see Table 5.1.

Although Lula's Brazil compares favorably to Cardoso's Brazil, the picture looks less impressive when compared to the rates of growth of other large Latin American countries. Table 5.2 shows these statistics. Within the group of the largest economies of the region, Brazil's economic growth only surpassed that of Mexico between 2003–09.[15] Although Mexico reached an average rate of growth of 2.1 percent, Brazil attained only the slightly higher average rate of 3.4 percent during Lula's administration.[16] Even after taking into account the variable effects of the economic crisis on the region, the performance of the

---

[14] First, Lula's administration made it easier for residents of Brazil to keep deposits or investments abroad (*outward transactions*). Second, Lula's administration conceded fiscal incentives to foreign investors to acquire public debt, Carneiro (2006).

[15] The rate of growth employed for 2009 is an estimation of the IMF's staff.

[16] This result also indicates that despite the negative effect of the international crisis on the Brazilian economy (an estimated contraction of 1.3 percent in 2009), the net balance of Lula's government continues to be positive.

TABLE 5.2. *Comparing Brazil's Performance with the Rest of Latin America (during Lula's Government)*

Indicators/Countries

GDP Growth (annual %)[a]	2003	2004	2005	2006	2007	2008	2009e	Average
Brazil	1.1	5.7	3.2	4.0	5.7	5.1	-1.3	3.4
Argentina	8.8	9.0	9.2	8.5	8.7	7.0	-1.5	7.1
Bolivia	2.7	4.2	4.4	4.8	4.6	5.9	2.2	4.1
Chile	4.0	6.0	5.6	4.6	4.7	3.2	0.1	4.0
Colombia	4.6	4.7	5.7	6.9	7.5	2.5	0.0	4.6
Mexico	1.7	4.0	3.2	5.1	3.3	1.3	-3.7	2.1
Peru	4.0	5.0	6.8	7.7	8.9	9.8	3.5	6.5
Venezuela	-7.8	18.3	10.3	10.3	8.4	4.8	-2.2	6.0

Inflation[a]	2003	2004	2005	2006	2007	2008	2009e	Average
Brazil	14.8	6.6	6.9	4.2	3.6	5.7	4.8	6.7
Argentina	13.4	4.4	9.6	10.9	8.8	8.6	6.7	8.9
Bolivia	3.3	4.4	5.4	4.3	8.7	14.0	6.5	6.7
Chile	2.8	1.1	3.1	3.4	4.4	8.7	2.9	3.8
Colombia	7.1	5.9	5.0	4.3	5.5	7.0	5.4	5.7
Mexico	4.5	4.7	4.0	3.6	4.0	5.1	4.8	4.4
Peru	2.3	3.3	1.6	2.0	1.8	5.8	4.1	3.0
Venezuela	31.1	21.7	16.0	13.7	18.7	30.4	36.5	24.0

Indicators

GDP per Capita Growth (annual %)[b]	2003	2004	2005	2006	2007	2008	Average
Brazil	-0.3	4.2	1.8	2.6	4.3	3.7	2.7
Argentina	7.8	8.0	8.1	7.4	7.6	5.9	7.5
Bolivia	0.4	1.9	2.3	2.6	2.4	4.0	2.3
Chile	2.8	4.9	4.5	3.5	3.6	2.1	3.6
Colombia	3.1	3.1	4.3	5.5	6.2	1.3	3.9
Mexico	0.6	3.2	2.3	3.7	2.2	0.2	2.0
Peru	2.8	3.7	5.6	6.5	7.6	8.6	5.8
Venezuela	-9.4	16.3	8.5	8.0	7.1	3.1	5.6

Per Capita Social Public Expenditure, Total (% of GDP per capita)[b]	2003	2004	2005	2006	2007	2008	Average
Brazil	22.0	21.9	22.0	23.7			22.4
Argentina	19.3	19.1	19.9	20.9			19.8
Bolivia	18.4	18.3	17.8				18.2
Chile	14.4	13.5	12.8	12.1			13.2
Colombia	11.1	10.6	11.7	11.3			11.2
Mexico	27.1	27.7	28.8				27.9
Peru	5.3	5.4	5.0	5.1			5.2
Venezuela	8.2	9.0	9.4	11.6			9.6

Sources: (a) IMF, World Economic Outlook Database, April 2009, (e = estimated by the staff of the IMF); (b) Economic Commission for Latin America and the Caribbean (constant 2000 US$). All data were retrieved in July 2009.

Brazilian economy in terms of growth remains slightly lower than the Latin American mean (see Table 5.2).

The weakness of Brazil's performance stems from the high interest rates and appreciated currency necessary for inflation targeting. But it also reflects deeper structural weaknesses in the economy. The lack of, or incompleteness of, structural reforms in the Brazilian economy helps explain the disappointing average rate in Brazil. Major tax reforms, trade reforms, labor market reforms, and pension reforms are still on the long-term Brazilian agenda. But neither Cardoso nor Lula has advanced far in these domains (discussed further later). Brazil's relatively modest growth also means that GDP per capita growth remains one of the lowest of the region, at only 2.7 percent between 2003–08.

By contrast, Brazil's performance in controlling inflation and economic stability compares well to the achievements of the other Latin American countries. Lula's average annual inflation rate from 2003–09[17] (6.7 percent) approaches the averages of most of the larger Latin American countries, such as those of Argentina (8.9 percent), Mexico (4.4 percent), Colombia (5.7 percent), and Chile (3.8 percent). However, the macroeconomic achievements of 2007, 2008, and the expected inflation rate for 2009 suggest that Brazil could soon rank among the outstanding economic performers among Latin American countries, such as Chile and Peru. As shown in Table 5.2, these two countries were able to combine the lowest inflation rates with the highest rates of growth between 2003–08.

As the editors note (and the specific country chapters elaborate on), the moderate left's greater commitment to macroeconomic stability is one of the key economic differences with the radical left cases and a crucial reason for the moderate left's better economic performance. This is becoming particularly salient with the onset of the global economic crisis. As Javier Corrales notes in Chapter 2 of this volume, Venezuela faces both economic and political risks from declining oil revenues and years of macroeconomic profligacy. By contrast, the economic stability and predictability achieved by Lula's government has left the Brazilian economy arguably poised to ride out the crisis better than many other economies in the region. In fact, as Table 5.1 shows, Brazil has been able to keep intact its international reserves. This has fostered confidence in the ability of the Brazilian economy to successfully face the international crisis and has given Brazil space to stimulate its economy in the face of the crisis. Thus, countercyclical and expansive public policies such as greater public investment (e.g., through the PAC) are helping to promote economic recovery.[18]

Social Indicators and Policy

As noted previously, Lula da Silva's campaign promises of social justice and an "inversion of priorities" have not been the centerpiece of his administration. In

---

[17] The rate of inflation employed for 2009 is an estimation of the IMF's staff.
[18] The Programa de Aceleração do Crescimento (Program for Accelerating Growth, or PAC) is programming investments of more than US$200 billion in infrastructure.

fact, Lula's administration has consistently limited social expenditures in order to maintain its main priorities: macroeconomic balance and low inflation rates. Social spending has increased, but not dramatically, and a considerable part of the increase is accounted for by increased spending on Brazil's highly regressive social security system. Nevertheless, as we show in Table 5.3, poverty and inequality (Gini Index) measures have registered considerable improvements during Lula's time in office. Thus, Lula's social policy performance presents something of a paradox.

As with the country's macroeconomic performance, the good results are partially a consequence of good fortune and partially the outcome of explicit policy decisions. The reduction in poverty (at an annual average of 7.9 percent between 2003–07)[19] seems to stem from Brazil's moderate economic growth, discussed previously, and from a large increase in the number of beneficiaries of Brazil's innovative income transfer programs, particularly the conditional cash transfers associated with the Bolsa Família (Barros Silva et al. in Chapter 6 of this volume note that there is some controversy over whether the Bolsa Família has had real effects on income and poverty). It should be noted, however, that the conditional cash transfers began under President Cardoso and in any event do not represent significant increases in social expenditures. In short, Bolsa Família is a low-cost, high-visibility program that increases low-income families' purchasing power but is less promising with respect to creating fundamental changes in Brazil's social and economic structure (Hall 2007).

As Table 5.3 shows, the macroeconomic improvements in the country stand in contrast to the modest efforts made in public social expenditure. In general, social spending as a percentage of GDP per capita has slightly increased between 2002, when Cardoso's administration concluded, and 2006. Social spending rose only slightly after 2004 mainly due to pension costs and the expanded coverage of the Bolsa Família. This fact again underscores the pragmatic stability orientation of Lula's administration (which has been concerned more with the fiscal accounts) and its not particularly leftist character – at least by the standards of traditional or populist modes of leftism (Ponce 2007).

In addition, some relevant components of this social expenditure – for their implications for human development and the categorization of what a leftist party is – present only limited improvements, confirming the continuity of the status quo (inherited from Cardoso) during Lula da Silva's government in the scope of social policies. Specifically, public expenditure in social security, education, and health as a percentage of GDP per capita show similar behaviors. First, per capita public expenditure in social security has experienced an increase from 12.2 (as a percentage of GDP per capita) in 2002, when Cardoso's administration concluded, to 12.9 in 2006. Second, per capita public expenditure in both education and health as a percentage of GDP also experienced small increases during the same period. In the case of education, the rate

---

[19] This calculation is based on the features provided by the Instituto de Pesquisa Econômica Aplicada (IPEA).

TABLE 5.3. *Comparing Cardoso's and Lula's Performance: Social Indicators and Policy*

Social Indicators	1995	1996	1997	1998	1999	2000	2001	2002	Average Cardoso	2003	2004	2005	2006	2007	2008	Average Lula
Unemployment (% of total labor force)[a]	4.6	5.4	5.7	7.6	7.6	7.1	6.2	11.7	6.9	12.3	11.5	9.8	10.0	9.3	7.9	10.1
Minimum real wage (constant R$)[c]	242	248	255	270	260	274	299	289	267	315	321	353	400	414	424	371
Per capita social public expenditure, total (% of GDP per capita)[a]	20.2	19.5	19.2	21.6	21.4	20.9	21.0	21.4	20.7	22.0	21.9	22.0	23.7			22.4
Per capita social public expenditure, social security (% of GDP per capita)[a]	10.3	10.7	10.5	11.7	11.6	11.2	11.0	12.2	11.1	11.4	11.7	12.0	12.9			12.0
Per capita social public expenditure, education (% of GDP per capita)[a]	4.8	4.5	4.0	5.5	5.5	4.9	5.0	4.2	4.8	5.1	4.5	4.5	4.8			4.7
Per capita social public expenditure, health (% of GDP per capita)[a]	4.4	3.6	3.9	3.7	3.9	3.9	4.2	4.1	3.9	4.5	4.6	4.5	4.9			4.6
Adult literacy rate (% age 15 and above)[b]						86.4				88.4	88.6		89.6	90.5		

(*continued*)

TABLE 5.3 *continued*

Poverty/Inequality Indicators	1995	1996	1997	1998	1999	2000	2001	2002	2003	2004	2005	2006	2007	2008
Poverty[a]		35.8			37.5		37.5		38.7	37.7	36.5	33.3	30.3	
Poverty (% of households)[c]	27.0	27.0	27.0	26.0	27.0		26.0	26.0	27.0	25.0	22.0	19.0	17.0	
Extreme poverty rate (% of national population)[a]		13.9			12.9		13.2		13.9	12.1	10.6	9.0	8.5	
Extreme poverty rate (% of households)[c]	10.0	11.0	11.0	10.0	10.0		11.0	9.0	11.0	9.0	8.0	6.0	6.0	
Gini index (100 = perfect inequality, 0 = perfect equality)[d]	59.2	59.1	59.3	59.2	58.5		58.6	58.2	57.6		56.3		55.0	
Gini index[c]	59.8	60.0	60.0	59.8	59.2		59.3	58.7	58.0	56.9	56.7	56.0	55.3	

Sources: (a) Economic Commission for Latin America and the Caribbean; (b) UNESCO Institute for Statistics, Global Education Database; (c) Instituto de Pesquisa Econômica Aplicada (IPEA); (d) World Bank, World Development Indicators. All data were retrieved in July 2009.

increased from 4.2 percent in 2002 to 4.8 percent in 2004. Likewise, the rate for health expenditures rose from 4.1 percent in 2002 to 4.9 percent in 2004 (as a percentage of GDP per capita) (see Table 5.3).

The increase in social security expenditures – a regressive system in Brazil, but one tightly connected to the PT's traditional base in the public sector unions – stemmed from the system Lula inherited, which could not sustain itself. In fact, resources from the federal government, states, and municipalities were diverted to compensate for the deficit in the social security sector. For example, in 2002, the federal state spent R$22.9 billion to cover the deficit of the pension system, an amount that surpassed federal expenditures on health or education (Berzoini 2003: 180).

To ensure the sustainability of the Brazilian social security system, Lula da Silva introduced a reform against the preferences of the PT and its base. The reform included several important measures from a fiscal and actuarial perspective: It increased the number of years one had to work in order to retire with full benefits; it established a limit to those benefits (pensions); and it set a limit of R$2,400 for future public or private employees (Sallum and Kugelmas 2003: 31). In general, the reform enacted in the Brazilian social security system focused on reversing the continuous loss of capacity of the Brazilian state to pay pensions in the future (Berzoini 2003; Brant 2003; Iwakami Beltrão and Sugahara 2003; Rocca 2003).[20]

Nevertheless, the limited increases in the levels of per capita social expenditure in education and health, coupled with the appreciation of the *Real* during Lula's administration, might pose a threat to the levels of competitiveness and future economic growth of the Brazilian economy. These weaknesses within the current Brazilian strategy will have to be addressed in the future if higher rates of growth and productivity become the priority.

Despite the somewhat regressive policies adopted by Lula's administration, poverty experienced consecutive reductions from 2003–07. We now turn to evaluate those characteristics that have helped reduce poverty in Brazil. We address economic growth, more progressive types of social spending such as income transfer programs, and finally public investment.

ECONOMIC GROWTH AND POVERTY

Within the context of a stable economy with relatively low rates of growth and inflation, Brazil experienced moderate reductions in both its poverty rate and its

---

[20] Before the reform, Brazil had two different types of regimes: the *Regime Geral de Previdência Social*, managed by the Instituto Nacional do Seguro Social, serves workers belonging to the private sector and some public entities, while *Regimes Próprios de Previdência dos Servidores* (RPPS) assists public workers hired by the state. Of the two types of systems, the RPPS was relatively more costly. In 2002, its costs represented 7 percent of GDP, of which worker contributions covered only 1 percent, leaving 6 percent of GDP to be contributed by the state. Moreover, the average benefit for this regime reached R$2,000, which was far superior to the R$382 of the *Regime Geral* (Brant 2003: 186).

extreme poverty rate during Lula da Silva's administration. Both lower inflation rates and higher economic growth rates under Lula contributed to increase average wages. Likewise, the real value of the Brazilian minimum wage grew at an average annual rate of 6.6 percent during Lula's administration – well above the 2.6 percent it had grown in the Cardoso years (see Table 5.3). Finally, as shown in Table 5.3, levels of unemployment dropped from 12.3 percent in 2003 to 7.9 percent in 2008. In general, the reduction of the poverty rate corresponds strongly to the economic growth, decreasing unemployment, and rising minimum wages experienced by the Brazilian economy.

INCOME TRANSFER PROGRAMS AND POVERTY (NONLABOR INCOME)

As noted previously, levels of poverty have experienced a consistent decline during Lula da Silva's government. The reduction in the poverty rates seems to respond not only to the moderate economic growth experienced between 2003–08 but also to the implementation of the program of conditional cash transfers collectively called Bolsa Família.

In general, all the income transfer programs[21] to the poor experienced an increase of 24 percent between 2002–05. In total, these transfers – excluding administrative costs – represented 2.58 percent of the gross domestic product, compared to the average rate of 1.90 percent registered during Cardoso's administration (Mercadante 2006: 122). Although this amount increased from Cardoso to Lula, it is still modest for a government that is in theory leftist and committed to social justice.

At the start of his term, Lula da Silva implemented one highly visible antipoverty program: the Fome Zero (Zero Hunger) program. The initial budget of the program for 2003, the year in which it was launched, was R$1.8 billion. According to the *Folha de São Paulo*, at the end of the first semester of the program, less than 6 percent of this budget had been spent, and the program was increasingly unpopular. The failure of Fome Zero led the administration to salvage it by wrapping four existing stipend programs[22] under the banner of Bolsa Família, the centerpiece of which was the widely acclaimed Bolsa Escola, a program begun at the end of the Cardoso administration. Bolsa Família provides subsidies and income support to people with monthly income below the minimum wage, measured at R$50 for each family member (Tavares Soares, Sader, Gentili, and Benjamin 2004: 30–4). In general, the initial budget for the program was limited by two factors: the tight federal fiscal policy imposed by Lula's administration and the limited capacity of the Brazilian state to spend the budget and distribute the resources efficiently – especially its limited ability

---

[21] These include Abono Salarial, Bolsa Qualificação, Seguro-Desemprego, Previdência Rural, Seguro-Safra, Bolsa Família, Benefício de Prestação Continuada, Renda Mensal Vitalícia, Agente Jovem, and PETI.

[22] Bolsa Família unified four programs: Bolsa Escola, Bolsa Alimentação, Vale Gás, and Cartão-Alimentação (Prata 2006).

to identify the poor and the inefficient intervention of the local municipalities (Tavares Soares, Sader, Gentili, and Benjamin 2004: 36).

Perhaps Lula da Silva's most important social policy contribution has been the development of a single unified registry (*cadastro único*) of program beneficiaries, which has allowed the government to overcome the initial problems with the implementation of Bolsa Família. As a result, the program has been expanding since 2004, with the number of beneficiaries growing consistently. Thus, in 2003, the number of benefited families was 3.6 million, rising to 6.5 million families in 2004, 8.7 million in 2005 (Mercadante 2006),[23] and 11.1 million in 2006 (Hunter and Power 2007: 19). Since then, the program has provided coverage to more than 11 million families. According to official figures, 11.6 million families were taking part in the program in May 2009.[24] Bolsa Família has been considered the largest cash transfer program internationally in terms of both coverage and financing (Rawlings and Rubio 2005). In terms of the resources spent, Lula's administration raised the amount transferred by Cardoso from R$2.148 billion in 2002 to R$3.141 billion in 2003, then to R$5.152 billion and R$6.476 billion in the following two years (data taken from Caixa in Prata 2006).

As the Bolsa Família program has expanded since 2004 (together with the requirement that the children of families receiving benefits attend school), the rate at which poverty declined sped up. Thus, poverty rates fell 7.4 percent in 2004, 12 percent in 2005, 13.6 percent in 2006, and 10.5 percent in 2007 (IPEADATA Statistics). Likewise, extreme poverty rates fell 12.9 percent, 12.4 percent, 15.1 percent, and 5.6 percent in these same four periods, respectively (IPEADATA Statistics). These figures may suggest that the program to combat extreme poverty may now be in a situation of diminishing returns, just as they may suggest the future limited real effect of the program in reducing extreme poverty rates. However, it is reasonable to argue that Bolsa Família played a role in the reduction of poverty in Brazil.[25] In sum, pragmatism and fiscal caution have characterized the social policy focused on eradicating poverty during Lula's administration.

PUBLIC INVESTMENT AND POVERTY

As Table 5.4 shows, access to basic services such as household water and electricity (as a percentage of national population) has not experienced a substantial increase during Lula da Silva's administration (Lopreato 2006). One

[23] The data was taken from the Ministério do Desenvolvimento Social e Combate à Fome.
[24] The source for these data is the Ministério do Desenvolvimento Social e Combate à Fome. Data retrieved on 9 July 2009, from http://www.mds.gov.br/adesao/mib/matrizviewbr.asp?
[25] Analyzing data of the Brazilian National Household Survey from 1995 to 2004, Nanak Kakwani, Marcelo Neri, and Hyun Son (2006) concluded that the combination of both labor (as a function of salary, productivity, and levels of unemployment) and nonlabor income (social security and especially income transfer programs) contributed to reduce poverty and inequality in Brazil.

TABLE 5.4. *Comparing Cardoso's and Lula's Performance: Public Sector and Gross Fixed Capital Formation*

Indicators	1995	1996	1997	1998	1999	2000	2001	2002	Absolute Change	2003	2004	2005	2006	2007	2008	Absolute Change
Tax burden (% of GDP)^a	28.4	28.6	28.5	29.3	31.1	30.3	31.8	32.3	3.9	31.9	32.7	33.7	34.1			2.2
Total public debt (% of GDP)^a	27.9	30.7	31.8	38.5	44.5	45.5	49.8	51.3	23.4	53.5	48.2	47.9	45.8	43.8	38.8	−14.7
Gross fixed capital formation (% of GDP)^a	20.6	19.3	19.9	19.7	18.9	19.3	19.5	18.3	−2.3	17.8	19.6	19.9	20.9	22.9		5.1
Total public investment (R$ billions)^b						27.4	33.3	34.1		29.6	37.9	45.3	57.2	72.8	93.7	
Public investment in infrastructure (R$ billions)^b								11.5		8.2	21.2	22.7	30.3	36.1	49.3	

Other Indicators	1995	1996	1997	1998	1999	2000	2001	2002	Absolute Change	2003	2004	2005	2006	2007	Absolute Change
Access to household water (% of national population)^c	76.0	77.4	77.5	78.7	79.6	80.9	81.8		5.8	82.4	82.1	82.2	83.0	83.1	0.7
Access to household electricity (% of national population)^c	91.5	92.6	93.1	94.0	94.6	95.8	96.5		5.0	96.8	96.7	97.0	97.5	97.9	1.1

Sources: (a) IPEA; (b) Tesouro Nacional, Ministério de Fazenda; (c) Economic Commission for Latin America and the Caribbean. All data were retrieved in July 2009.

characteristic sometimes associated with leftist governments is that they employ the public sector to carry out aggressive public investment in human capital through aggressive education and health programs.[26] To that extent, Lula's administration does not look like a leftist administration.

However, unlike these disappointing features in investment in human capital and basic services, the Lula da Silva government has made some advances in infrastructure development. For example, a new industrial policy was implemented in 2004 (and a new coordinating agency created in 2005) to advance private–public partnerships in the development of key sectors, such as semiconductors, computer software, and capital goods. This built on already existing initiatives to promote research and investment in critical utilities, such as energy and water (Rodríguez-Clare and Melo 2007). Despite these new efforts, both public and private domestic investment levels remained relatively low during most of Lula's administration, consistent with Brazil's modest pace of economic growth.

More recently, Lula da Silva has been able to take advantage of the country's macroeconomic stability and fiscal surplus to launch a more ambitious plan. In January 2007, Lula's administration announced a four-year program to accelerate economic growth called the Programa de Aceleração do Crescimento (Program for Accelerating Growth, or PAC) based on investment of US$236 billion in infrastructure – especially focused on roads, electricity, sanitation, and housing. As Table 5.4 displays, in following the goals of this program, the Brazilian government has already significantly increased the amounts of public investment in infrastructure since 2007 – in addition to another substantial increase in total public investment. This plan, which is to be funded by the public sector, aims to increase the modest levels of public investment in Brazil seen in the last few decades (Hall 2007).

PT Performance vis-à-vis Institutions

There is probably no area in which the PT has been as disappointing as it has been in its political conduct. The PT has stood since its inception for democratic, participatory decision making and honest governance. During its years in the opposition in Congress, it stood clearly and explicitly against corruption, and Lula da Silva's 2002 presidential campaign played on public anger over successive corruption scandals during Cardoso's two terms in office. The PT and Lula's stance on corruption and good governance was not merely rhetoric, as the public widely perceived the party as standing for these as well. But the PT in power at the national level has been a different party, at least to some degree as a consequence of Lula's choices about macroeconomic policy.

Our understanding of the PT provides further nuance to the editors' characterization of moderate left parties. The editors observe that the radical left is willing to incur polarization and to use antagonistic approaches to politics

[26] Consult Lange and Garrett (1991) and Boix (1998).

to mobilize support and exclude the opposition. The radical left undermines existing institutions and democratic procedures to advance its political and economic program. By contrast, the moderate left is more oriented to negotiation with the opposition and is willing to make concessions to preserve the institutional and procedural aspects of democratic governance. To a large extent, this does characterize the PT under Lula da Silva and makes it similar to Chile under the *Concertación*, while sharply differentiating it from the regimes of Evo Morales and Hugo Chavez. However, Huber and Pribble note that the Chilean left has been constrained by its own coalition partners within the *Concertación* and by the right in Congress. Those constraints have limited the government's more ambitious and progressive social policy programs. By contrast, the PT has largely abandoned its more far-reaching proposals. It has pursued such a moderate economic program more out of internal acceptance than due to external constraints emanating from congressional opposition. In this regard, the basis of the PT's moderation differs somewhat from that of the Chilean left.

Arguably the worst element of the PT's performance has been the party's abandonment of its distinguished history as a champion of clean government. The Lula da Silva administration has been tainted by some of the worst corruption scandals in Brazilian history (Cason 2006; Flynn 2005). The most serious allegations center on the so-called *mensalão* (monthly salary or stipend) scandal, in which opposition members of Congress received monthly payments (roughly US$12,000) in exchange for voting for Lula's policy program. The scandal erupted in 2004 and led to parliamentary investigations that ultimately brought down some of Lula's closest allies – notably José Dirceu, a longtime party stalwart and one of Lula's chief political strategists. Discovery of the *mensalão* scandal led to further revelations about illegal campaign financing, offshore accounts, and a vast public contracting kickback scheme that had begun under PT mayors and governors well before the 2002 presidential election. The PT's previous corruption differed from other cases, as it appears to have been oriented primarily toward party building rather than personal enrichment, and it grew in response to the PT's relative fund-raising disadvantages vis-à-vis more right-wing and business-friendly parties. Nevertheless, it is appalling in its scope and scale, as well as in the damage it has done to the only clean reputation in Brazilian party politics, and it has been made worse by Lula's mostly cavalier attitude toward the various scandals.

The *mensalão* scandal, however, was not about party building and not a response to a campaign finance disadvantage. The question, then, is why did the Lula da Silva government enter into this arrangement? The answer stems from the way the PT chose to manage its governing coalition. Brazil's fragmented party system makes it extremely unlikely that any executive will hold a majority from his or her party in the legislature. As a result, all presidents in the New Republic have had to cobble together coalitions. Traditionally, coalitions have been stitched together by dividing cabinet positions among coalition members, with the expectation that such positions offered control over resources that could then be used for patronage purposes (*fisiologismo*) by the individual cabinet members and their parties. In addition, *fisiologismo* was an important source of political leverage with the Congress. Members of Congress depend on patronage spending for their electoral success and have typically bargained with the executive over the release of specific patronage spending items inserted into the budget in exchange for legislative support.

Lula da Silva faced two difficulties with this strategy. First, his own party did not want to share control with coalition supporters (Sola 2008). Instead, the party divided up cabinet posts among its own members and left crucial coalition supporters out (Couto and Baia 2006). Brazilian presidents typically fill tens of thousands of bureaucratic appointments – another crucial element of patronage, and one typically shared among coalition members. But the PT was reluctant to share control over this crucial resource, too. Instead, Lula dramatically expanded the number of cabinet posts to a record thirty-five members and filled the bureaucracy with thousands of the PT faithful. The PT's unwillingness to share control over resources led Lula's administration to rely on alternative means of securing legislative support for government policies: the *mensalão*.

But Lula da Silva faced a second problem as well. Core members of the PT opposed central elements of Lula's orthodox policy program, especially the reform of the social security system (Couto and Baia 2006). Moreover, tensions between Lula and his own party over the government's agenda led to internal squabbling, weak direction, and a concentration of decision making in the executive that angered both the Congress (especially the PT delegation within it) and members of the social movements that had long been the strongest base of PT support. "*O modo petista de governar*" (the PT mode of governing) – the PT phrase for describing the participatory style of decision making made famous by its participatory budgeting process (*orçamento participativo*) – had given way to traditional, executive-dominated, closed decision making, greased by pork and corruption.

The social security reform particularly highlights the difficulty Lula da Silva faced with his own party. Brazilian presidents had been under pressure to reform the country's cumbersome and highly regressive social security system for years. The system had been a fiscal burden (in deficit more than 4 percent of GDP), placing significant pressure on government efforts to maintain a balanced budget. Cardoso passed only a limited reform, largely due to intense PT-led opposition (Kingstone 2003). The PT claimed that the system was not in deficit and that the reform was an IMF-inspired assault on the nation's seniors (*os velhinhos*). However, once in office, Lula moved quickly to pass the very reforms he had helped defeat under Cardoso. Lula faced intense opposition from public sector unions and his own party and ultimately was able to pass the reform in late 2003 only through patronage and threats of expulsion. In the end, four PT deputies did defect (another seven abstained) and were expelled from the party. Lula's shift on social security was perhaps the most important evidence for the left of his abandonment of the party's most cherished principles and of his collusion with the financial sector (e.g., Bianchi and Braga 2005).

Social movement actors also felt bitterly betrayed by Lula da Silva as his administration followed the Cardoso precedent of subordinating policymaking to macroeconomic priorities and insulating key macroeconomic decision makers (notably the minister of finance) from outside pressure. As a result, the inclusive mode of decision making long championed by the PT and actually implemented in a number of PT-led municipalities through participatory budgeting was simply abandoned at the national level. For some time, social movement organizations, most dramatically the Landless Movement (*Movimento dos sem Terra* or MST), held off in their criticisms and avoided confrontational tactics. But by the end of Lula's first term, key movements like the MST had decided that the PT–social movement alliance was over and renewed their activities as separate groups (Hochstetler 2008).

The combination of vigorous *fisiologismo*, appalling corruption, and closed-door decision making might have been more tolerable if the Lula da Silva administration had more legislative accomplishments to its credit. Unfortunately, that is not the case. Lula and the PT largely abandoned their historic platform to continue Cardoso's pragmatic neoliberal agenda. As a result, they inherited the same set of structural reforms that Cardoso wrestled with during his two terms, most importantly labor market, tax, and deeper pension system reforms (Samuels 2004). From a neoliberal perspective, these are crucial reforms to improve the fiscal health of the state and thereby allow lower interest rates, with direct consequences for the competitiveness and dynamism of the domestic economy. But Lula's administration has made little to no progress on any of these key reforms, with its most recent failure occurring in December 2007, when it failed to renew the Tax on Financial Transactions (CPMF). To some extent, this is a reflection of the difficulty of reforming policies tied to patronage resources in a political system greased by patronage. It is also a reflection of the PT's political weakness in the Congress, particularly in the wake of the corruption scandals and their impact on crucial PT leaders.

CONCLUSION

In sum, Brazil's performance under Lula da Silva has been mixed, and its assessment varies somewhat depending on the measure one chooses to use. By the yardstick of traditional leftist concerns, the Lula administration has been a considerable disappointment. Judged as a constrained leftist government, the picture has been mixed. The question, then, of what the left has done right in Brazil is a difficult one. It is hard not to take into account Brazil's tumultuous years between 1985 and 2002. The governments of José Sarney, Fernando Collor, and Itamar Franco were all serious failures of one kind or another. Cardoso accomplished a great deal but ended his second term in a cloud of disappointment and scandal. Given that record, Lula deserves considerable credit for embracing a centrist, pragmatic market orientation that has become the linchpin of virtually unprecedented economic stability. Moreover, that stability has helped reduce poverty and has provided a base for ongoing improvements, both in Lula's second term and under future presidents.

But in other ways, it is hard not to be disappointed with the Lula da Silva administration. On the social policy front, the Lula government has shown little imagination or initiative regarding the need to build human capital for the long term. Bolsa Família may reach ever-larger numbers of poor families and boost family income, but it does not otherwise address Brazil's severe quality issues in education and health, and it does not build on the innovative efforts of the Cardoso administration (Arretche 2004; Draibe 2004; Weyland 2007; Hunter and Sugiyama 2009). In this regard, our conclusions are very similar to Barros Silva et al. in Chapter 6 of this volume. Macroeconomic stability has sparked growth but has done little to address the country's critical infrastructure needs or to address the drags on economic competitiveness and dynamism that come from the very mechanisms used to secure stability. Finally, the Lula administration has done nothing to begin to reverse the country's history of corruption and exclusion – and indeed may have made matters worse.

These shortcomings matter because the exceptional international economic context has not lasted. During this exceptional period, all of Latin America profited from India and China's surging demand for goods and from the weakness of the U.S. dollar. Brazil appears to be well positioned to ride out the crisis, although it is still too early to make predictions about the global economy and the durability of Chinese demand for Brazilian goods. In any event, the Brazilian economic model continues to suffer from limits to its competitiveness – and most importantly – limits to its capacity to address the country's enormous social inequities. The jury is still out for the Lula da Silva administration. Stability, predictability, and low inflation create ample opportunity to promote the kind of sustainable economic growth with democratic institutions best exemplified by Chile's successful market model. But the danger of allowing the country to sink into its familiar patterns of corruption, exclusion, and boom-bust economic cycles is ever present.

6

Lula's Administration at a Crossroads

The Difficult Combination of Stability and Development in Brazil

Pedro Luiz Barros Silva, José Carlos de Souza Braga,
and Vera Lúcia Cabral Costa

The present chapter examines what Brazil's so-called leftist governments have done right for the development of the country.[1] It seeks to identify the principal policy issues and decisions of the Fernando Henrique Cardoso and Luiz Inácio Lula da Silva administrations from 1994 until the middle of 2008. Our main argument is that a new pattern of capital accumulation that was beginning to be established by the Cardoso government has been extended and consolidated under the Lula da Silva administration. At the same time, a new set of social policies, particularly programs for the very poor, were implemented by the Cardoso government and have been expanded and deepened under the Lula administration. In other words, a significant change in Brazil's social policy strategy (Draibe 2003) that had been initiated between 1996 and 2002 was intensified and strengthened between 2003–08.

Our purpose in this chapter is to show that these new social and economic tendencies have shaped the most important priorities of government action and state intervention from 2003 until now, with three principal results: First, the government's actual agenda[2] has diverged in key ways from the program presented in 2002 by Lula da Silva's political coalition in the campaign for the national elections of that year. The electoral platform of the Workers' Party (Partido dos Trabalhadores – PT) reflected long-standing party goals, but the government's policy approach has differed significantly from that platform. Second, the government's adoption of the new agenda did not reduce the popularity levels of the Lula administration or of the president himself, except among elements of the middle class. Third, but as a result of its divergence from historic PT goals, the Lula government has not been able to restructure Brazil's pattern of capital accumulation in a way that could overcome the country's peculiar type of underdevelopment.

---

[1] We would like to thank the conference organizers, Wendy Hunter, Raúl Madrid, and Kurt Weyland, for their written comments and suggestions, which helped us to improve this chapter.

[2] The classic book on the concept of public agenda is Kingdon (1995).

This chapter is divided into three parts, plus some concluding remarks. The first part proposes a new interpretation of the economic and social policy strategy that Brazil has pursued during the last few decades. Our views differ both from more pessimistic predictions of the problematic effects of leftist administrations and from optimistic visions that by 2010, Brazil will have completed the necessary macroeconomic adjustments to maintain and improve a long-term pattern of economic growth with social justice. Instead we argue that the Lula da Silva administration has been successful in maintaining Brazil's hard-won economic stability and achieving a modest level of economic growth, but not in initiating a dynamic process of development that could diminish and eventually overcome the manifold economic limitations and social deficits plaguing the country.

After the first section has examined the Lula government's mixed economic policy record, the second part uses opinion polls to analyze popular performance ratings of the president and his administration. This section shows that despite the Lula government's high degree of continuity with the socioeconomic policy approach of the Cardoso administration – whose performance many citizens had criticized – large sectors of the Brazilian population evaluate the current administration and the president favorably. This high level of popularity reflects the government's decision to extend and upgrade significantly a number of income transfer and family support programs (most prominently Bolsa Família) that directly reach many millions of destitute people. Strong approval from public opinion and support from some important scholars and intellectuals who have a substantial presence in the media[3] have allowed the president to overcome the political obstacles and corruption scandals faced by his administration, particularly in 2005,[4] and to win a convincing reelection victory in 2006.

Although this section highlights the striking political success of the Lula da Silva administration, the third part of the chapter discusses some of its limitations and deficiencies on the economic and social front. This section examines the development strategy that Brazil has consolidated during the last two decades and emphasizes the changes that must be made if Brazil is to create a more equitable and well-integrated society. In particular, we enumerate the most important characteristics of a new pattern of capital accumulation that could overcome the asymmetries and heterogeneities of Brazil's peculiar version of social and economic underdevelopment.

---

[3] See the conclusions of the seminar organized by IPEA in 2006 (IPEA 2006) and the recent volumes compiled by Paes de Barros, Foguel, and Ulyssea (2007) about the economic effects of the type of cash transfer benefits adopted by the Lula government and their impact on the decline of income inequality in Brazil. See also the analysis of the Bolsa Família program in the second part of this chapter.

[4] These political difficulties and the decline of Lula's popularity in 2005 were not caused by the government's unambitious agenda in economic and social policy. Instead, they were due to scandals involving executive-legislative relations. For perceptive comments on this situation, see Coimbra (2007).

THE CONSOLIDATION OF A NEW PATTERN OF CAPITAL
ACCUMULATION

The recent debate about Brazilian development has been centered around two
positions, which for the sake of clarity will be presented in ideal-typical distinct-
ness. The first position is that from the 1990s to the present, Brazil has been
experiencing a process of socioeconomic regression. In this view, the country
has again taken on the international role of agrarian exporter (Paula 2005;
Bresser Pereira 2007; Gonçalves and Filgueiras 2007) – a development strategy of very limited promise. Other authors advance the opposite view, arguing
that the adjustments already made to the Brazilian economy allow for its com-
fortable, beneficial insertion in ample international trade networks. Additional
measures to redirect public expenditure could place the country on a steady
path toward economic growth, provided that the government prioritizes investments in economic infrastructure (energy and transport) and contains current
spending, especially expenditures on social security and health care (Pinheiro
and Giambiagi 2005; Franco 2006).

    This chapter argues that neither of these two positions correctly and fully
describes the political and economic developments that have taken place in
Brazil during the past 18 years, which include the administrations of presidents Fernando Collor de Mello (1990–2), Fernando Henrique Cardoso (1995–
2002), and Lula da Silva (2003–present). Our view is that a new, typically capitalist development scheme is being fully consolidated in Brazil. This new pattern
of capital accumulation has been built step by step since the beginning of the
1990s, replacing the preceding nationalist, heavily state-interventionist development model. The transition to and consolidation of this market-oriented
strategy was put on a firm track in 1994 with the enactment of the landmark
Plano Real, which expanded and accelerated an economic liberalization program initiated in more haphazard ways in 1990. Because sufficient time has
passed, this chapter can examine the structural characteristics of the new economic strategy. Our findings contradict both of the theories of contemporary
Brazilian development described previously.

    It is worth clarifying from the outset that Brazil's new, market-oriented
development model is certainly subject to fluctuations and instability, as are
all capitalist accumulation patterns, especially those in the global periphery
during the era of financialization, which entails the dominance of the financial
system in the economy.[5] Moreover, it is a pattern whose underlying private
logic has produced and, if left unchanged, will continue producing a strong

---

[5] The dominance of finance in the economy that the term "financialization" denotes (Braga 2000)
means that financial assets grow at higher rates than productive assets. Therefore, even productive
corporations engage in financial speculation. Banks are transformed in financial "supermarkets"
that promote different kinds of speculation through ever newer schemes and mechanisms. Central
banks become hostage to the financial system. They have to do whatever is necessary to attract
and retain capital inflows and thus avoid recessions.

concentration of income and wealth. The new model has also allowed for the creation of productive, financial, as well as speculative capital wealth. The word "speculative" here refers to values that do not reflect productivity and profitability. In the authors' view, this speculative component of Brazil's new development scheme has helped to induce well-off sectors of the population to support a government that – due to its leftist roots – had been expected to diverge from capitalist interests. Ironically, however, business sectors have been the major beneficiaries of the political–economic strategy adopted so far.

If, as this chapter claims, a dynamic, internationalized growth pattern has emerged and consolidated during the last two decades, then a new political and economic foundation for Brazilian development has been built that has managed to overcome – with strong state and international support – the setbacks arising from considerable international volatility (such as the Asian financial crisis of 1997). Brazil's capacity to deal with different types of crises does not derive from the automatic movement of internal or external markets but from an innovative type of economic and political imposition that is typical of financial globalization. The double-sidedness of this process – namely that Brazil has managed to overcome crises, but at serious socioeconomic and political cost – has been ignored or minimized by analysts, who mostly adhere to the two distinct views described previously.

Thus, the new, fuller insertion in capitalist globalization has enabled the Brazilian economy to overcome crises that paradoxically arise from the instability and fluctuations caused by globalization itself. This capacity for crisis management has rested on the increasingly complex interaction among public and private, national and international forces. In particular, the new relations between state and market that have been established over the course of the past twenty years have curbed the propagation of crises.

The sociopolitical coalition that was forged under the Collor, Cardoso, and Lula administrations succeeded in dismantling the well-entrenched development scheme centered around economic nationalism and state interventionism and replacing it with a more economically liberal pattern of accumulation integrated with greater depth into the global economy. Specifically, this coalition made a set of policy decisions feasible that unfolded with very suitable timing and sequence.[6]

First was the creation of a currency, the *Real*, which reunified the three functions of money that are crucial for economic stability: to be a means of payment, a reference for prices, and an instrument for storing value in Brazil. The Plano Real thus managed to recreate a currency for the accumulation of profits in Brazil, avoiding dollarization. In these ways, the Plano Real restored economic stability after many years of high and hyperinflation. The *Real* is not internationally convertible, however, which therefore requires the accumulation of huge international currency reserves by the Brazilian Central Bank.

[6] For further discussion of these concepts, see Pierson (2004).

Between 2004–07, Brazil's international reserves grew from approximately fifty to eighty billion U.S. dollars.

Second was the restructuring and capitalization of the public and private banking system, which then expanded the offer of credit in response to the increase in demand and the reduction of interest rates that resulted from economic stabilization. Together with the ample credit provided by Brazil's Economic and Social Development Bank (BNDES) and with international financing, the self-financing of large industrial holdings on the capital market helps fulfill the function of funding productive investment. Indeed, Brazil's domestic capital market has started to expand. On the international front, Brazil liberalized capital movements for both its citizens and for foreigners. A Central Bank with a high level of effective independence, which serves as a guardian of price stability, is another linchpin of a financial system that generates trust in investors. This new institutional configuration has allowed Brazil to achieve considerable economic growth in recent years although the economic authorities, in a strikingly conservative posture, have maintained high interest rates.

Third, large companies are liquid and profitable and have been expanding their productive investment in response to growing internal consumption. These business sectors have made not only operational but also financial gains. The latter opportunity arises from the process of financial globalization and helps explain why high interest rates did not forestall the accumulation of monetary profits, especially by large companies. For big business, the classic separation between the productive and the financial spheres has faded or completely disappeared. Brazil's small and medium-sized businesses, however, have very limited if any access to these financial opportunities.

Fourth, the expansion and upgrading of Brazilian agribusiness, which has achieved high levels of international competitiveness, has generated a significant increase in exports and made a positive contribution to the country's balance of payments. Because agribusiness relies on technical innovations, its production requirements diversify and expand demand for machines and other types of equipment, and thus provide an important stimulus for the domestic industrial sector. Brazil's dynamic agriculture, therefore, does not supplant industry as the main engine of economic growth – but on the contrary – enhances the opportunities for industrial development. Seen from this perspective, there is no evidence that an unavoidable and irreversible process of deindustrialization is taking place – contrary to the pessimistic claims mentioned previously.

Fifth, the external vulnerability of the Brazilian economy has been reduced, as suggested by the fall in the external debt coefficient in relation to exports, among other indicators. Although this reduction is reversible, Brazil has acquired an additional cushion of protection through the growing accumulation of international reserves and assets, which since January 2008 have been greater than the amount of the nation's external debt. Thus, an economic constraint that used to impose tremendous limitations on Brazil's economic and social development during the 1980s and 1990s has lost its stringency.

Sixth, and finally, under the current conditions, the players with financial power may have incentives to support lower interest rates and higher growth. The reason is that changes in these indicators would increase the chances of improving Brazil's investment grade,[7] which major international investors nowadays regard as synonymous with profitable business opportunities.

All of these elements have the capacity of guaranteeing Brazil's economic stability and of producing steady growth at reasonable levels. But it is also worth noting that the timing and sequence of these decisions has created a pattern of capital accumulation that makes the generation of formal-sector employment problematic and that maintains a highly unequal distribution of income and wealth. Even under the leftist Lula da Silva administration, Brazil continues to have one of the starkest gulfs between the rich and poor in the world. And if left to its own devices, the economic development model that has been consolidated over the last fifteen years is unlikely to bring any drastic improvement on this indicator.

Certainly, for the first time in decades, the 2000s brought a modest reduction in income inequality. To explain this new, albeit slight, trend, scholars point to new or improved social policy initiatives, which target benefits toward the poorest layer of the population. These programs, which have been initiated by the federal government, yet with the decisive support of states and municipalities, include the retirement system for rural workers without previous requirement of contribution or official labor registration. By extending pension coverage beyond the formal sector of the workforce, which enjoys a reasonable level of wages and social protection, this program benefits a segment of the population that suffers from particularly severe material deprivation. The guaranteed cash benefits established by the Organic Law of Social Assistance for other needy groupings and the family grant program (Bolsa Família), which pays destitute families a monetary subsidy for sending their children to school and obtaining basic medical care, fulfill similar functions. All of these transfer schemes have been implemented in a very competent manner by established state agencies, namely the ministries of social security and social development. As a result, these payments tend to reach their intended beneficiaries. And unlike their counterparts in Venezuela and Bolivia, these welfare programs are protected by strong state institutions against financial cuts and political backlash.

A more skeptical interpretation, by contrast, questions that even modest improvements in income distribution have in fact occurred. These voices claim that the annual data from the National Household Survey (Pesquisa Nacional por Amostra de Domicílios) can only provide valid and reliable measurements of income concentration between rich and poor sectors inside the formal labor sector. For various reasons, these surveys are incapable of ascertaining income

---

[7] Statements made by President Lula da Silva throughout 2008 signal a move in this direction: Brazil's bias should be toward growth. This priority is evident in Lula's references to the Growth Acceleration Program of 2007, which announces a wide range of public and private investments in economic and social areas.

shifts in the informal sector and of estimating the real differences of wealth concentration between the world of capital and the world of labor.[8]

Even if this skepticism is incorrect and there has actually been a slight improvement in income distribution, it resulted only from compensatory measures that seek to alleviate the socially deficient operation of Brazil's new development model. To the present day, there has been insufficient attention to public policies that combat the root of the problem through effective interventions in strategic areas, especially primary and professional education, health care, basic sanitation, and job and income generation. Although there have been some efforts to this effect, they have been characterized by significant regional and sectoral differences. As a result, inequality in policy outputs and outcomes has continued to prevail among the country's regions, inside these regions between different states and municipalities, and even inside depressed municipalities. Whereas some local and regional governments have been able to enact successful strategies to generate social assistance, jobs, income, and access to basic social services, others have failed on this front.

These serious social problems and deficits, however, do not necessarily depress economic growth or threaten the new market-oriented pattern of capital accumulation. Although they may eventually become a political problem of national reach, that does not seem to be taking place under the Lula da Silva administration, as the next section demonstrates.

PUBLIC PERCEPTIONS OF BRAZIL'S SOCIOECONOMIC AND POLITICAL SITUATION

Interestingly, most of the Brazilian population does not seem to be aware of the structural deficiencies in the country's development model, many of which – including pronounced social inequality – have plagued the country for decades. No public perception of structural problems at the macroeconomic and social levels appears in the systematic surveys that have assessed the performance of President Lula da Silva and his government from 2003 onward.[9] These polling data show instead that, for the most part, common citizens as well as business leaders have evaluated the country's social and economic conditions positively. Data from polls commissioned by the National Confederation of the Transport Sector (Confederação Nacional do Transporte) and conducted by the SENSUS

---

[8] Márcio Pochmann, current president of the governmental think tank IPEA (Instituto de Pesquisa Econômica Aplicada), has conducted research on this topic. The special edition of IPEA's *Boletim de Políticas Sociais* in 2007 (IPEA 2007), in its chapter about work and income, adopted the same criteria of analysis.

[9] With the exception of mid-2005, polls on the performance of President Lula da Silva and his administration, such as those administered by CNT/SENSUS (discussed in the second section of this chapter), Confederação Nacional da Indústria (CNI), and Instituto Brasileiro de Opinião Pública e Estatística (IBOPE), consistently show higher levels of positive evaluation than under the Cardoso administration.

TABLE 6.1. *Lula's Performance Ratings by Level of Family Income*

	Up to 1 Minimum Wage		From 1 to 5 Minimum Wages		From 5 to 10 Minimum Wages		From 10 to 20 Minimum Wages		Above 20 Minimum Wages		Total	
	Qt	%	Qt	%	Qt	%	Qt	%	Qt	%	Qt	%
Approve	307	81.4	759	66.0	184	59.5	63	52.5	22	50.0	1335	66.8
Disapprove	57	15.1	342	29.7	106	34.3	48	40.0	19	43.2	572	28.6
Doesn't know/ Didn't answer	13	3.4	49	4.3	19	6.1	9	7.5	3	6.8	93	4.7
TOTAL	377	18.9	1150	57.5	309	15.5	120	6.0	44	2.2	2000	100.0

Source: CNT/SENSUS, April 2007.

Institute suggest that the chief executive and his administration have enjoyed increasing support in public opinion over time.

Assessment of President Lula da Silva and his Government

Survey assessments of the Lula administration and the president's own performance from 2004–08 show that after the most turbulent period in 2005, when the government was beset by corruption scandals, approval ratings recovered and climbed even higher than they had been at the beginning of Lula's term.[10] For example, whereas in October 2007 approval of President Lula's administration stood at 46.5 percent while disapproval was 16.5 percent, by February 2008 the positive assessment had climbed to 52.7 percent while disapproval had dropped to a mere 1.7 percent. And whereas in October 2007 Lula's presidential popularity had stood at 61.2 percent versus 32.5 percent disapproval, in February 2008 his personal performance had an approval rating of 66.8 percent versus 28.6 percent disapproval.

Certainly there is a significant portion of the Brazilian population – 28.6 percent – that does not evaluate Lula's performance as successful. As shown in Table 6.1,[11] this disagreement is much more widespread among families with higher incomes than among the poor, although those better-off sectors are relatively favored by Brazil's stark income inequality. At the same time, a poll conducted in April 2008 revealed that the popularity of the president himself had grown even among families with higher incomes.

Prospects of Future Economic Growth

Also, a February 2008 CNT/SENSUS study asked if people believed their country's current economic growth was sustainable. Most interestingly, the vast

[10] CNT/SENSUS, February 2008.
[11] The classification of income levels used in this type of poll is based mostly on salaries and wages. People who receive capital income, that is the wealthy, are not reached by this poll.

majority of respondents, a whopping 60.9 percent, believed that Brazil's economic growth would not stop in the future, whereas 5.2 percent replied that Brazil's growth would last another six months, 5.3 percent that it would last one more year, 4.3 percent expected two years, and 11.6 percent predicted four years. In September 2004, optimism had also been strong, though not quite as widespread: A majority of 51.7 percent had responded that growth would not stop, 8.7 percent thought it would last for six months, 7.8 percent for one year, 10.5 percent for two years, and 9.0 percent for four years. Thus, despite the looming threat of a global economic crisis, Brazilians became ever more sanguine about their country's future growth prospects.

Overall Assessment of the Socioeconomic and Political Situation

Based on these and other findings, the February CNT/SENSUS 2008 poll concluded: "President Lula remains 'bullet-proof.' His popularity ratings are still high due to good economic outcomes and results in social programs, in addition to the fact that his political discourse is easily grasped by the population."[12] This finding confirms one of our principal claims, namely, that the strategy adopted by the Lula da Silva administration of extending and deepening the macroeconomic choices of the Cardoso administration elicits support not only from well-off Brazilians, especially wealthy business people, but also from the general population, especially poorer segments. In particular, the extension of social programs, especially transfer schemes that distribute income to the lower rungs of the social pyramid, has produced excellent results in bolstering Lula's popularity and thus strengthening his powers of negotiation with the National Congress. Interestingly, the president has commanded this widespread support although he has not resolved a number of the structural problems plaguing Brazil's economy and society, especially the previously mentioned deficits in employment generation and income distribution.[13] Similarly, as Huber, Pribble, and Stephens note in Chapter 4, the absence of changes that would reduce inequality in income and wealth constitutes one of the most serious failures of the Chilean left in government.

Obviously, then, the Lula administration's favorable poll results are based on short-term indicators of economic and social policy performance. This situation constitutes a marked contrast to the assessments of the Cardoso administration carried out at the end of its second term in office. Although Lula's predecessor had pursued similar economic policies and enacted more substantial reforms in social policy (see Draibe 2003; Melo 2005), President Cardoso's popularity ratings during the early 2000s were far less generous. Due to this

---

[12] *Sumário Executivo Pesquisa 91°*, CNT/SENSUS, 18 February 2008.
[13] When Journalist José Nêumanne analyzed data from the CNT/SENSUS survey in an *Estado de São Paulo* article in February 2008, he characterized this strategy as "filling the pockets of the rich and the stomachs of the poor" (Nêumanne 2008).

weak standing, he did not succeed in getting his chosen candidate elected in the 2002 presidential contest.

The Lula da Silva administration did not obtain these high approval ratings by presenting to the public an agenda of innovative structural reforms for transforming the new market model, which provides disproportionate benefits to business and better-off sectors while opening up only limited opportunities for poorer segments of the population. Contrary to the traditional, fairly radical program of his Workers' Party, the Lula government has not pursued this type of profound change. But popular perception has not noticed that meaningful reforms that would stimulate economic and social development, for example through a thorough revamping of the education system, are not taking place.

Instead, President Lula da Silva has demonstrated political savvy and an impressive capacity to interact with the least privileged social classes. These skills have helped to ensure support from these poorer segments throughout most of his two administrations. Lula's political cleverness was demonstrated by his capacity to promote rapid adjustments in the social Priority Program that the government had announced at the beginning of its first term. These modifications changed a complex set of policies and programs that proved difficult to implement into the successful, highly visible Bolsa Família program. In 2006, this program alone reached 51.4 million beneficiaries with cash transfers and 11.8 million with various types of social services. It was entrusted to a new ministry, which commanded the institutional capacity and organizational conditions for implementing this kind of conditional cash transfer scheme effectively. The creation of the Ministry of Social Development and Fight against Hunger has allowed for the fulfillment of a longstanding demand that a comprehensive system of social assistance and welfare be established in Brazil. This system currently comprises a number of social service programs and income transfer schemes such as the Bolsa Família. It considerably strengthens Brazil's regime of social protection by guaranteeing benefits as a matter of public policy and a right of citizenship, not as clientelistic favors, which was the case in earlier time periods.

In sum, the social protection system, which the Cardoso administration had begun to update and transform, was strengthened under the Lula government with the creation of the Ministry of Social Development. Furthermore, it gradually acquired a great deal of broader political significance. Large parts of Brazilian society came to see it as a safety net that was capable of reaching even the poorest citizens, whom earlier governments had largely seemed to neglect. The widespread perception that Lula, who himself had risen from dire poverty, was the first Brazilian president to care about these underprivileged segments of the population has undoubtedly helped to boost his popularity and ensure the legitimacy of the ruling alliance. The resulting political clout has given the Lula government greater bargaining power in its complex relations with the legislative branch and with social movement actors.[14] Moreover, the expanded

---

[14] For an interesting analysis of social movements see Houtzager, Acharya, and Lavalle (2007).

system of social protection helps to immunize Brazil's market-oriented pattern of capital accumulation against political challenges while requiring only a limited amount of fiscal resources, and thus not creating a significant drain on the economy. Therefore, business and other better-off sectors are content with Lula's approach as well. With fine irony, journalist José Nêumanne synthesized the thoughts of the wealthy in Brazil: "The millionaires can sleep in peace, as long as the poor can eat" (Nêumanne 2008).

THE LIMITATIONS OF THE CURRENT PUBLIC AGENDA

As this chapter has demonstrated so far, the Lula da Silva administration has not transformed the new market model established under the preceding Cardoso government, but has furthered its political consolidation by expanding compensatory social programs that have guaranteed popular support. As a result, the new pattern of capital accumulation has not faced serious questioning and challenges in contemporary Brazil, despite its difficulties in generating employment and ensuring a fairer distribution of income. Instead, public opinion has focused on a rather narrow set of issues. In particular, the predominant discussion in the media concerns the question of sustainable growth and the need for long-term fiscal balance to guarantee it. The prevailing assumption seems to be that such growth would automatically be accompanied by continual improvements in the distribution of wealth, without any need for structural reform.

The concerns of Brazil's propertied classes are particularly limited. They are interested simply in the smooth functioning and proper management of the new market model, which they regard as the best development option for the country because it rests on the foundations of private property, free initiative, and competition. In their view, there is no point in worrying about a range of tricky issues, such as the question of the denationalization of the Brazilian economy as a result of multinational investment and other effects of economic globalization. Similarly, the social question – especially going beyond measures to reduce poverty and to address Brazil's profound inequality – is distinctly secondary on the government's agenda. Even less controversial issues, such as what type of development the country should pursue or how the relations between the state and the private sector should be structured, are swept under the rug. The standard response to all these questions is the advocacy of private, business-friendly solutions, which in the eyes of Brazil's better-off sectors can take care of any problems.

With these limitations, the range of topics open for discussion has been defined. The chapter by Kingstone and Ponce in this volume makes this point as well. In the eyes of Brazil's better-off sectors, there is no doubt that the country will continue to have a capitalist pattern of development whose economic dynamism will be supported by the international financial institutions, such as the World Bank and the International Monetary Fund. These sectors do not foresee a structural rupture of the established growth model but highlight the need for continuous adjustment, designed especially to safeguard Brazil's fiscal balance. Evidence of this constant insistence on macroeconomic equilibrium has been the recent business demands that the government balance its fiscal accounts, especially through expenditure containment, and that it correct the exchange rate in order to achieve high and sustainable growth. In this vein, the leadership of the powerful association of São Paulo industrialists lobbied hard against renewing a provisional tax on financial transactions that the government had used to boost fiscal revenues.

Thus, from the perspective of Brazil's financial and business sectors, the Lula da Silva government and its future successors merely need to administer the established development model in a competent fashion. A particularly important task will be to bring about a substantial reduction of net government debt relative to GDP, which would prove the government capable of honoring its obligations and would thus boost investor confidence.

In the eyes of Brazil's upper classes, issues that other sectors of the population may regard as highly relevant deserve only limited, mostly rhetorical support. These issues include the egregious inequality in the distribution of income and wealth between capital and labor – a topic that business people do not like to raise. Instead, they call attention to the inequality between better-paid and poorer sectors among dependently employed people, which is actually less important. To the extent that social issues do come up, Brazil's wealthy sectors claim that the solutions to these problems would come from growth itself and from purely compensatory social policies;[15] in their eyes, there is no need for any structural reform.

But contrary to this very limited perspective, it is obvious that any government that wants to effect a significant reduction in Brazil's terribly skewed income distribution would have to turn this effort into one of its main economic, social, and political priorities. Interestingly, it is not for a lack of ideas that the Lula da Silva administration has not effectively done so. Inside Brazil's political parties and in civil society, there are groups that have designed promising development projects. These projects are both production-oriented and distribution-oriented.

The Lula da Silva government has announced an ambitious plan to stimulate production, but its execution has been quite deficient. If fully implemented, the Growth Acceleration Program launched in January 2007 holds the potential of moving Brazil in a new, more promising direction. A total investment of R$503.9 billion by the government and private sector from 2007–10 would create a foundation for boosting socioeconomic development. The plan foresees investments in roads, railroads, airports, ports, waterways, various types of energy production, and social and urban infrastructure. But these investments are not happening at the speed required for producing a structural change in Brazil's socioeconomic development pattern.

[15] For an excellent overview of this very complex subject, see Paes de Barros et al. (2007).

Only if Brazil were to adopt an economic model that turns production with fair distribution into the central priority could the country break the path dependence established by the new, market-oriented pattern of accumulation from the 1990s onward. Of course, pursuing this kind of structural change should be a central goal of any center-left or left government. Such a government would need to create a support coalition that would make it politically feasible to move in new structural directions. Based on this alliance, both the socioeconomic structure and the economic and social policy regimes would need to be revamped. Issues such as fiscal adjustment, which business often demands to tie the government's hands, would not be allowed to impede this kind of transformation. The current fiscal and exchange rate problems and the difficulties arising from exorbitant interest rates would need to be resolved in a way that does not stifle production and development.

In other words, a new development pattern is necessary to change the growth and distribution outcomes produced by the market-oriented development model that Brazil has established during the past fifteen years. This new pattern requires a significant adjustment in the management of the economy to create a solid fiscal foundation for sustained production and growth. Of course, such a transformation is in no way easy. The current development pattern ensures profits for better-off segments of Brazilian society, who have strong political interests and considerable clout to defend the status quo.

THE NEED FOR A NEW DEVELOPMENT MODEL

This essay adheres to the general view that a market-oriented pattern of capital accumulation does not automatically help a country to overcome underdevelopment. It is well known that a market economy as such does not guarantee full employment, an equitable distribution of income and wealth, and the effective sovereignty of the nation. But as a new departure during the 1990s, such a market-oriented system has been established and consolidated in Brazil, even under a left government. Starting with the Plano Real, which resolved the country's monetary crisis, Brazil enacted a series of liberalization measures that substantially reshaped its development strategy. This economic transformation was accompanied by the creation of a social protection system that extends into the poor informal sector and by the redefinition of intergovernmental relations. As a result of all these changes, Brazil's new pattern of capitalist growth in the context of financial globalization has definitively replaced the preceding nationalist development model and has acquired powerful economic and political bases of support (Torres Filho et al. 2007). The market model is by now secured in its strategic foundations and is subject only to tactical criticism from business people, such as incessant complaints about the tax burden, the government's current spending levels, and social security outlays. It is notable that a government headed by a left party has played a key role in consolidating this model.

But the fact that Brazil has consolidated a new, viable pattern of capital accumulation does not imply that this market model is bringing about true development by overcoming the numerous economic and social problems plaguing the country. A development model that would really hold that promise and bear out historic left ideals would be one in which innovation is generated domestically; monetary and financial flows are organized so as to diminish international dependence; dynamic production and fair distribution go hand in hand; regional issues are resolved in line with national priorities; and the country asserts its national interests and assumes a leadership position on the global stage. Admittedly, it would be difficult to identify a country that has already achieved these goals, especially in Latin America.

If Brazil does not construct a new development scheme along those lines, it may achieve growth but make other problems of underdevelopment more intractable – precisely what happened for decades before the debt crisis of the 1980s. These features of underdevelopment include a high level of international monetary and financial dependence; a low domestic capacity for technological innovation; structural heterogeneity among productive sectors and regions of the country; pronounced inequality in the distribution of income and wealth; structural unemployment; and limited international influence. Given this multitude of problems and deficits, the construction of a socioeconomic model capable of overcoming underdevelopment would be a very complex task, both politically and economically. As one of Brazil's leading development theorists, Celso Furtado, used to say in the early 2000s: "The country has never been so far from what it dreamed." Similarly, many historic figures within the PT no doubt reflect on how far the policies of the Lula da Silva government are from those envisioned by the party in earlier years.

Specifically, an accumulation pattern that leads to genuine development must have the following main characteristics:

(1) It must overcome international monetary and financial fragility. For that purpose, and because Brazil does not have a national currency that is internationally convertible, it must facilitate the consistent accumulation of international reserves in strong currencies. Consequently, the pattern must generate a structural surplus in the balance of trade and services and in the current account. To accomplish this goal, in turn, the country's productive structure must be innovative, competitive, and dynamic, internally and externally.

(2) This development model must also maintain the strong link between investment and domestic production through efficient long-term financing. Only in this way can Brazil achieve growth and productivity increases without creating inflationary pressures. Lula da Silva's policies have been moving in that direction during his second term through the launching of the "Productive Development Policy" by the BNDES, Brazil's national development bank. Through this and other programs,

Brazil has resumed its earlier efforts at pursuing a strategic industrial policy coordinated among several governmental agencies. The steps listed in the preceding two paragraphs would make it possible to generate high-quality employment at growing average real wages, increase the size of the formal sector of the economy, and create a better distribution of income.

(3) The size of Brazil's population and territory, and the complex social issues affecting the country require a great deal of public spending and investment. Existing spending must also be reprioritized or else socioeconomic inequality and related problems of underdevelopment cannot be overcome (Hunter and Sugiyama 2009). A number of policy reforms that have been postponed since the 1980s finally need to be tackled. Compensatory schemes such as Bolsa Família or other social assistance programs cannot make up for their absence. These urgently needed albeit difficult measures include a financial and fiscal reform of the state. Any effort to bring about a fairer distribution of income and wealth – a cornerstone principle of the left historically – requires a transformation of Brazil's financial system, which has been characterized by an ever greater concentration of capital. In fact, the market-oriented accumulation pattern established from 1994 onward has exacerbated this problem. Indeed, the current financial system has forced the federal government to spend on average 8 percent of GDP per year on the payment of interest. This huge drain on resources forestalls public spending on urgent development problems and provides additional gains for well-off sectors.

(4) On the social front, the distribution of land must be altered to improve the welfare of the rural poor albeit in a manner that does not disrupt the achievements of agribusiness. Brazil must combine its tremendous achievements in agribusiness with attention to ecological sustainability, and to the needs of depressed areas and poor segments of the population in different regions of the country. Notwithstanding some advances – such as a noncontributory pension scheme for rural workers established by the military regime and land reform measures implemented under President Fernando Henrique Cardoso – the nation still has not solved the historic problem of poverty in the countryside. Moreover, divergences among regions must be reduced to ensure the integrated development of the country.

(5) Brazil has maintained the development of its industrial capacity, which it built up over decades, to a degree unique in Latin America. Contrary to the pessimistic view mentioned at the beginning of this chapter, the country has not suffered any deindustrialization process, as occurred in Argentina, Chile, Mexico, and other nations. Moreover, Brazil has several well-endowed public banks that have been restructured and are on solid footing, such as the national development bank BNDES, the Bank of Brazil, and regional banks for the Northeast and the Amazon region. Furthermore, there are public sector institutions that can be reorganized

to strengthen planning capacity. Thus, in terms of sheer resource availability, Brazil has the economic and institutional wherewithal to institute a socioeconomic model that can overcome underdevelopment.

Certainly, however, domestic and international interests that have gained strength over the years during which the liberal pattern of global financial insertion has been hegemonic impose serious political impediments to changing the country's accumulation pattern. These differences in orientation between conservative and progressive sectors have led to tensions inside the Lula da Silva government. As a result, the administration has been at a crossroads in its attempts to marry stability with development. The Central Bank's efforts in mid-2008 to combat renewed inflationary pressures through a significant increase in the basic interest rate reflect those tensions. Once again, the concern over economic stability won out over the promotion of growth and development. But this kind of outcome is not set in stone. Politics can make a difference and assert itself over and against economic pressures and constraints. The depth of income inequality and the variety of serious social and economic problems plaguing Brazil can certainly provide a strong stimulus for not abandoning the fight against the perpetuation of underdevelopment.

7

The Policies and Performance of the Contestatory and Moderate Left

Raúl L. Madrid, Wendy Hunter, and Kurt Weyland

INTRODUCTION

The preceding chapters have provided wide-ranging assessments of the economic and social policies, the political strategies, and the performance of four left governments in contemporary Latin America. The authors have examined rich and thorough information on ongoing transformation processes that have attracted a great deal of attention from academics and other observers, including the U.S. government. Capturing the dynamics and grasping the direction of political and socioeconomic change in midstream is always a difficult undertaking. The editors therefore commissioned renowned country experts whose deep familiarity with the national and international context and the long-term development trajectories of these countries allow for a grounded and nuanced interpretation of leftist reform efforts. The chapters examine recent reform efforts and policy programs as well as their potential impact on each country's development model. In these ways, the present volume seeks to capture new political experiences and interesting policy experiments in a comprehensive fashion.

As the introduction explained, the main purpose of this volume is to examine the differences in policy and performance among Latin America's contemporary left. Precisely for that reason, it bears emphasizing that these obvious differences have played out inside broad bounds of similarity. Although Venezuela's Hugo Chávez and Bolivia's Evo Morales have clearly diverged from the path followed by Brazil's Luiz Inácio Lula da Silva and the Chilean *Concertación* governments headed by Ricardo Lagos and Michelle Bachelet, all of these administrations have stayed within an economic and political–institutional framework that has become fairly consolidated in the region. In particular, all of the current left-leaning governments have kept their countries open to foreign trade and investment. Despite a number of nationalist measures, even Venezuela's Hugo Chávez has relied on increased export proceeds and presided over an import boom. As a result, Venezuela's trade dependence – a frequently used indicator of globalization – has actually grown. Similarly, all left-wing governments have maintained the basic institutions of electoral democracy. Even Chávez's proclaimed "revolution" has not proceeded to a violent overthrow of the existing socioeconomic and political order. Thus, the four administrations share some important similarities that distinguish them from earlier incarnations of the left in Latin America, such as the Castro regime in Cuba, the Allende government in Chile, and the Sandinista regime in Nicaragua, all of which sought to carry out more thoroughgoing transformations of their societies and economies. Above all, these similarities among the current leftist governments reflect fundamental economic and political constraints that set limits to these governments' degree of radicalism.

Despite these constraints, however, the case studies assembled in this book show that the four administrations have differed significantly in their policy course. The Lula da Silva and *Concertación* governments have clearly been more moderate than the Morales and especially the Chávez administrations. While the preceding chapters focused on specific country cases, this conclusion seeks to draw out comparative perspectives, not only among the four countries analyzed in depth in this volume, but also among other left-leaning governments in Argentina, Ecuador, Nicaragua, and Uruguay. It contrasts the policy outputs of these left-wing administrations and evaluates their outcomes, drawing on the ample evidence offered in the case studies. Has the moderate or the contestatory left been more successful in achieving economic growth and development and in avoiding inflation? Which type of government has done better in combating social problems such as poverty and inequality? And what achievements are more sustainable, supported by regular budget revenues rather than exceptional windfall rents derived from temporarily high export prices? Last but not least, which government has performed better on measures of democratic quality, such as accountability, responsiveness, and citizen participation?

While the political and policy differences between the two kinds of left-wing governments constitute the central theme of the present volume, the case studies also yield a finding not anticipated at the outset of this project: These differences are sharper in some policy areas than in others. The clearest divergence appears in political strategy. Whereas moderate governments in Brazil and Chile have respected existing political institutions and sought out common ground with the opposition, the contestatory governments of Bolivia and Venezuela have tried to sweep away the established political framework and eliminate institutional bastions of the opposition. They have used constituent assemblies to rewrite the political rules and concentrate power in the executive. Seeking to enhance their political strength, they have also pursued a polarizing, mobilizational form of politics.

It is not by chance that Latin America's contestatory left governments have prioritized power enhancement. Political strength has proven useful in the pursuit of a socioeconomic agenda that contains transformative elements. Morales in Bolivia and especially Chávez in Venezuela have substantially increased state intervention in the economy. They have also undertaken some far-reaching social policy pursuits, including land reform. While neither set of reforms has been as profound as those pursued by leftist radicals in the 1960s and 1970s, presidents Chávez and Morales have been decidedly more ambitious in their goals than their Brazilian and Chilean counterparts. By contrast, the center-left governments of presidents Lula da Silva, Lagos, and Bachelet have remained squarely within the rules of the liberal democratic game, maintaining the market-oriented framework bequeathed to them by their predecessors and extending the programs of social assistance and broader social protection that they left behind. There are some signs that Lula da Silva would like to maintain more state control in the economy and Bachelet would prefer to enact more robust and universal social protection, yet neither appears willing to push beyond the boundaries of liberal democracy and market economics to achieve these outcomes. The Workers' Party in Brazil and the Chilean Socialists have a higher intrinsic commitment to liberal, representative democracy than their contestatory counterparts, and they also have far less of a need to concentrate political power since they do not intend to enact radical economic and social policies.

Based on these divergent goals and approaches, the policies of moderate and contestatory left governments have yielded different results, with the clearest differences appearing in democratic performance. The contestatory governments have undermined horizontal accountability and increased social and political polarization (albeit within the broader context of reasonably free and fair elections and an uncensored press). But they have also enhanced the political influence of traditionally marginalized groups, such as the indigenous population, and in this way boosted political participation and satisfaction with democracy. By contrast, the moderate left governments have respected existing democratic institutions and proceeded by cooperation and consensus building. Yet the moderate left governments have made little progress in incorporating traditionally marginalized groups; nor have they typically been able to prevent the decline or stagnation of political participation and satisfaction with democracy among the citizens of their countries.

The moderate and contestatory governments have also achieved divergent macroeconomic performance. The *Concertación* and the Lula da Silva administration have presided over steady, reasonably strong economic growth and low levels of inflation. By contrast, inflation has risen noticeably under the Chávez and Morales governments, although it still remains below historical levels in those countries. The Morales and especially the Chávez government have enjoyed high growth in recent years, but growth rates under Chávez have been erratic, and in both countries growth has been driven by factors that may not be sustainable, namely high international oil and gas prices. Similar differences have characterized social policy performance. Moderate governments in Brazil and Chile have managed to reduce poverty and, to a lesser extent, social inequality in a gradual, cumulative fashion. Venezuela, meanwhile, has achieved striking success in boosting popular well-being in the course of a few years, but this followed upon an initial aggravation of poverty and unemployment during the first five years of the Chávez administration. It is also unclear whether the recent progress made in reducing poverty in Venezuela is sustainable, given its dependence on the high level of spending and growth fueled by the oil boom.

In sum, the contestatory left has undertaken more ambitious initiatives on the political, economic, and social front and has managed to achieve considerable progress toward its goals in recent years. But it is unclear whether these accomplishments – especially the economic and social achievements – are sustainable. By contrast, the moderate left has taken smaller steps, yet on a more solid foundation. These steps have added up to considerable progress over time. This patient approach may yield greater achievements in the long run, as Chile's track record suggests.

A subsequent section of this concluding chapter examines the track record of other left-leaning governments in Latin America, focusing on Argentina, Ecuador, Nicaragua, and Uruguay. We find that the administrations of Rafael Correa in Ecuador and, to a lesser extent, Daniel Ortega in Nicaragua fit our definition of a contestatory left government in that they have concentrated political power and significantly expanded social programs and state intervention in the economy. The government of Tabaré Vázquez, by contrast, is clearly a moderate left government in that it has respected the country's existing political institutions and largely maintained the liberal economic policies of its predecessors. The governments of Néstor Kirchner and Cristina Fernández de Kirchner in Argentina fall somewhere in between. Like the contestatory left, the Kirchner and Fernández administrations have pursued state interventionist economic policies, but they have not sought to dramatically overhaul their country's political institutions.

These four secondary cases provide additional support for the arguments advanced in this book. Overall, cautious and gradualist policies have outperformed more radical and contestatory policies. Of these administrations, the clearest success story is the Vázquez government in Uruguay, which has generated strong economic growth while maintaining a low rate of inflation and a high level of respect for the political rights and civil liberties of its citizens. The governments of Néstor Kirchner and, to a lesser extent, Cristina Fernández, also have been relatively successful, particularly in economic terms. By contrast, the Correa administration in Ecuador and the Ortega administration in Nicaragua have generated a mixed record, especially in light of their problematic posture toward democratic institutions and practices.

CHARACTERISTICS, ENVIRONMENTS, AND STRATEGIES
OF THE TWO LEFTS

As indicated in the introduction, the differences in policy approach and results reflect the divergences in the historical origins and organizational characteristics of the moderate versus contestatory left. The two strands of leftism are of entirely different generations. The moderate left emerged from the gradual but thorough deradicalization of left-wing parties that had been formed many years before. These parties shifted to the center and embraced market reforms during the late 1980s and 1990s in the wake of the debt crisis and the decline of Communism. By contrast, the contestatory left burst onto the political scene during the mid-to-late 1990s, when growing disaffection with market economics stimulated renewed radicalism. Whereas the moderate left is composed of older, more institutionalized parties with a relatively well-consolidated organizational apparatus, the contestatory left consists of younger, more fluid and personalistic movements that have not yet had time to develop organizational rules, cadres, and structures.

As the introduction discusses, the contestatory and the moderate left developed in very different types of countries. Whereas the contestatory left emerged in states that suffered from high levels of instability, inefficiency, and corruption, the moderate left arose in states that enjoy a reputation for stability, efficiency, and low levels of corruption by Latin American standards. Similarly, although the contestatory left has emerged in settings where the opposition is weak and the existing party system has largely fallen apart, the moderate left has developed in relatively well-institutionalized party systems with vibrant opposition parties (Flores Macías 2008). Finally, the contestatory and the moderate left have experienced very different economic pressures. The contestatory left has arisen in energy-exporting, rentier economies that benefited massively from the boom in energy prices in the mid-2000s. By contrast, the moderate left has emerged in much more diversified economies that have not benefited from the commodity price boom to the same degree (Weyland 2009).

The characteristics of the moderate versus contestatory left and the political–institutional and economic settings in which the two different strands rose to power deeply shaped their divergent policy orientations as well as their economic, social, and political performance. In a nutshell, the contestatory left found more room for maneuvering and has been eager to use it for ambitious initiatives. Its comparatively radical efforts have attained considerable short-term success, but also provoked a good deal of political conflict, suffered from implementation problems, and run up against limits of sustainability, especially with the sharp decline in energy prices in late 2008. The moderate left, by contrast, encountered more economic and political constraints and was unwilling to challenge these restrictions aggressively. As a result, its reform program – more circumspect to begin with – has also advanced in a more piecemeal fashion. Yet while unexciting, the resulting progress has been more economically sustainable and protected against political backlash, adding up to a solid, cumulative long-term trajectory, especially in Chile.

In other words, the movement nature of the contestatory left and the opportunities it encountered for establishing hegemony in collapsing party systems have produced bursts of activism designed to bring political and socioeconomic breakthroughs. This more radical vision seeks to challenge economic constraints, revamp institutional structures, and defeat the forces upholding them. The leader's promise of a new start motivates a large mass following, integrates hitherto "excluded" or disaffected sectors into politics, and rewards them with material and symbolic benefits. But this very activism and ambition can spark polarization and conflict, and it tends to weaken rather than strengthen institutional capacity and administrative performance.[1] The short-term accomplishments of the contestatory left, which in Bolivia and especially Venezuela have depended on an unusually large influx of energy revenues, therefore lack a firm institutional foundation. Whereas the more radical left can attain dramatic advances, it also runs the risk of serious setbacks. Living dangerously can yield considerable payoffs in the short run, but also incur significant costs and losses, especially in the long run.

By contrast, the firm organization of the moderate left and the fact that it is embedded in relatively institutionalized, competitive party systems have induced it to proceed with caution and stay inside the confines of the more market-oriented system that Brazil and Chile have established. Yet while unwilling to rock the boat, the moderate left has sought to use the available margin of maneuver, which is significantly larger than strict "neoliberals" claim. In particular, it has enhanced the regulation of economic forces, used the state to provide more public goods, and improved social protection and investment in human capital. Eschewing mass mobilization, it has made better policies *for* the people yet not *with* the people. This technocratic approach has yielded well-designed, innovative programs, facilitated their faithful implementation, and ensured their institutional consolidation (see Boeninger 2007 on Chile). It also has avoided the political backlash and economic crisis that activism often ends up provoking. But although this strategy has produced substantial results, especially in the Chilean case, it has not given the citizenry a sense of political inclusion. The "slow boring of hard boards" (Weber 1971: 560) may be crucial for overcoming obstacles and attaining lasting progress, yet it does not inspire the enthusiasm that bold activism does.

POLITICAL STRATEGIES AND PERFORMANCE

As mentioned at the outset of this conclusion, there are particularly clear differences between the moderate and contestatory left in their political strategies and their projects for institutional change. The first major initiative of contestatory left parties has been a determined push to overhaul the existing institutional order and concentrate political power. The contestatory left has been highly critical not only of the policies pursued by previous parties, but also of the political institutions that helped these parties maintain their hold on power. It has viewed these institutions as corrupt, self-serving, politically biased, and impervious to the needs of the people. Thus, presidents Chávez and Morales have sought to reform these institutions radically, as the chapters by Corrales and Gray Molina discuss. In particular, the contestatory left has

[1] On the importance of the state's institutional capacity, see Huber (1995) and Lora (2007).

viewed the concentration of power as necessary to carry out sweeping reforms of economic and social policy. It believes it must wrest control of the legislature, the judiciary, the state bureaucracy, and other governmental institutions from the traditional parties in order to prevent these parties from blocking or eviscerating its economic and social policy agenda.

Moderate left parties, by contrast, typically believe that it is possible to find common ground with the opposition. Because their policies represent more continuity than rupture with the past, moderate left parties have often been able to attain their goals through negotiation, rather than imposition. The moderate left also tends to have a more benevolent view of the existing state institutions than does the contestatory left. Although it has voiced criticisms of these institutions and sought to make them more efficient and democratic, it has not typically seen a need for radical reform. Therefore, the moderate left has avoided dramatic departures and has maintained liberal, representative democracy. It has undertaken major reform initiatives only to eliminate the last vestiges of undemocratic, authoritarian rule (such as appointed senators in Chile). In sum, the moderate left has employed cautious and pragmatic political strategies, whereas the contestatory left has opted for a more radical and revisionist approach.

INSTITUTIONAL REFORM EFFORTS

The contestatory left governments have adopted a bold political strategy that focuses on overhauling their country's political institutions in an effort to strengthen their hold on power. They have rewritten the constitution to allow for their own reelection, dissolved or manipulated the legislature, and stacked traditionally nonpartisan institutions with their supporters. And they have used frequent elections and referenda as well as street demonstrations to weaken and demoralize the opposition and legitimize their reforms. These measures have undermined horizontal accountability and hollowed out democracy. Yet at the same time, the contestatory left has helped to boost mass satisfaction with democracy and has expanded the participation and representation of some traditionally marginalized groups.

As the chapter by Corrales discusses, the Chávez administration in Venezuela has taken the greatest steps to rework political institutions to its advantage. Immediately after taking office in 1999, Chávez convened a Constituent Assembly that dissolved the legislature, rewrote electoral laws, and devised a new constitution. The new constitution expanded the powers of the president and allowed for consecutive reelection while also introducing plebiscitary mechanisms, such as the possibility of recalling executive and legislative officeholders. Since that time, Chávez has expanded the Supreme Court and stacked it with his supporters, politicized the National Electoral Council, the Comptroller's Office, and the Central Bank, and used his control over military and diplomatic promotions and assignments to reward his allies and purge his opponents. In 2007, Chávez sought to enact additional constitutional reforms to obtain even more powers, including the right to be reelected indefinitely, but the proposals were defeated in a popular referendum. Undeterred, the president in late 2008 called and triumphed in another referendum to lift the ban on presidential reelection.

The Morales administration in Bolivia has adopted a similar political strategy, as the chapter by Gray Molina details. Shortly after the new president took office in early 2006, he convened a Constituent Assembly to overhaul Bolivia's political institutions. This body drafted a new constitution that would allow Morales and future presidents to run for two consecutive five-year terms. The new charter also establishes direct elections to the Supreme Court, expands the size of the Senate (where the Movimiento al Socialismo – MAS – did not have a majority), and lowers to a simple majority the percentage of congressional votes needed to confirm members of nonpartisan institutions such as the National Electoral Institute and the Comptroller's Office. All of these measures should enable Morales to strengthen his hold on power by placing more of his supporters in key governmental institutions. The Constituent Assembly approved the constitution in a highly controversial proceeding that was boycotted by the opposition (Lehoucq 2008: 117–20).

The moderate left, by contrast, has played by the existing rules of the game and has eschewed major reforms of political institutions. As the Huber, Pribble, and Stephens chapter discusses, the center-left coalition in Chile has respected institutions of horizontal accountability as well as basic political rights and civil liberties. Under the 1980 constitution, the Chilean president has substantial unilateral powers, but recent chief executives have largely declined to use these powers in favor of negotiating policies with the legislature. The *Concertación* governments also have respected the independence of the judiciary, and both the judiciary and the legislature have served as effective veto players, often acting against the wishes of the president. The only controversial constitutional reforms undertaken in Chile were aimed at eliminating authoritarian relics that the Pinochet regime had introduced with its 1980 constitution. Above all, the Lagos administration finally managed in 2005 to eliminate appointed senators and restore the president's right to dismiss the chiefs of the armed services, as Huber, Pribble, and Stephens discuss. Thus, the institutional reforms pushed by center-left governments in Chile have sought to complete the reconstruction of liberal, representative democracy, rather than to concentrate power in the executive branch or introduce plebiscitary mechanisms.

Similarly, the Lula da Silva administration in Brazil has maintained liberal democratic institutions. Like all Brazilian governments since 1985, it has respected civil rights and has presided over free and fair elections. In contrast to the contestatory left in Bolivia and Venezuela, Lula da Silva has not undertaken any major constitutional reforms designed to concentrate power in the executive branch. Horizontal accountability is somewhat weaker in Brazil than in Chile, though. The judiciary is independent and has successfully resisted government initiatives on a number of occasions, but it is also severely overburdened. Overall, like the *Concertación* in Chile, the PT administration has been committed to liberal, representative democracy and has not pushed in a majoritarian direction.

RELATIONS WITH THE OPPOSITION

Bold reform efforts tend to provoke resistance. The moderate left accepts the need to safeguard political space for such opposition, but the contestatory left seeks to overpower it and push it aside. Accordingly, Chávez, Morales, and their movements have behaved quite aggressively toward the political opposition, although the opposition has engaged in numerous aggressive and, sometimes, undemocratic practices as well. They have regularly denounced opposition leaders harshly and have pursued controversial criminal charges against some of them, driving a few of them into exile. Even rank-and-file supporters of the opposition at times have been subject to harassment, including the loss of government jobs and state social benefits, especially in Venezuela. The Chávez and Morales administrations also have regularly denounced the media. Both governments have been accused of using regulatory measures, advertising budgets, and tax audits to punish media outlets that are critical of the government, and the Chávez administration has steadily expanded state ownership of the media industry (Human Rights Watch 2008).

In addition, social movements allied with and, in some cases, controlled by the government have used demonstrations to intimidate the political opposition and other critics of the government. The Morales administration, for example, has used protests, particularly by indigenous groups, to put pressure on the opposition to pass legislation, including the new constitution. Similarly, the Chávez administration has used the mass-based organizations it created, like the Bolivarian Circles, to bully the opposition.

The contestatory left governments thus have undermined some of the fundamental principles of liberal democracy. While they have upheld the formal core institutions of representative democracy, such as free and more or less fair elections, they have squeezed the political pluralism that gives them substance. For democracy to thrive, there need to be ample opportunities for open, undisturbed public debate, including criticism of government officials and their performance. In its quest for political hegemony, the contestatory left has frequently infringed on this maxim. Civil society has become less civil as debate and deliberation have increasingly been replaced by mass mobilization, extrainstitutional pressure, and the occasional recourse to intimidation and even violence. The willingness to compromise has given way to polarization and mutual recrimination.

As Corrales's chapter stresses for the case of Venezuela, liberal democracy is at risk of turning into a façade as the majoritarian concentration and exercise of power makes checks and balances ever less effective. Chávez quickly won hegemony in the Constituent Assembly and therefore managed to advance his reform project via the new institutional mechanisms that he had created. But in reaction to its virtual exclusion from the formal political arena, the new opposition resorted to extrainstitutional and sometimes clearly undemocratic mobilization, including a crescendo of mass demonstrations in 2001–02, a military coup attempt in April 2002, and a ruinous economic strike in 2002–03. In Bolivia, the opposition has had a stronger foothold due to its regional concentration in the eastern lowlands where the country's recent economic growth and its new natural gas deposits have been concentrated. The MAS's majoritarian push has begun to overwhelm this opposition and take advantage of its divisions to establish predominance in formal institutional arenas. It remains to be seen whether this emerging hegemony will induce the opposition to resort even more to extrainstitutional means than some of its sectors have already done. Given fierce polarization, violence could erupt (Lehoucq 2008). Thus, the prospects for vibrant democratic pluralism are not good.

Moderate left governments have avoided these conflicts and convulsions and have preserved ample political pluralism. In Brazil and Chile, opposition forces can advance their criticisms and attacks without any harassment by the government or its allied organizations and social movements. There are a wide variety of venues for public debate, and freedom of speech is guaranteed without any infringements. The opposition can compete with the government in all arenas without any restriction. In Congress and other institutional settings, there is a good deal of negotiation and cooperation between these contenders. By putting its institutional influence to full use, the opposition often hinders or downsizes government projects, as Huber, Pribble, and Stephens demonstrate in their analysis of progressive social reform efforts in Chile. The Lula da Silva, Lagos, and Bachelet governments have nevertheless respected the opposition, helping to maintain a lively pluralist democracy.

EFFORTS AT MASS INCLUSION

Despite – or in some sense, because of – their illiberal edge, the political reform efforts of the Chávez and Morales administrations also have important positive aspects, especially in fostering popular participation. With their revamping of constitutions and their conflicts with the opposition, the majoritarian leaders of the contestatory left seek to mobilize large sectors of the mass citizenry and promote their "inclusion" into politics. For this purpose, they create or extend mechanisms of political participation, such as referenda, popular recall elections, and community councils. Moreover, Chávez and Morales frequently mobilize their mass following to demonstrate their overwhelming support and thus intimidate the opposition. In his first few years in office, for instance, the Venezuelan president deliberately convoked one election or referendum after the other, constantly keeping his political base activated. This dynamic strategy was politically successful as each new contest ended up boosting Chávez's popularity. Evo Morales seems to be pursuing a similar course of action, albeit not quite at the hyperactive pace of his Bolivarian counterpart.

These mobilizational efforts of the contestatory left have had some positive effects on democracy, which warrant emphasizing. First, they have enhanced the political participation and influence of some traditionally marginalized groups. In Bolivia, indigenous leaders and organizations for the first time have a substantial presence and influence in the government.[2] Moreover, the Morales administration consults regularly with the diverse set of social movements that make up the MAS. In Venezuela, Chávez has encouraged the participation of social actors that had long felt unrepresented, particularly the urban poor. These efforts have been especially intense at the local level. For instance, from 2006 onward the Chávez administration has helped create twenty thousand community councils (Ellner 2008: 127–8).

Second, the contestatory left governments have increased satisfaction with democracy at the mass level. In Venezuela, in particular, the percentage of survey respondents who were very or somewhat satisfied with democracy rose from 30 percent in 1996 to 59 percent in 2007, according to Latinobarometer polls (Corporación Latinobarómetro 2007: 91). Indeed, the latter figure was the second highest in all of Latin America that year. Surveys by the Latin American Public Opinion Project also report a significant increase in popular satisfaction with democracy in Bolivia, from 58.5 percent in 2004 to 68.5 percent in 2006 (Madrid 2008). These improvements in contentment with democratic performance probably reflect both the contestatory left's efforts to promote popular participation and support for the president more generally. The fact that for the first time the president hails from the popular sectors has probably helped boost support for Chávez and Morales. Mass identification with the president is especially strong in Bolivia, given that Evo Morales often portrays himself and is portrayed by others as an indigenous leader.

The high level of satisfaction with democracy in Venezuela is noteworthy, given that many observers, including Corrales in his chapter, highlight the top-down nature of popular mobilization in the Bolivarian movement. Chávez has clearly been the main instigator of mobilization in Venezuela, where social movements lack the autonomy and importance of their counterparts in Bolivia. Moreover, the available evidence suggests that the Bolivarian movement has used material incentives and even the veiled threat of sanctions to stimulate mass involvement. But although part of these participatory activities could therefore be driven by instrumental considerations, there also seems to be a good deal of genuine appreciation for Chávez's efforts. Although outside observers are legitimately concerned about populist manipulation, many citizens themselves identify with the new political style and the course that Venezuelan democracy has taken in recent years.

In contrast to these efforts and accomplishments, the principal weakness of moderate left governments is that they have done little to expand the political

---

[2] The category of "indigenous" and its relationship to "mestizo" are highly ambiguous and contested in Bolivia, as Toranzo Roca (2008) and Zavaleta Reyles (2008) analyze in considerable depth.

participation and influence of marginalized sectors of the population and to boost satisfaction with democracy. Huber, Pribble, and Stephens show that the *Concertación* has largely shied away from incorporating popular organizations and encouraging citizen participation. One reason has been the desire to avoid the kind of social mobilization that spiraled out of control under the presidency of Salvador Allende (1970–3).

The left in Brazil has a stronger mass base, but it has not included this base in the policymaking process. As Kingstone and Ponce discuss, the Lula da Silva administration has created a high-level economic and social development council, but this assemblage of organization leaders and notables has not had a large influence on actual decision making. Instead, the PT government has resorted mostly to the closed and executive-dominated policymaking procedures that have characterized Brazilian democracy. Even more surprisingly, the Lula da Silva government has not undertaken any effort to spread to the rest of the country the innovative mechanisms of popular involvement, such as participatory budgeting, that had sprouted up in a number of PT-run cities, especially Porto Alegre. While during its long years in the opposition at the national level, the party had advertised these novel schemes of participatory governance with much fanfare, it did nothing to promote them once it managed to take over the federal government.

As a result of the absence of significant participatory initiatives, the gradual political exhaustion of the long-ruling *Concertación* in Chile, and the corruption scandals plaguing the Lula da Silva administration and the allegedly "clean" PT, the moderate left has failed to increase citizen satisfaction with democracy. According to Latinobarometer, only 30 percent of Brazilians were very or somewhat satisfied with democracy in 2007, down from 36 percent in 2001. In Chile, only 36 percent of the population stated that they were satisfied with democracy in 2007, down from 42 percent in 2001 (Corporación Latinobarómetro 2007: 91).[3] Thus, although the *Concertación* has by many standards had a very good economic and social policy performance, and although contemporary Chile leads Latin America in rankings of the quality of democratic governance (Mainwaring and Scully 2010), many Chileans are not very happy with the ruling coalition and the functioning of democracy. To a significant segment of the citizenry, majoritarian mobilization feels better than the sober, technocratic decision making of liberal democracy.

OVERALL ASSESSMENT OF DEMOCRATIC PERFORMANCE

As the preceding examination shows, the contestatory and moderate lefts have taken divergent positions on the trade-off between the liberal and majoritarian components of modern democracy. Conceptualized in Dahl's classical treatise as the distinction between "participation" and "opposition" (Dahl 1971), these

[3] Satisfaction with democracy was higher in both Brazil and Chile in 2007 than it was in 1996, however.

two sets of principles have traditionally stood in particularly pronounced contradiction in Latin America's highly unequal societies and relatively exclusionary democracies. In that setting, the liberal insistence on checks and balances, careful debate and deliberation, and respect for basic rights and established institutions hinders reform efforts and effectively protects existing privileges. But it also forestalls rash, imprudent changes and the undemocratic concentration of power. By contrast, majoritarian mobilization, often led by personalist leaders, has a greater chance of effecting reform, yet at the risk of undertaking ill-conceived initiatives, disregarding legitimate criticism, worsening social and political polarization, and bending to the will of a strongman with increasingly autocratic leanings.

These tensions have shaped the political strategies of the moderate versus contestatory left: They have set opposite priorities in Dahl's trade-off. Whereas Lula da Silva, Lagos, and Bachelet have sided with political liberalism, Chávez and Morales have relied on majoritarianism. The outcomes have been predictable. The PT and *Concertación* governments have preserved and, via Chile's 2005 constitutional reforms, enhanced pluralist, representative democracy, and significantly improved government for the people, achieving average Freedom House scores of 1.25 (Chile, 2000–08) and 2.15 (Brazil, 2003–08). But they have not boosted participation, despite the PT's base-democratic origins and continuing links with social movements. By contrast, the Bolivarian movement and the MAS have involved mass actors more in politics, via bottom-up mobilization in Bolivia and more top-down promotion in Venezuela, and they have sought to attain more freedom of action by revamping established institutions and concentrating power in a leader. But this assault on political liberalism has triggered strong opposition and created the risk of a slide into nondemocratic rule, especially in Venezuela, as the average Freedom House score of 4.2 for civil liberties (1999–2008) suggests.[4]

Overall, the threats emerging from majoritarianism are more problematic for democracy than the limitations imposed by political liberalism. In its emphasis on preventing the worst, liberalism is unexciting – but it also helps avoid the sort of economic and political catastrophes that twentieth-century Latin America suffered with striking frequency. By contrast, majoritarianism looks attractive in its ambitious effort to combat problems such as poverty and inequality, which are also abundant in the region. Yet while popular mobilization can sometimes be helpful in breaking obstacles to change, as Gray Molina's chapter argues, its actual track record is mixed at best, as Latin America's experiences with populism suggest. And the potential price, an involution toward authoritarianism, is high and can hinder the correction of mistakes. Therefore,

[4] Venezuela's average political rights score during these years was 3.4. Bolivia achieved an average of three on both dimensions in 2006–08. All data were computed from Freedom House (2008 and 2009).

the cautious strategy of the moderate left looks more promising and more compatible with the maintenance and strengthening of democracy than the bold efforts of the contestatory left.

ECONOMIC POLICY AND PERFORMANCE

As in the political sphere, there are clear differences between the contestatory and moderate left governments with regard to economic policy. Their movement character and absence of a firm institutionalized membership base has predisposed the Bolivarian movement and the Bolivian MAS to pursue relatively expansionary economic policies designed to provide benefits to vast sectors of the population. After years of recession and economic difficulties from 1999–2003, the windfall rents produced by sky-high energy prices have allowed President Chávez to pursue this goal during the last few years. As a result, Venezuela has recently achieved exceptionally high growth and a remarkable import boom, though at the price of significant inflation. President Morales has moved in a similar direction, but with greater caution because the Bolivian gas industry is much less developed. By contrast, Brazil's much more diversified economy has not yielded windfall rents, and in Chile, a resource stabilization fund has sterilized the extraordinary influx of copper proceeds. The Lula da Silva, Lagos, and Bachelet administrations have therefore faced greater constraints, and their more institutionalized party organization and the competitive pressures exerted by the centrist and conservative opposition have enabled and induced these leaders to discipline their mass base and limit appeals for economic expansion. Therefore, these governments have followed fairly orthodox macroeconomic policies.

Similar differences have characterized the stance of the contestatory versus moderate left toward their country's economic development model. The more radical political impulse of Chávez's and Morales's movements and the increased bargaining leverage provided by huge energy reserves at a time of global scarcity have led to substantial efforts to reverse some of the market reforms enacted during the 1990s, especially in the area of privatization. Both governments have significantly expanded state intervention in the economy, including the takeover of more and more productive activities – a remarkable departure from the economic liberalism prevailing during the 1980s and 1990s. By contrast, the moderate left forces governing Brazil and Chile have accepted the basic outlines of the market model and have undertaken only limited initiatives to regulate and direct economic forces, for instance through new industrial policy programs in Brazil.

Although the contestatory left has attained considerable success in recent years, such as sky-high growth in Venezuela, the sustainability of these accomplishments is highly uncertain – especially given the recent decline in energy prices. Having relied much less on this temporary bonanza, the efforts of the moderate left to build a more solid foundation for economic development and diversify the Brazilian and Chilean economies look more advantageous in a long-run perspective.

MACROECONOMIC POLICY

The contestatory left has taken advantage of economic opportunities to pursue expansionary economic policies, whereas the moderate left has insisted on strict fiscal discipline. Even the contestatory left, however, has not increased public expenditures indiscriminately. During the difficult economic times at the beginning of his presidency, when international oil prices were at record lows, Hugo Chávez embraced austerity, as he indicated by keeping his predecessor's "neoliberal" finance minister in office in 1999. But the Bolivarian leader opened the purse strings widely as soon as Venezuela emerged from this initial recession and from the economic difficulties caused by mass demonstrations and business strikes from 2001–03, and he kept them open as international petroleum prices skyrocketed from 2003 onward. As Corrales's chapter documents, the central government's spending rose from 18 percent of GDP in 1998 to 34 percent in 2008. This expenditure explosion placed Venezuela toward the top of Latin American countries. Predictably, it also sparked inflation, which reached 22.5 percent in 2007 and 30.9 percent in 2008, the highest levels in Latin America during those years (BCV 2009). Although not dramatic by the region's historical standards, this rate of price increases is unusual for the postadjustment period. Moreover, inflation would have been even higher had it not been for the Chávez administration's decision to allow for a tremendous import boom. Some experts are convinced that the current spending levels require international petroleum prices that are two to three times as high as they were at the end of 2008 (El Universal 2008; Jessop 2008).

Bolivia's Morales has also increased public spending, yet at a lower rate, given more meager resources. The government's new development plan adopted in 2006 foresaw a wide range of ambitious public investments, but the underdeveloped state of the gas industry has restricted the influx of revenues and made it difficult for the Morales administration to implement its goals. Although heading in a similar direction as Venezuela, Bolivia has therefore gone down that path much less far. As a result, economic distortions have been much less pronounced; for instance, inflation ran at 11.7 percent in 2007 and 11.9 percent in 2008 (La Razón 2009) – high for contemporary Bolivia, but much lower than in Bolivarian Venezuela. Also, the Morales government has not felt compelled to impose heavy-handed regulations, such as the price controls adopted in Venezuela.

By contrast, the moderate left governments of Chile and Brazil have proceeded with much greater caution. As the chapter by Huber, Pribble, and Stephens discusses, the Concertación has practiced fiscal restraint, a policy on which the powerful conservative opposition has insisted as well. The Lagos administration even went so far as to establish a rule that under normal conditions the government should plan to run an annual surplus of 1 percent of GDP, and it enacted a fiscal responsibility law to help facilitate this commitment. The *Concertación* has refrained from tapping into the extraordinary revenues produced by the international copper price boom of recent years. To finance public spending in fiscally responsible ways, it has instead raised taxes on a few occasions. But it has maintained low tax rates overall and has relied heavily on indirect taxation, such as the value-added tax. Monetary policy also has been quite conservative under the *Concertación* governments, and the Lagos administration's efforts to strengthen the independence of the Central Bank should ensure the continuation of these conservative policies in the future.

As the chapters by Kingstone and Ponce and by Barros Silva, Braga, and Costa highlight, the Lula da Silva administration in Brazil also has embraced economic orthodoxy. The government's fiscal, monetary, and tax policies have been quite conservative. The Lula administration has increased its annual budget surplus and reduced the primary nominal deficit, and it has maintained the same low income tax rates of the Cardoso administration (Flores Macías 2008: chap. 3). It also has boosted interest rates and practiced conservative monetary policies in order to comply with relatively stringent inflation targets. As Kingstone and Ponce explain, this cautious approach emerged in response to investor fears about the PT's potential radicalism and fiscal irresponsibility, which led to a bout of capital flight in 2002. To reassure Wall Street, in particular, Lula da Silva committed to a fairly orthodox macroeconomic approach. Thus, when running up against international economic constraints, the moderate left has chosen to work inside these confines, rather than challenging them, as the contestatory left has done.

EFFORTS TO TRANSFORM THE MARKET MODEL

Even more clearly and importantly, there have been substantial differences in the approach of the two strands of leftism toward the newly established, more market-oriented development model. Both presidents Chávez and Morales have taken measures that are distinctly radical by the standards of the present world-historical juncture, after the international collapse of state socialism and the worldwide wave of market reforms. By contrast, presidents Lula da Silva, Lagos, and Bachelet have accepted the new framework and enacted only changes that do not contradict its logic.

Aided by their heightened power in domestic politics and by the economic clout emanating from huge energy reserves, the contestatory left governments have increased state intervention in their economies significantly. Certainly, Chávez and Morales have not nationalized the entire economy as the Castro regime in Cuba did. But they have greatly boosted state interventionism and have nationalized some important state-owned firms, especially in the natural resource sector. In particular, they have restored public sector activities in the sphere of economic production, flouting one of "neoliberalism's" most fundamental goals. In a dramatic, deliberately defiant step, Evo Morales called in the military to occupy foreign oil and gas installations on 1 May 2006. And in Venezuela from 2005 onward, nationalization measures and similar kinds of initiatives have been rhetorically justified with official praise for "socialism." Thus, the contestatory left has ostentatiously announced and proceeded toward a partial reversal of the market reforms enacted during the 1990s.

The Chávez administration has gone the furthest of Latin America's new left governments in expanding state intervention in the economy. As the Corrales chapter discussed, the Bolivarian leader has increased the state's role in almost every economic sector. The government has nationalized a number of firms, such as the country's telecommunications giant, a steel company, and an electrical company, and it has created new state-owned firms, such as airlines and telecommunications companies. It has also expanded its control over the oil industry, not only by increasing taxes and royalty payments, but by forcing private companies to sell majority ownership to the state.

Interestingly, however, Chávez's rhetorical embrace of "twenty-first century socialism" has at least up to now not amounted to a full-scale transition to socialism. While nationalizing important foreign-owned firms, the government has left most domestically owned companies alone, and the private sector continues to control a large share of the Venezuelan economy. The Chávez administration has also not followed through on threats to default on its external debt or withdraw from international financial institutions such as the World Bank and the International Monetary Fund (IMF). Nor has it enacted significant barriers to foreign trade. On the contrary, Venezuela has experienced an import boom in recent years. Even the government's efforts at trade diversification have had only limited success; Venezuela continues to depend heavily on the United States.

Thus, Chávez's departures from the market model have remained partial and have not led headlong into state socialism. Indeed, his vision of "twenty-first century socialism" has remained nebulous. In fact, Corrales argues that Chávez's economic initiatives are not guided by a new blueprint, but represent a return to the country's long-standing tradition of state interventionism fed by oil rents. As during earlier boom times, especially the 1970s, the state has expanded its role as producer and distributor of windfall gains, investing in new economic and social projects, and using its increased clout to drive a harder bargain with investors and assume a more nationalist posture. And as on earlier occasions, the Venezuelan economy has become ever more dependent on oil as the overvalued exchange rate and flood of imports triggered by the recent boom has further undermined alternative economic sectors. In this way, Chávez's various initiatives are closer to variations on an old theme than to a fundamental change of course.

As the chapter by Gray Molina details, Morales has also increased state intervention in the economy, although not as much as Chávez. The Morales administration has used the high-profile nationalization decree to force foreign-owned gas companies to renegotiate their contracts and enormously increase the taxes, royalties, and fees that these companies pay to the Bolivian state.

The government also has nationalized a few private firms, such as the phone company and some gas companies. Moreover, like the Chávez administration, Morales has rejected a free trade agreement with the United States and aggressively pursued new trade relationships in Europe, Asia, and the Middle East. The Morales administration has not uniformly departed from market economics, however. The government has maintained liberal trade policies for the most part and has tried to maintain its access to U.S. markets, pushing for the renewal of its trade privileges through the Andean Trade Promotion and Drug Eradication Act (ATPDEA). In sum, the Morales government has not initiated anything resembling a transition to socialism, despite its vocal rejection of "neoliberalism."

Compared to the transformatory efforts undertaken in contemporary Venezuela and Bolivia, the moderate left has proceeded with much greater caution. The Lula da Silva, Lagos, and Bachelet governments have eschewed nationalization of privately owned companies, refrained from dramatic tax hikes, kept their economies open to foreign trade and investment, and maintained close economic relations with the United States and its allies. They do differ from the more conservative regimes that preceded them, however, in slowing down or halting privatization, expanding the government's role in public goods provision, and resuming industrial policy efforts. These programs use the maneuvering room provided by the market model but do not seek to push its limits aggressively.

As the chapter by Huber, Pribble, and Stephens discusses, center-left governments in Chile have largely kept in place the market model established under the Pinochet regime. The *Concertación* has even privatized some state-owned enterprises, though at a slower pace than the military dictatorship. Various *Concertación* governments, including the Lagos administration, have also lowered tariffs and signed free trade agreements with a number of countries, including the United States.

At the same time, however, the center-left coalition has sought to promote economic and social development more proactively than the neoliberal Pinochet regime. The *Concertación* has undertaken or maintained a number of export promotion initiatives, seeking to strengthen Chile's diversified insertion in the global economy (e.g., Nelson 2009: chap. 3). Over the years, these measures have helped to reduce the relative weight of the copper industry in GDP, exports, and state revenues. The *Concertación* has also sought to invest in human capital and upgrade Chile's labor force, both through general education reforms and through specific labor training programs. Perhaps most significantly, the first *Concertación* government established capital controls to avoid volatile short-term financial flows. For years, this innovative program shielded the Chilean economy from some of the vicissitudes of globalization (Ffrench-Davis 2002: chap. 10). But under the pressure of the Asian, Russian, and Brazilian financial crises, Chile felt compelled to lower these restrictions, and the Lagos administration suspended them altogether.

Pursuing a similarly moderate course, Lula da Silva has also refrained from nationalizing foreign firms or forcing them to renegotiate their contracts. Indeed, administration officials protested against the Bolivian oil and gas "nationalization," which imposed the highest costs, ironically, on Brazil's state-owned Petrobras. On the domestic front, the PT government has also proceeded with prudence. Contrary to initial plans, for instance, it has not imposed a significantly tighter regulatory regime on privatized utility companies. The international economic policies of the Lula da Silva administration have also stayed close to market principles. For example, the government has expanded Brazil's openness toward international capital and has maintained fairly liberal policies toward foreign trade, although it has eschewed a free trade agreement with the United States.

Brazil, however, has gradually strengthened the state's role in guiding economic development. Soon after coming to office, the Lula government resumed industrial policy programs, albeit confined to four high-priority sectors, as Kingstone and Ponce mention. In 2008, this scheme was extended to a much larger range of productive activities (IEDI 2008). Sustained by the abundant loan capital of Brazil's national development bank, these initiatives constitute a significant departure from "neoliberalism," as the chapter by Barros Silva, Braga, and Costa emphasizes. In particular, these industrial policies are designed to help prevent the economic opening of the 1990s from confining Brazil increasingly to an agro-export model. Instead, they support and further expand a highly diversified export sector and a broad industrial base.

EVALUATION OF ECONOMIC PERFORMANCE

The divergence between the moderate and contestatory left in macroeconomic and development policy has led to different patterns of economic performance. Although the moderate left has preserved economic stability and achieved steady growth at solid but unspectacular rates, the contestatory left – at least in Venezuela – has had a much more checkered record as stretches of deterioration have been followed by striking growth spurts. Due to these fluctuations, the contestatory left's economic policies have yielded mixed results to date. Economic growth was negative during the first years of the Chávez administration owing in part to domestic political instability, especially the 2002–03 oil industry strike and the capital flight triggered by ideological polarization. Between 1999 and 2003, the Venezuelan economy shrank by an annual average rate of 3.1 percent (Weisbrot and Sandoval 2006: 9). In late 2003, however, a recovery began, thanks in part to high oil prices, which contributed to a phenomenal average growth rate of 11.8 percent between 2004–07. The Morales administration, meanwhile, has only been in office since the beginning of 2006, but economic growth has been relatively strong so far. The Bolivian economy grew by 4.5 percent in 2006, 4.2 percent in 2007, and 6.0 percent in 2008, due largely to high energy prices and the renegotiation of natural gas contracts, which boosted Bolivia's revenues considerably.

High growth has come at a cost, however. Inflationary pressures have been strong in both countries. As mentioned previously, prices rose by 11.9 percent in Bolivia in 2008, and by 30.9 percent in Venezuela, with a continuing upward trend. Inflation tends to disproportionately hurt poorer sectors, the contestatory left's core constituencies and proclaimed beneficiaries. Moreover, as we have seen, it is unclear whether Bolivia's and Venezuela's recent growth spurts are sustainable, given that this economic expansion has been fueled to a large extent by sky-high oil and gas prices. Indeed, the dramatic decline in prices during the second half of 2008 is likely to hurt their economies. The renewed glut on international energy markets also lowers the bargaining leverage of state-owned companies in Bolivia and Venezuela and makes it harder to attract future foreign investment, given the recent nationalization measures and renegotiation of contracts.

Even more basically, the analyses by Corrales and especially Gray Molina, question the mono-export strategy pursued by the Chávez and Morales administrations. Under Chávez, Venezuela has increased its dependence on oil, a product whose price is highly volatile. At the same time, "Dutch disease" has ravaged other economic sectors. As Gray Molina argues, the Morales government seems to be heading in exactly the same direction, betting on the gas industry, and inadvertently weakening alternative lines of production and export. Bolivia's acrimonious relationship with the United States, for example, has threatened trade preferences for Bolivian small industry, artisan production, and natural products. As both Venezuela's and Bolivia's painful experiences with boom and bust cycles suggest, a mono-export strategy does not constitute a promising development model. Despite its economic, social, and political innovations, the contestatory left is, paradoxically, returning to an economic development model that has repeatedly failed.

By contrast, the efforts of the moderate left to further diversify the Brazilian and Chilean economies through intensified engagement with economic globalization look more promising. Based on this prudent, noncontroversial strategy, the *Concertación* and the Lula da Silva administration have achieved a good economic performance. Both countries have enjoyed fairly strong growth in recent years. The Chilean economy has expanded at an average annual rate of 5.4 percent under the *Concertación* (1990–2007), an impressively long stretch; and it has grown at a rate of 4.4 percent during the Lagos and Bachelet years (2000–07). By contrast, Latin America as a whole grew at an annual average rate of only 1.5 percent from 1990 to 2007. As Kingstone and Ponce stress, Brazil has also performed reasonably well in recent years, growing at an average annual rate of 3.8 percent during the Lula da Silva administration (2003–07), as opposed to 2.3 percent during the Cardoso years (all figures from IDB 2008). At the same time, inflation has remained very low in Chile and in Brazil.

Moreover, economic growth under the moderate left appears to be more sustainable than the recent spurts achieved by contestatory left governments. The recent expansion of the Brazilian and Chilean economies is not as closely tied to a commodity price boom as it is in Bolivia and Venezuela. Chile has sterilized a large share of exceptional copper revenues through a stabilization fund, and Brazil does not have a rentier economy at all. Both the Brazilian and Chilean economies are more diversified than are the Bolivian and Venezuelan economies. The resumption of industrial policies in Brazil provides additional incentives for the development of novel sectors, and Chile has for many years pursued the upgrading of its export model, although with less success than anticipated. The economies of the moderate left governments are not without their problems as the chapters in this volume discuss, but they nevertheless appear to be better positioned for long-term growth and stability than do their counterparts in Bolivia and Venezuela. Indeed, under the *Concertación*, Chile has had the most stable and fastest growing economy in Latin America.

SOCIAL POLICY AND PERFORMANCE

Social justice has always been a central goal of the left, and it has motivated both the contestatory and the moderate left in contemporary Latin America. In fact, the social policies pursued by all the governments under investigation have certain features in common that distinguish them from their nonleft counterparts in the region. Committed to using public financing and active state intervention to address fundamental needs, such as enhancing health, education, and social security, all have increased social expenditures considerably and moved away from a prior emphasis on private social provisioning. Moreover, both the contestatory and moderate left governments have adopted new programs that include universalistic as well as targeted benefits.

Despite these common features, however, there also are important differences in the social policy approach of the two strands of leftism, which reflect their distinct political strategies, institutional settings, and fiscal revenue bases. As in the political and economic sphere, the contestatory left has faced increased latitude and diminishing constraints in social policy and has pursued particularly ambitious and far-reaching change, yet on a relatively precarious economic and institutional basis and, in Bolivia, at a low level of absolute resource availability. By contrast, the moderate left has enjoyed less room for political maneuvering, has submitted to the economic strictures of the market model, and has therefore pursued a gradual, sequential path toward reform, yet with a greater chance of attaining sustainable progress.

DETERMINED REDISTRIBUTION?

The social policy goal that is most distinctive of the left involves combating social inequality through programs designed to "soak the rich" in order to give to poorer sectors. And given the materialistic focus of the traditional left, the redistribution of productive assets used to be regarded as particularly important. But reflecting the constraints of economic globalization and the political restrictions arising from democratic institutions, none of the governments under investigation has started a major offensive on this front. Even during the march toward "twenty-first century socialism" in contemporary Venezuela, there has been no confiscation of industrial enterprises or takeover of urban property. Where nationalizations have occurred, the previous owners received reasonably fair compensation and thus did not have to bear significant losses. Similarly, none of the leftist governments have enacted substantial increases in direct taxation. There has not been much redistributive revamping of entitlement schemes either. For instance, Lula da Silva's retrenchment of Brazil's highly regressive pension system for public sector employees, which provides considerable privileges to better-off groups, was rather limited in scope. And neither Lula nor any of the other presidents has dared to reform the costly system of virtually free education at public universities, which primarily benefits the middle and upper classes.

The only exception to this cautious avoidance of direct redistribution has been land reform, which the contestatory left has promoted. The land reform measures enacted by President Chávez provoked a great deal of political conflict, less because of their effective impact on Venezuela's wealth distribution but more because of their infringement of property rights. Despite this resistance, the Bolivarian president has taken over a number of landholdings and handed them to peasants and their cooperatives (Wilpert 2007: 110–15; Ellner 2008: chaps. 5–6). But since Venezuela is an exceptionally urbanized country, these measures, which are rather radical for the present "post neoliberal" conjuncture, will not make much of a dent in the overall distribution of property. In fact, at the same time that Chávez has squeezed large landowners, the governmental distribution of oil rents and the profit opportunities created by distortionary regulations have enriched the financial sector and a new state-dependent "Boli-bourgeoisie" (Scaglione 2008: 67–8, 76, 81–3, 88). As a result, the overall trends in income distribution under "twenty-first century socialism" remain unclear; the massive import boom of sophisticated and expensive consumer goods suggests that many well-off people have benefited considerably from Chávez's "revolution."

Evo Morales has also pushed hard for significant land reform. Given the much greater weight of agriculture in the Bolivian economy, this measure is actually more important for Bolivia than for Venezuela. Yet the clout of agribusiness and its regional concentration in the opposition-controlled lowlands make this initiative even more controversial (Gamarra 2008: 137–8). Although the Morales government has enacted land reform legislation, implementation efforts have been slow and highly conflictual.

The moderate left, by contrast, has not raised the banner of land reform. In Chile, memories of the fierce conflicts under the Marxist Allende government (1970–73) help to keep this issue off the current political agenda. In Brazil, there was an active and rather successful land redistribution program under the centrist government of Fernando Henrique Cardoso (1995–2002; see Ondetti 2007), but it has slowed significantly under the Lula da Silva administration. President Lula has had a greater ability to discipline his own party's mass base, including the PT-affiliated Movement of Landless Rural Workers (MST), and thus avoid trouble – such as land invasions – that could scare off investors in Brazil's booming agro-export sector. The PT government has sought to avoid expropriations, instead distributing land that the state had already owned.

In sum, there is a clear contrast between the contestatory and the moderate left in their land redistribution programs. But the actual outcome of this divergence has so far remained limited because agriculture does not play a large role in Venezuela, where redistribution has advanced, and because it has not yet advanced very far in Bolivia, where agriculture does have greater significance for popular well-being.

EQUITY-ENHANCING PROGRAMS

Instead of placing priority on direct redistribution, all left-wing governments have concentrated largely – the moderate left, entirely – on schemes to reduce poverty, strengthen social protection, and raise human capital. The most innovative initiatives have combined these goals in the form of conditional cash transfer programs, which provide income support for poor families who maintain their children in school or health care programs (Rawlings 2005). In Brazil's high-profile family grant program (Bolsa Família), which has been widely copied by other countries including Bolivia, destitute mothers are paid a monthly stipend if they guarantee their children's consistent classroom attendance. These types of antipoverty programs are attractive to left-wing governments for several reasons. By alleviating abysmal poverty and contributing to human capital formation, they pursue noncontroversial goals; by focusing on the least well-off, they can have a significant impact on popular well-being without undermining budget discipline; and by benefiting large numbers of citizens, they can yield a significant vote boost for the incumbent party. Therefore, such programs have turned into flagship initiatives of leftist governments across the contestatory versus moderate divide. Both the Morales and especially the Lula da Silva administration have instituted or expanded conditional cash transfer programs with great fanfare.

Yet despite this specific commonality and the broader shared emphasis on equity enhancement over direct redistribution, the contestatory and the moderate left have conducted social policy reforms in different ways that reflect their divergent organizational characteristics and the political–institutional and economic constraints they face. In a nutshell, the moderate left has concentrated on enacting or continuing reforms in the institutionalized social programs administered by line ministries and other established state agencies, especially in the areas of health care, social security, and education. By contrast, the contestatory left has prioritized the creation of ad-hoc schemes, especially the vast system of "missions to save the people" in Bolivarian Venezuela. And both Chávez and Morales have made many new social programs dependent on extraordinary revenues, especially the windfall rents produced by the recent international energy price boom. The advantage of this more flexible strategy, which corresponds to the movement character of the contestatory left, is that it can reach its beneficiaries more quickly than the ossified, sclerotic existing state institutions could. But the disadvantage is that the lack of institutionalization exposes these initiatives to the risk of administrative chaos and to the danger of retrenchment should windfall rents dry up, for instance with the looming severe recession in the global economy. By contrast, the slow, sequential advance of the moderate left may produce more lasting accomplishments.

Accepting the need for budgetary balance and facing a vigilant right-wing opposition, the *Concertación* in Chile has pursued social policy reform in prudent yet determined ways. After taking office in 1990, it raised social spending in a steady and sustained fashion in order to reverse the underfunding of public health and education produced by the austerity measures of the Pinochet regime. These expenditure increases were financed through a tax reform negotiated with the center-right. Thereafter, Socialist President Ricardo Lagos enacted more structural change. As the chapter by Huber, Pribble, and Stephens stresses, the Plan AUGE introduced basic health care coverage for all Chileans, regardless of their affiliation with the private or public health sector. This universal publicly-provided floor counteracted the shift toward the private provision of health care imposed under the dictatorship. In the same way, Socialist President Bachelet expanded pension guarantees for less well-off people, even citizens who had not contributed to social security. Her effort to reduce regressive subsidies in the education system foundered in the wake of conservative and centrist opposition, however. All of these reforms, which significantly improve Chile's system of social protection and human capital investment, were phased in gradually, funded solidly through regular budget outlays, and administered by the line ministries and other established state agencies. Thus, while sequential and slow, the social change achieved by Chile's moderate left promised to be sustainable and irreversible. The practice of negotiating reform with the conservative opposition eliminated some more progressive, redistributive proposals, such as a solidarity fund in Plan AUGE, as Huber, Pribble, and Stephens discuss. But compromise and consensus also protected these advances against a political backlash.

In a similar vein, the Lula da Silva administration in Brazil has continued and expanded the efforts of the preceding Cardoso government to improve mass education and basic health care, which benefit poorer sectors the most (Hunter and Sugiyama 2009). For instance, the PT government has further increased coverage of a family health program that prioritizes preventive and simple curative measures. Moreover, the new president combined and extended several conditional cash transfer programs that the Cardoso administration had created (partly by building on innovations introduced by regional PT governments). In this way, the Lula administration created its high-profile family grant scheme, Bolsa Família. This novel program for simultaneous poverty alleviation and human capital formation also has firm institutional foundations. Created by law, it has been administered by the Social Development Ministry. Although President Lula da Silva received tremendous electoral payoffs

from Bolsa Família, there is no indication that the federal government allo-
cates funding or selects beneficiaries according to political criteria. Because the
Lula administration has not boosted social spending overall, and the family
grant costs a mere 0.5 percent of GDP (despite benefiting an estimated 45 million Brazilians), its reform initiatives appear economically sustainable. Because
they have not been characterized by politicization and conflict, they seem to be
protected against political backlash as well.

In line with the mobilizational nature of the Bolivarian movement and his
charismatic personal leadership, President Chávez has pursued a very different approach to equity-enhancing reform. Above all, he has used windfall
rents from Venezuela's oil boom to create a welter of ad-hoc programs, the
famous "missions" (see the extensive overview in Azzellini 2006: 129–73),
while advancing much less in the reform of institutionalized social policy programs. For instance, Chávez's tailor-made constitution of 1999 mandated a
comprehensive restructuring of the health system, but this project still has not
passed, despite the president's political hegemony and current monopoly control over the legislature. By contrast, he responded to opposition pressure and
the risks of electoral competition in 2003 by creating a variety of social policy campaigns and schemes, which provide benefits ranging from subsidized
food to health services and university scholarships (Ellner 2008: 120–2). These
missions, staffed in part by Cuban health workers and educators and evok-
ing revolutionary themes (e.g. Misión Che Guevara), expanded very fast and
boasted quick success on several fronts. For instance, the Chávez government
soon claimed to have eradicated illiteracy in Venezuela.

The missions are the largest social fund experiment in contemporary Latin
America. While beneficiaries are not means-tested, mission services tend to go
to poor people and poor areas of the country. These schemes are financed
through opaque mechanisms outside of the regular budget. Oil revenues are
transferred directly from the state petroleum giant PDVSA to a special fund
managed by the presidency. The missions also lack firm institutionalization,
and the existence of many cases of political screening of beneficiaries as well
as ideological self-selection give them a politicized character (Hsieh, Ortega,
Miguel, and Rodríguez 2008). In all of these ways, the missions stand on a
shaky financial, institutional, and political foundation and reports suggest that
their activities and performance fluctuate significantly. Should Venezuela's economic fortunes or Chávez's political fortunes be endangered, due for instance
to a decline in oil prices such as the one that occurred during the second half
of 2008, the fate of the missions is uncertain.

The social policy approach of President Morales and the MAS lies in between
the two poles discussed so far. Although their plans are closer to his Bolivarian counterpart, the fiscal restrictions arising from the underdeveloped state of
Bolivia's economy, including the gas industry, and the political strength and
institutional anchoring of the conservative opposition have prevented them
from fulfilling these ambitions. The new government has used gas tax revenues
to emulate Brazil's PT government and introduce a conditional cash transfer

program designed to promote school attendance. It has also expanded a universal pension plan that guarantees all Bolivians a minimal base of financial sustenance. Ironically, however, this progressive measure had initially been introduced by the first government of Gonzalo Sánchez de Lozada, Morales's most prototypically neoliberal predecessor, and thus does not constitute a leftist innovation (Müller 2009).

Moreover, the Morales government has pursued an enormous extension of another innovation of the Sánchez de Lozada administration, namely a program for covering basic health needs by the state. While the existing scheme provides only basic care, predominantly for poorer people, the MAS has proposed to turn this program into universal health insurance that would eventually treat the health problems of all Bolivians free of charge. Given the highly generous nature of this project, which experts regard as financially unviable and administratively infeasible in a poor country with an institutionally weak, dilapidated state, the government has so far submitted only one part of this project for congressional deliberation. But the conservative opposition, entrenched in the eastern lowland departments and concerned about the drain on departmental resources, has so far blocked this change. Thus, the MAS government's approach to equity-enhancing reform has rivaled Hugo Chávez's in its ambition, but has run up against immediate economic and political constraints. Even if the Morales administration succeeds in passing its initiatives, it is unclear whether the Bolivian state can effectively implement the gamut of new benefits.

PERFORMANCE ON SOCIAL INDICATORS

The different political strategies and social policy approaches of the moderate and contestatory left have produced diverging accomplishments on the social front. Essentially, the moderate left has attained steady yet unspectacular progress in poverty alleviation and human capital formation that looks sustainable. With its conflict avoidance, however, it has made little dent in stubbornly high inequality. By contrast, in the last few years the contestatory left, especially Hugo Chávez, has managed to achieve much faster success in reducing poverty and, perhaps, inequality as well. But these recent accomplishments follow upon an earlier period of actual deterioration, emerge mostly from the international oil price boom, and – due to their precarious financial and institutional foundations – seem vulnerable to reversals.

Over the years, the Chilean *Concertación* has overseen a constant and overall impressive reduction of poverty. When it took office in 1990, 38.6 percent of citizens qualified as poor. This number fell to 20.2 percent in 2000, when Socialist Lagos assumed the presidency, and then dropped further to 13.7 in 2006 (CASEN 2006). Extreme poverty declined from 13 percent to 5.6 percent and eventually 3.2 percent in these same years. Remarkably, progress continued throughout the international economic turbulence and domestic recession of the late 1990s and early 2000s. This fact suggests that the social programs created or improved by the center-left coalition, not only economic growth or the recent boom in international copper prices, played an important role in poverty alleviation (Olavarría Gambi 2005; Lustig 2009: 13). Social inequality, by contrast, has not diminished much. After rising slightly from 0.554 in 1990 to 0.564 in 2000, Chile's Gini Index fell to 0.522 in 2006 under Socialist President Lagos, as Huber, Pribble, and Stephens mention.

Brazil has followed a similar trajectory, yet for a shorter time period. Although 37.5 percent of the population lived in poverty in 2001, this number dropped to 30 percent in 2007. Indigence afflicted 13.2 percent of Brazilians in 2002 but only 8.5 percent in 2007, representing a reduction of more than 6 million people (CEPAL 2008: 81). For the first time in many years, social inequality has also started to decline in a sustained fashion under the Lula da Silva government. Brazil's Gini Index coefficient fell from 0.639 in 2001 to 0.59 in 2007 (CEPAL 2008: 85). Its educational and health indicators have also improved, but probably due mostly to the innovations introduced under the centrist Cardoso government. In sum, Brazil's performance has been solid but far from outstanding and, as Kingstone and Ponce stress, the Lula administration could certainly have done more in these social policy arenas.

The social performance of the contestatory left, by contrast, has been much more volatile, as evidenced by the experience of the Chávez government, the only more radical administration with a sufficiently long track record to allow for an assessment. Bolivarian Venezuela underwent years of social deterioration before achieving rapid success after 2003 in diminishing poverty and boosting other social indicators as well. An economic recession caused by low oil prices and severe conflicts with the opposition – including a two-month business strike – significantly exacerbated destitution and unemployment during Chávez's first four years in office. As even sympathetic observers admit (Weisbrot, Sandoval, and Rosnick 2006: 815), the poverty headcount rose from 49.99 percent of Venezuelans in early 1999 to a staggering 61 percent in early 2003. It was only the turnaround in global petroleum prices and the rapid recovery of the Venezuelan economy after 2003 that allowed for a dramatic expansion of social programs and helped reverse this situation. As a result, the percentage of people living in poverty fell greatly from 48.6 percent in 2002 to 28.5 percent in 2007. By official statistics, inequality also dropped considerably from a Gini Index coefficient of 0.5 in 2002 to 0.427 in 2007 (CEPAL 2008: 82, 86).

Given the Bolivarian government's lack of transparency, however, all of these figures need to be interpreted with caution. Regarding social inequality, for instance, Venezuela's recent import boom, which has led to a tremendous influx of sophisticated and expensive consumer goods, suggests that richer sectors have done very well under "twenty-first century socialism," as Corrales discusses. Indeed, the relative share of capital income compared to labor income has actually increased in the 2000s (Scaglione 2008: 79). Similarly, academic researchers have disputed some of the government's proclaimed social accomplishments, such as the elimination of illiteracy (Ortega and Rodríguez 2008).

An even larger question mark concerns the base and sustainability of Chávez's undisputed accomplishments, including the significant reduction in poverty. Under the Bolivarian administration as well as earlier governments, Venezuela's social (and economic) performance has tracked international petroleum prices closely. A new statistical investigation suggests that the recent social improvements were due not to the "missions" and similar social programs, but to the oil price boom (Lustig 2009: 13). Therefore, the decline of petroleum prices since late 2008 and the global recession, which has affected Venezuela with special severity, may well lead to another increase in poverty and inequality. As mentioned previously, the precarious financial and institutional base of Chávez's social policy schemes and the oil dependence of his development scheme provide little insulation against renewed economic and social problems.

In conclusion, the gradual reform strategy of the moderate left seems to hold better prospects for lasting success. While advancing in a painfully slow fashion and leaving social inequality largely unchanged, the *Concertación*, in particular, has brought sustainable improvements in the well-being of millions of people. The contestatory left, especially the Chávez administration, has sought to force a breakthrough toward much greater absolute and relative equity, but its mixed record and stark performance fluctuations are cause for concern.

THE PERFORMANCE OF OTHER LEFT-LEANING GOVERNMENTS IN LATIN AMERICA

To what extent do this book's findings, which are based on the study of governments in Bolivia, Brazil, Chile, and Venezuela, apply more broadly? Have other left-leaning governments in Latin America pursued policies that are characteristic of the moderate or the contestatory left, as we have defined them? And have these policies had the expected effects?

This section examines the policies and performance of left-leaning governments in Argentina, Ecuador, Uruguay, and Nicaragua. Given the significance of the Argentine case, it is included in this comparative analysis, although presidents Kirchner and Fernández hail from the ideologically amorphous Peronist Party and their leftist credentials are therefore debatable, as the introduction to this volume has mentioned. The following examination focuses on these four countries because other left governments, such as the administrations of Fernando Lugo in Paraguay and Mauricio Funes in El Salvador, are of too recent vintage to allow for even preliminary conclusions about their policies and performance. This section also excludes governments headed by presidents who used to identify with the left but do not do so any longer, such as the administrations of Alan García in Peru and Oscar Arias in Costa Rica.

In their economic and social policies as well as their political strategies, the administrations of Rafael Correa in Ecuador and Daniel Ortega in Nicaragua follow the approach of the contestatory left, whereas Tabaré Vázquez in Uruguay leads a moderate left government. Although these three administrations neatly fit the classification scheme applied in the present volume, the governments of Nestor Kirchner and Cristina Fernández de Kirchner in Argentina constitute a mixed case. The presidential couple has pursued interventionist, nationalist economic policies that resemble those of the contestatory left, but has been more moderate in its political strategies. Thus, the Kirchner and Fernández administrations represent hybrids that combine moderate and contestatory features.

These four additional cases provide support for the book's central argument that the moderate left, by and large, has outperformed the contestatory left. The most successful of the four has been the moderate Vázquez government. Under this administration, Uruguay has enjoyed strong economic growth, low inflation, and high levels of popular participation, mass satisfaction, and respect for the institutions and principles of democracy. The Kirchner and Fernández governments with their mix of moderate and contestatory policies have also been relatively successful in political and economic terms. By contrast, contestatory governments in Ecuador and Nicaragua have undermined liberal democracy and exacerbated inflation, although they have generated some economic growth and boosted mass satisfaction with democracy.

The government of Rafael Correa in Ecuador, elected in late 2006, has adopted a highly contestatory economic and political strategy. Like Chávez and Morales, Correa has concentrated power, denounced the opposition and media in strident terms, and used social mobilizations to intimidate his opponents (Conaghan and de la Torre 2008). Correa also has undertaken major institutional reforms. Shortly after taking office, he convoked a Constituent Assembly that shut down the existing Congress and drafted a new constitution. The new charter, which was approved by a large majority in a referendum in September 2008, permits presidential reelection, enabling Correa potentially to stay in office until 2017. It also expands the powers of the presidency, giving the chief executive the ability to dissolve Congress, dominate constitutional oversight bodies, and restrict the media (Montúfar 2008: 5). In addition, the new constitution will recentralize power in the national government by stripping authority from local mayors and forming new regional governments that may be dominated by the executive.

The Correa administration also has increased state intervention in the economy substantially during the short time it has been in power. For example, the government has moved to assert greater control of the oil industry, issuing a decree to increase the state's share of windfall oil profits from 50 percent to 99 percent, and forcing companies to renegotiate their contracts. The country's new constitution, meanwhile, prohibits land concentration, eliminates the autonomy of the central bank, gives priority to local investors over foreign investors, and provides for a larger state role in strategic sectors such as oil, mining, telecommunications, and water. The Correa administration also has boosted government spending, especially on social programs. Government expenditures increased from $9.8 billion in 2007 to $13.2 billion in 2008. The president even raided the country's stabilization fund, although it is supposed to be used only when oil prices are low.

In addition, this contestatory left administration has reoriented the country's international economic policies. It has taken a tough line on the country's foreign debt, threatening repeatedly to default on its loans, which has scared foreign creditors and enabled Ecuador to pay back some of its existing loans at steeply discounted prices. Correa also has raised tariffs, established quotas on some imports, and rejected a free trade agreement with the United States, although he has maintained Ecuador's membership in the World Trade Organization and sought to retain its existing trade privileges with the United States through the ATPDEA. Finally in June 2009, Correa announced that Ecuador would be joining the Bolivarian Alternative for the Americas (ALBA), the economic association created by Chávez in an effort to offset the power of U.S.-friendly, market-oriented regional organizations such as the Inter-American Development Bank. Thus, the Correa administration's economic policies have much in common with those of contestatory left governments in Bolivia and Venezuela.

These interventionist, nationalist policies have had mixed results so far. Despite the international oil price boom, Ecuador grew only 2.5 percent in 2007, the first year of the Correa administration, but economic growth jumped to 5 percent in 2008. The International Monetary Fund, however, is predicting a contraction in 2009 because of the decline in oil prices and the recession in the global economy. Poverty has declined in recent years, but the government may find it difficult to maintain this trend if the economy falls into a recession, particularly because nearly half of the public budget comes from oil revenues. Inflation, which had been quite low since Ecuador adopted the dollar as its currency, rose sharply in 2008, reaching 8.87 percent, up from only 3.3 percent in 2007.

The Correa administration's contestatory political strategy also has had mixed results. On the negative side, the president's confrontational approach has worsened polarization and weakened horizontal accountability. Correa also has undermined freedom of the press and freedom of speech more generally with his aggressive attacks on the media and any politicians who dare to criticize him. On the positive side, however, this charismatic leader has mobilized some poorer sectors of the population, which have traditionally been excluded from active involvement in politics. Moreover, the Correa administration's policies have been relatively popular to date, which has helped boost satisfaction with democracy. According to Latinobarómetro surveys, 37 percent of the population reported being very or somewhat satisfied with democracy in 2008, up from only 14 percent in 2005 (Corporación Latinobarómetro 2005 and 2008).

The administration of Daniel Ortega, which was elected in 2006, also applies a contestatory left approach, especially in its political strategies. The new government has regularly harassed its critics, including members of the media, and it has mobilized its supporters to intimidate and bully the opposition (Burbach 2009). Ortega has not yet sought to undertake major institutional reforms of the kind enacted in Bolivia, Ecuador, and Venezuela, but he has clearly sought to centralize power. His Sandinista party already controls the judiciary, the Supreme Electoral Council, and a significant sector of the media, and he has pushed measures that give the president more authority over the Central Bank and the security forces. Like his counterparts in Bolivia, Ecuador, and Venezuela, Ortega has stated that he would like to revise the constitution to enable him to run again for office. This is particularly worrisome given that there have already been serious concerns about the legitimacy of elections held under the Ortega administration. In 2008, the Sandinista-controlled Supreme Electoral Council banned two important opposition parties from participating in the municipal elections, a move condemned by the Organization of American States. The council also prevented some traditional election-monitoring organizations from overseeing the contest. In the wake of the election, there were numerous allegations of fraud, leading to the suspension of economic aid from the United States and the European Union.

Nicaragua's recent social policies also have more in common with the contestatory left than the moderate left. Since taking office, Ortega has eliminated educational matriculation fees, established a literacy program with Cuban assistance, sought to expand agricultural cooperatives, and created an antipoverty program with Venezuelan aid (Burbach 2009: 34; Kendrick 2009). The new administration also has sought to expand the political participation of the poor by creating citizen power councils that will oversee social programs and distribute government aid at the local level. Opponents have criticized these initiatives on the grounds that they politicize social programs because many of the councils are controlled by the Sandinistas (McKinley Jr. 2008: 6). The government's social policies also have been faulted for their lack of transparency and their centralization in the president's office.

The Ortega administration's economic policies are not as contestatory, however. During his electoral campaign, the Sandinista leader vowed to keep Nicaragua open to foreign trade and investment. Since taking office, he has kept his pledge to implement the free trade agreement the country had signed with the United States, other Central American nations, and the Dominican Republic. The Ortega administration also signed a loan agreement with the International Monetary Fund, which committed it to restrain spending, and it has largely complied with this condition. Nevertheless, the government also has launched a number of initiatives that are more in line with the contestatory left, and its rhetoric is frequently anticapitalist. Ortega has forged an economic alliance with Hugo Chávez, joining the Bolivarian Alternative for the Americas (ALBA). The Venezuelan government, in turn, has offered Nicaragua oil, power plants, factories, and tractors for sale at discount rates or with cut-rate loans. In addition, the Nicaraguan government has boosted social spending and public sector wages and provided fuel subsidies for buses and taxis. The Ortega administration, moreover, has threatened to take over the Esso Standard oil company in part because the firm has been unwilling to refine the petroleum that Nicaragua is purchasing at a discount from Venezuela (Rogers 2007).

These policies have generated mixed results so far. The Nicaraguan economy grew by 3.8 percent in 2007 and 3.0 percent in 2008, but growth is not expected to exceed 1 percent in 2009. Inflation, meanwhile, rose to 16.9 percent in 2007, up from 9.4 percent in 2006. It declined to 13.8 percent in 2008, but this figure still remained above the rate prevailing when Ortega took office. In recent months, the Nicaraguan economy has been hurt not only by the worldwide economic recession, but also by the previously mentioned decisions of the United States and the European Union to suspend aid to the country.

The Ortega administration's political strategies, meanwhile, have clearly undermined liberal democracy. Freedom House (2008b), for example, reported that Nicaragua had grown less free under the Ortega administration in part because of its excessive concentration of power in the executive branch. Many of Ortega's former supporters have become estranged from him and a variety of observers decry the regime's growing authoritarianism (Burbach 2009). Nevertheless, mass-level satisfaction with democracy has risen under the Ortega administration as it has under other contestatory left governments. In 2008, 39 percent of Nicaraguans reported they were satisfied or very satisfied with democracy, a significant increase from 2006 (Corporación Latinobarómetro 2008: 109). The Ortega administration is not nearly as popular as its counterparts in Bolivia, Ecuador, and Venezuela, however. In fact in 2008, only 32 percent of Nicaraguans reported that they approved of their government, which represented a decline from 54 percent in 2007 and constituted the second lowest level in Latin America that year (Corporación Latinobarómetro 2008: 91).

By contrast, the administration of Tabaré Vázquez in Uruguay, which was elected in 2004, has employed moderate policies. The government's political strategy has been cautious and pragmatic and it often has pursued its goals through negotiation rather than imposition. The Vázquez administration, in marked contrast to the contestatory left governments, has largely refrained from denouncing the media or demonizing the opposition. It has respected the independence of the judiciary and has not sought to concentrate power or revise significantly the existing political institutions. Nevertheless, it has tried to gain more seats on some of the key accountability institutions, such as the Electoral Court and the Comptroller's Office, which are dominated by the opposition (Chasquetti 2007: 261–2).

The Vázquez administration's economic policies also have more in common with the moderate left than the contestatory left. The government has largely eschewed increased state intervention in the economy, and although not privatizing state-owned companies, it has not undertaken nationalization measures either. It has restrained spending, maintaining a large annual budget surplus, and has kept the economy largely open to foreign trade and investment (Flores Macías 2008: 111–13). Indeed, environmental groups and the Argentine government have criticized Vázquez for his decision to allow European companies to build two major cellulose plants on the Uruguay River in spite of concerns about their environmental consequences. Uruguay's new government also signed an investment agreement with the United States. It initially sought to negotiate a free trade agreement with the United States as well, but scaled back these plans in the face of intense criticism from its left-wing supporters and partners in Mercosur (Chasquetti 2007: 252–53; Flores Macías 2008: 113).

At the same time, the Vázquez administration has pursued reforms that might traditionally be expected of the left. For example, it enacted a major tax reform that created a progressive individual income tax and reduced the size of the regressive value-added tax. Thus, the Vázquez government's policies are not strictly market-oriented, but seek significant modifications in a gradualist, negotiated manner, as is typical of the moderate left.

The Vázquez administration's economic policies have yielded relatively strong results so far, aided by the healthy international and regional economy. Between 2005–08, the Uruguayan economy grew at an average annual rate of 7 percent, emerging from the recession that it suffered under the previous government. GDP growth reached 11 percent in 2008, but was expected to be only 2.5 percent in 2009 because of the worldwide economic downturn. Foreign reserves and foreign investment have also increased significantly. Inflation, meanwhile, is down, averaging only 7.25 percent between 2005–08.

Uruguay's moderate left has also been quite successful in political–institutional terms. The Vázquez administration has maintained the country's traditionally strong democracy and has received very high marks for respecting the civil and political rights of its citizens. Interestingly, satisfaction with democracy has been high, in marked contrast to the generally low levels prevailing under other moderate left governments. In 2008, 71 percent of Uruguayan citizens reported that they were satisfied or very satisfied with democracy, by far the highest level in Latin America (Corporación Latinobarómetro 2008: 109). Among the moderate left, the Vázquez administration has gone the furthest in encouraging popular participation. Drawing on its close ties to labor unions and other grassroots organizations, it reactivated the tripartite salary councils that regulate wages and working conditions, and created a National Economic Council that included representatives from business, labor, and civil society. It also has proposed a political decentralization and a citizen participation law (Goldfrank 2008: 19). Thus, the Uruguayan case demonstrates that it is possible for a moderate left government to stimulate popular participation and enjoy high levels of satisfaction with democracy, without sliding into the plebiscitarian majoritarianism of the contestatory left.

In contrast to the clear-cut cases of Correa, Ortega, and Vázquez, the administrations of Néstor Kirchner (2003–07) and Cristina Fernández de Kirchner (2007–present) are more ambiguous. Whereas some scholars have included the Argentine governments among the more radical left (Castañeda 2006; Leiras 2007), others have placed them in the moderate camp (Petkoff 2005), and still others have located them in between the two groupings (Lanzaro 2008; Vargas Llosa 2007). In fact, it is questionable whether the Kirchner and Fernández administrations constitute left governments at all because they have been based in the Peronist Party, which has traditionally been a catch-all populist movement with more centrist and right-wing than leftist elements. In line with this lack of a clear ideological identity, the Kirchner and Fernández administrations represent a mixture of moderate and contestatory orientations. In their political strategies, the two administrations align more closely with the moderate left, but their economic and social policies resemble those of the contestatory left.

Like the moderate left in Brazil, Chile, and Uruguay, the Kirchner and Fernández administrations in Argentina have generally respected civil and political rights, including freedom of the press, although there have been complaints that the government has directed its advertising to reward allies and punish its critics. Both governments have used some social mobilization to put pressure on the opposition but usage of this tactic has decreased in recent years (Etchemendy and Garay 2008). Moreover, neither the Kirchner nor the Fernández administration has sought to overhaul Argentina's political institutions in order to concentrate power. Indeed, the institutions of horizontal accountability are arguably stronger now than under Carlos Menem, the market-reforming president of the 1990s. Argentina maintains an autonomous judiciary, which was strengthened by the Kirchner administration, and a freely elected legislature, which has grown increasingly assertive. Both governments have pursued fairly inclusive strategies in the legislature, reaching out to members of the opposition in order to pass legislation. They also have maintained or built ties to a variety of social organizations, especially unions.

In contrast to their political moderation, the Kirchner and Fernández administrations resemble the contestatory left in their economic policies. The Argentine state has intervened significantly in the economy in recent years. It has placed controls on exports and on the prices of some products, such as meat, milk, gas, and electricity. The government also renationalized some formerly privatized companies, such as the national post office, the main water utility company, the national airlines, and the manager of the airwaves used by cellular phone companies, and it created new state-owned airlines and oil companies (Flores Macías 2008: 99–102). The state also recently took over the assets of the private pension system, which was created in 1994. A similarly tough line was taken with foreign bondholders, withholding interest payments and pressuring them to accept a lengthier repayment period and a 55 percent reduction in the face value of their bonds (Etchemendy and Garay 2008: 14). In addition, the Kirchner and Fernández administrations have pursued expansionary monetary policies, although they have also kept public spending under control and have consistently run a fiscal surplus. Thus, overall, Argentina's recent economic policies have more in common with the Morales, Correa, and Chávez administrations than with the moderate left.

The Kirchners' economic strategy has yielded highly positive results so far, but there are some emerging signs of problems. The Argentine economy suffered a profound crisis in the early 2000s, but under their leadership it recovered from 2004 to 2007, growing at an average rate of 8.8 percent annually. Inflation rose during the Kirchner administration, however; it averaged 9.2 percent in official figures, but many independent economists are convinced that it has actually been considerably higher. The economy remained strong during 2008, the first full year of the Fernández administration, with growth of 7.0 percent and inflation of 7.2 percent. Nevertheless, growth is expected to decline considerably in 2009. The International Monetary Fund has predicted that the economy will shrink by 1.5 percent in 2009, with actual inflation running at approximately 18 percent.

In political terms the Kirchner and Fernández administrations have also performed relatively well. Argentine democracy has received reasonably high marks for respecting political and civil liberties. Elections have been free and fair, and freedom of speech and association has been largely respected. The Kirchner and Fernández administrations have been criticized, however, for centralizing power excessively and for politicizing the process of choosing Supreme Court justices. There also have been numerous complaints of corruption. Mass level satisfaction with democracy has declined in recent years, falling from 50 percent in 2001 to only 33 percent in 2007 and 34 percent in 2008. Nevertheless, overall the democratic performance of the Kirchner and Fernández administrations has been reasonably good.

Thus, the political strategies of these four additional left governments have largely had the expected effects. The more contestatory approach has undermined pluralism and democracy and has increased political polarization, although it has also led to an increase in mass satisfaction with democracy and the mobilization of some traditionally marginalized groups. By contrast, political moderation has reduced polarization and strengthened democracy and liberal rights. Overall, as Table 7.1 indicates, the governments that have pursued moderate strategies have received significantly better scores from Freedom House in terms of their respect for political rights and civil liberties, but, with the notable exception of Uruguay, these countries have registered lower than average levels of mass satisfaction with democracy.

The repercussions of economic policies are also in line with the findings derived from the book's four main cases. The state-interventionist, economic-nationalist approach adopted by more contestatory leftists has generated rapid growth in Argentina and modest growth in Nicaragua and Ecuador, but has also led to rising inflation in all three countries. By contrast, more market-friendly policies have created strong growth *and* relatively low inflation in Uruguay. Overall, as Table 7.2 indicates, the record of economic growth of the moderate left has been slightly better than that of the contestatory left and has demonstrated somewhat less variance over time.[5] Meanwhile, inflation has predictably been almost twice as high on average in the countries that

---

[5] Without the ambiguous case of Argentina, the moderate left's advantage in growth rates would be even more significant.

TABLE 7.1. *Democratic Performance of Leftist Governments*

Government (Years)	Mean Political Rights Score	Mean Civil Liberties Score	Percent Satisfied with Democracy
Bolivia (Morales 2006–08)	3	3	38
Ecuador (Correa 2007–08)	3	3	36
Nicaragua (Ortega 2007–08)	3.5	3	41
Venezuela (Chávez 1999–2008)	3.5	4.2	48
Mean of contestatory left	**3.25**	**3.3**	**41**
Argentina (Kirchner and Fernández 2004–08)	2	2	37
Brazil (Lula 2003–08)	2	2.3	30
Chile (Lagos and Bachelet 2000–08)	1.3	1.2	35
Uruguay (Vázquez 2005–08)	1	1	67
Mean of moderate left	**1.6**	**1.6**	**42**

Source: Freedom House 2008 and 2009; Corporación Latinobarómetro 2006, 2007, 2008.

TABLE 7.2. *Economic Performance of Leftist Governments*

Government (Years)	Average GDP Growth (Standard Deviation)	Average Inflation Rate (Standard Deviation)
Argentina (Kirchner and Fernández 2004–08)	8.5% (0.87)	8.8% (2.41)
Bolivia (Morales 2006–08)	5.1 (0.78)	9.5 (3.90)
Ecuador (Correa 2007–08)	3.8 (1.77)	6.0 (3.82)
Nicaragua (Ortega 2007–08)	3.4 (0.57)	15.4 (2.19)
Venezuela (Chávez 1999–2008)	3.7 (8.83)	20.7 (6.84)
Mean of contestatory left	**4.9 (2.56)**	**12.1 (3.83)**
Brazil (Lula 2003–08)	4.1 (1.80)	6.0 (2.20)
Chile (Lagos and Bachelet 2000–08)	4.2 (1.23)	3.8 (2.25)
Uruguay (Vázquez 2005–08)	8.0 (2.03)	7.3 (1.97)
Mean of moderate left	**5.4 (1.69)**	**5.7 (2.14)**

Source: Banco Latinoamericano de Exportaciones 2009; IDB 2009; ECLAC 2003.

have pursued state interventionism and economic nationalism than in nations governed by the moderate left.

In conclusion, the main results of the four country cases featured in this book also apply to other left-wing experiences in contemporary Latin America.

PRELIMINARY ANSWERS TO BIG QUESTIONS

The rich findings of the chapters on Bolivia, Brazil, Chile, and Venezuela and the comparison with Argentina, Ecuador, Nicaragua, and Uruguay suggest responses to the questions raised in the introduction to this volume. There has been a sufficient track record to allow for a provisional evaluation of the performance of Latin America's moderate versus contestatory left on the issues of economic development, social equity, and political democracy, although the economic volatility afflicting Third World countries and the fluid political situation prevailing especially in the nations governed by the contestatory left preclude definitive judgments.

Regarding the left's efforts to foment dynamic economic development, all the administrations under investigation have managed to achieve economic growth despite facing significant domestic and international constraints, but the moderate left has done so on a much more sustainable basis. The *Concertación* and the Lula da Silva administration have understood that they must maintain market-oriented policies in an era of economic globalization. In response to the investor panic and capital flight of 2002, even the initially quite radical Workers' Party in Brazil has embraced the new framework and proceeded cautiously in its efforts to attain socioeconomic change. Accepting the basic outline of the market model allows only for limited reforms at any one time. Yet the moderate left trusts that over time, a series of small steps add up to a significant, lasting, and irreversible advance. The successful Chilean experience shows how well this strategy can work. Gradual reforms can have cumulative effects, and economic prudence can yield significant payoffs over a long stretch of time. Yet the greater difficulties faced by Brazil suggest that these accomplishments are not easy to replicate.

The contestatory left, by contrast, has challenged neoliberalism and the constraints of globalization rather boldly. In the mid-2000s, this more radical strategy attained considerable success, as evident in high growth rates and a tremendous increase in export and tax revenues, which swelled state coffers. But the drastic drop in international energy prices during the second half of 2008 may well bring an end to this boom and its accompanying accomplishments. The maneuvering room that Hugo Chávez, in particular, has appeared to enjoy may be a temporary reflection of an unusual boom. Moreover, the polarizing political strategy pursued by the contestatory left has incurred tremendous costs, which seriously depressed Venezuela's socioeconomic performance from 1999 to 2003. The enmity created during those years also exposes "twenty-first century socialism" to the risk of reversal should Chávez's political fortunes plummet. Thus, Latin American leftists defy the constraints of globalization at their peril. They can achieve short-term success, but at the risk of long-term setbacks. On balance therefore, the gradual approach of the moderate left looks more promising.

Both currents of leftism, however, could do more to use the latitude left by economic globalization for promoting socioeconomic development. So far, none of the governments under investigation has designed and implemented a systematic, coherent strategy for active state intervention in the economy. The predominance of liberal economic thought in Chile and the pressures of the conservative opposition have prevented the *Concertación* from creating ambitious public schemes for upgrading the country's export model by moving towards productive activities of higher value-added. As Huber, Pribble, and Stephens emphasized, a sectorally focused industrial policy is missing, and the indirect efforts to enhance Chile's comparative advantages via investments in education and labor training have not had huge payoffs. Because economic liberalism never took as firm a hold in Brazil, the Lula administration was better positioned to resume an industrial policy program, which has a long tradition in the country. But for years, these initiatives were confined to a few sectors. Only recently have they been expanded and thus acquired the potential to foment Brazilian development noticeably, as the chapter by Barros Silva, Braga, and Costa explains.

Despite its push to expand the state's role in the economy, including direct involvement in production, the contestatory left has not designed and enacted a systematic, promising strategy for state guidance of socioeconomic development either. Chávez's disparate activities do not constitute a clear, coherent plan. In particular, a public investment program that would successfully diversify the economy is conspicuous by its absence. Venezuela has become even more dependent on oil, turning almost literally into a monoexport economy. The practice of milking the government's cash cow PDVSA for social purposes raises further questions about the sustainability and promise of the Bolivarian approach to development. Indeed, Corrales argues convincingly that Venezuela is repeating another cycle of its traditional, rather unsuccessful oil rentierism. As Gray Molina warns, President Morales is at risk of falling prey to the same temptation and foregoing chances for economic diversification. The underdevelopment of the gas industry and the institutional weakness of the Bolivian state create additional barriers to economic success.

Thus, in comparison to the impressive economic accomplishments of the moderate leftist government of Felipe González in Spain (1982–96; see Boix 1998), Latin America's contemporary left has performed rather poorly in designing and implementing a state-guided development strategy that could yield significantly higher economic and social payoffs than the globalized market model currently in place, as Barros Silva, Braga, and Costa highlight. Given its ambition to restructure the market system profoundly, this deficit is especially debilitating for the contestatory left. Although also missing opportunities for fomenting economic development through state initiatives, the moderate left – with its greater reliance on the private sector – is less affected.

Despite this partial disappointment on the economic front, all left-wing governments have attained progress on the social front, especially in reducing poverty and improving educational skills and health, that is, "human capital." These accomplishments clearly arise from the concern for social equity, a defining characteristic of the left. Nevertheless, none of the four countries has made a significant dent in persistently high social inequality. Even "twenty-first century socialism" has found it difficult to effect real redistribution, given the economic and political constraints prevailing in the era of market reform and democracy. Moreover, recent social progress has rested on the global economic boom of the mid-2000s, as the contrast with the deterioration of social indicators in the economically troubled early years of Chávez's presidency suggests. This observation, corroborated by a recent statistical study (Lustig 2009: 13), of course raises the question of sustainability, which is especially acute for the contestatory left governments given their heavy reliance on commodity rents.

Although the moderate left has also been helped by the international bonanza, its social achievements are more solid (Lustig 2009: 13), as suggested by Chile's steady progress in greatly reducing poverty over the last twenty years, despite various international financial crises and a domestic recession at the turn of the millennium. This noteworthy accomplishment shows that Latin American countries can attain social advances despite economic problems. Significant improvements in the well-being of the poorest sectors are not costly and therefore do not run up against stringent fiscal constraints. And democratic competition provides an incentive for this preferential option for the poor, who control a large share of votes. In shifting to a propoor strategy, rather than channeling most benefits to its core constituencies among the formal working class, the Latin American left has absorbed and productively modified (Huber 2009: 73–80) a claim initially advanced by neoliberalism (Castañeda 1990), which has long advocated that the state privilege the destitute with public resources (while requiring better-off sectors to buy social protection in the market). In sum, the Latin American left has produced substantial improvements in social indicators, albeit not in a very distinctive fashion. Centrist and even right-wing governments have undertaken similar initiatives, as is particularly obvious in the Brazilian case, where the administration of Fernando Henrique Cardoso (1995–2002) enacted more important social policy reforms than its leftist successor.

As the moderate left has shown stronger performance on the economic and social front, it has also attained better outcomes in politics, especially by living up to democratic principles. More clearly, even, than in the area of economic development, the activism and ambition of the contestatory left have proven counterproductive in politics, leading to creeping threats to full democracy. The efforts to promote political inclusion and mass participation have opened the door for plebiscitarian majoritarianism and increasingly infringed on pluralism and liberal safeguards, especially in Venezuela. The hegemonic tendencies of governing leftists in Bolivia, Ecuador, and Nicaragua are worrisome as well. Arguably, the contestatory left has ended up undermining democracy more than deepening it.

The moderate left, especially the *Concertación* and Lula da Silva, has not enacted many high-profile programs to eliminate barriers of discrimination and create novel mechanisms of political participation. Except for the removal of authoritarian residues from the Chilean constitution, it has not pushed for an overhaul of the institutional framework either. But its lack of ambition in political reform and its limited transformatory zeal in economy and society have prevented the emergence of risks to the checks and balances, pluralism, and competitiveness that are constitutive of democracy. Rather than putting pressure on the opposition and restricting public deliberation through attacks on the media (a common occurrence in contemporary Venezuela, Bolivia, and Ecuador), moderate left governments have submitted fairly to the judgment of public opinion and the electorate. This democratic posture has benefited accountability and responsiveness, and has reduced the danger of policy mistakes and failures. Respecting the institutional confines of pluralist democracy, the moderate left cannot produce magical solutions to national problems, but it can avoid disasters and catastrophes.

The contestatory left has rejected this prudence and boldly pushed for a refoundation of the political and institutional system, yet at the price of threats to democracy itself. Bolivia's Morales and the MAS have concentrated on incorporating the indigenous and poor *mestizo* sectors that had been politically marginalized. Venezuela's Bolivarian constitution of 1999 introduced several plebiscitary institutions and softened the principle of representation through recall elections. Moreover, both leaders, as well as Ecuador's Correa, have promoted a mobilizational style of politics, calling for one electoral contest after the other and using mass demonstrations to intimidate established "liberal" institutions. As mentioned previously, this movement strategy has helped to boost popular satisfaction with democracy and thus improve the quality of the political regime in the eyes of a good part of the citizenry.

But as a serious downside, the majoritarian push of the contestatory left has put strong pressure on the institutional framework of pluralist democracy. Claiming to advance the interests, needs, and demands of previously neglected, poorer, and ethnically discriminated sectors, Chávez and Morales have attacked the opposition and concentrated political power, dismantled checks and balances, and undermined horizontal accountability. Although contestatory leftists regard majoritarianism as the necessary instrument or unavoidable price for advancing the cause of the "subaltern," there is a real risk that power concentration could become consolidated and assume an ever more autocratic nature. This danger is especially acute in Venezuela, where Chávez's leadership has a pronounced top-down character. Earlier experiences in Latin America, as under the populism of Lázaro Cárdenas and Juan Perón, suggest that plebiscitarian mass incorporation can turn undemocratic – and as the Mexican case shows, mass incorporation can gradually give way to mass control, and eventually, mass exclusion.

Because power is ultimately decisive in politics, a reasonable degree of dispersal and a guarantee of pluralism and respect for opposition are part of the nonnegotiable core of democracy. Therefore, checks and balances and other liberal safeguards cannot be sacrificed on the altar of mass inclusion and popular participation. Although the contestatory left has made some accomplishments on the political front, they do not seem to be worth the risks.

THE WISDOM OF AESOP

Evaluating ongoing political experiences is always difficult, especially when they have elicited as much passion as Latin America's contemporary left(s). Information on many aspects of economic, social, and political performance is still spotty; the evolution of current trends – for instance, the eventual depth of the global recession and its impact on international energy prices – is hard to predict; and the very significance of new initiatives, decisions, and programs remains unclear: Are they formalistic symbols or do they constitute real change? But on the other hand, it is particularly interesting for researchers to take the pulse of current developments, precisely because they have inspired high hopes in some observers, and deep fears in others.

This volume has taken on the challenge by focusing on four high-profile experiments and assessing their performance in a comprehensive and thorough way. All four of these experiences combine light and shadow, even the comparatively successful Chilean case. None of them has turned into a beacon that – in the eyes of all observers – outshines the rest. And none of these experiments constitutes a model that would be unproblematic to emulate. Yet on balance, the case studies and the present concluding assessment suggest that the moderate left, especially in Chile, has charted a more promising, sustainable course that over time can produce greater economic and social progress in a well-functioning democracy than the more ambitious yet impatient approach of the contestatory left. As in the ancient fable, the tortoise once again ends up beating the hare.

Bibliography

ABI (Agencia Boliviana de Información). 2006. Bolivia: Desastres naturales dejaron una pérdida de $US 260 millones y 39.181 damnificados. 16 March.

Abramo, Laís, and María Elena Valenzuela. 2006. Inserción laboral y brechas de equidad de género en América Latina. In *Trabajo Decente y Equidad de Género en América Latina*, ed. Laís Abramo, 29–62. Santiago de Chile: Organización Internacional del Trabajo.

Agosín, Manuel, and Ernesto Pastén. 2003. Corporate Governance in Chile. Documento de Trabajo no. 209. Banco Central de Chile, May.

Agüero, Felipe. 2006. Democracia, gobierno y militares desde el cambio de siglo: Avances hacia la normalidad democrática. In *El gobierno de Ricardo Lagos: La nueva vía chilena hacia el socialismo*, ed. Robert Funk, 49–67. Santiago de Chile: Ediciones Universidad Diego Portales.

Alarcón, Carlos. 2008. Estatutos autonómicos en levitación. *La Razón*, 26 February.

Alberts, Susan. 2006. Subjecting Power to Rules: Constitutionalism and Democratic Survival in Latin America. Paper delivered at the 102nd annual meeting of the American Political Science Association, Philadelphia, PA, 31 August.

Alvarez, Angel E. 2008. Venezuela ¿La Revolución pierde su encanto? *Revista de Ciencia Política* 28, no. 1 (July): 405–32.

Arellano, José Pablo. 2006. Del déficit al superávit fiscal. *Estudios Públicos* 101 (Summer): 165–86.

Arnson, Cynthia, ed. 2007. *The "New Left" and Democratic Governance in Latin America*. Washington, DC: Woodrow Wilson Center.

Arretche, Marta. 2004. Toward a unified and more equitable system: Health reform in Brazil. In *Crucial Needs, Weak Incentives: Social Sector Reform, Democratization, and Globalization in Latin America*, ed. Robert R. Kaufman and Joan M. Nelson, 155–88. Washington, DC: Woodrow Wilson Center Press.

Auth, Pepe. 2007. Institucionalidad, democracia y transparencia en el Partido por la Democracia (PPD). Santiago de Chile: Secretaría General del PPD, October.

Averbug, André. 1999. O Brasil no contexto da integração hemisférica: Controvérsias em torno da Alca. *Revista do BNDES* 11 (June): 49–78.

Azzellini, Dario. 2006. *Venezuela Bolivariana: Revolution des 21. Jahrhunderts?* Cologne: Neuer ISP Verlag.

BADEINSO/ECLAC (Base de Datos de Estadísticas e Indicadores Sociales). Santiago de Chile: United Nations Economic Commission for Latin America and the Caribbean. http://www.eclac.cl/badeinso/Badeinso.asp. Accessed 19 December 2008.

Baer, Werner. 1995. *The Brazilian Economy: Growth and Development.* Westport, CT: Praeger.

Baiocchi, Gianpaolo. 2005. *Militants and Citizens: The Politics of Participatory Democracy in Porto Alegre.* Stanford, CA: Stanford University Press.

Baker, Andy. 2009. *The Market and the Masses in Latin America.* Cambridge, UK: Cambridge University Press.

Banco Central do Brasil. Statistics. http://www.bcb.gov.br. Accessed 8 July 2009.

Banco Latinoamericano de Exportaciones. 2009. Info Latin America. http://www.blx. com/ListarInfoLatam.aspx?CAT_ID=5&LAN_ID=2. Accessed 20 June 2009.

Barbosa Filho, Nelson. 2008. An unusual economic arrangement: The Brazilian economy during the first Lula Administration. *International Journal of Politics, Culture and Society* 19, no. 3 (April): 193–215.

Bardhan, Pranab, Samuel Bowles, and Michael Wallerstein, eds. 2006. *Globalization and Egalitarian Redistribution.* New York: Russell Sage Foundation; Princeton, NJ: Princeton University Press.

Barrios, Franz. 2008. Hacia un pacto territorial en Bolivia: Conflictos, conceptos, consensos en torno a las autonomías. Documento de trabajo. La Paz: PAPEP-PNUD.

BCV (Banco Central de Venezuela). 2009. Índice Nacional de Precios al Consumidor. http://www.bcv.org.ve/excel/4_5_2.xls?id=415. Accessed 9 January 2009.

Berzoini, Ricardo. 2003. A previdência: Reforma com justiça social. In *Governo Lula: Novas Prioridades e Desenvolvimento Sustentado*, ed. João Paulo dos Reis Velloso, 177–81. Rio de Janeiro: José Olympio.

Bianchi, Alvaro, and Ruy Braga. 2005. Brazil: The Lula government and financial globalization. *Social Forces* 83, no. 4 (June): 1745–62.

Blofield, Merike. 2006. *The Politics of Moral Sin: Abortion and Divorce in Spain, Chile and Argentina.* New York: Routledge.

Boeckh, Andreas, ed. 2007. Die lateinamerikanische Linke und die Globalisierung. *Lateinamerika Analysen* 17 (July): 69–197.

Boeninger, Edgardo. 2007. *Políticas Públicas en Democracia: Institucionalidad y Experiencia Chilena, 1990–2006.* Santiago de Chile: Uqbar/CIEPLAN.

———.1997. *Democracia en Chile: Lecciones para la Gobernabilidad.* Santiago de Chile: Editorial Universidad Andrés Bello.

Boersner, Demetrio. 2007. Dimensión internacional de la crisis venezolana. In *Venezuela en Retrospectiva: Los Pasos Hacia el Régimen Chavista*, ed. Günther Maihold. Madrid and Frankfurt: Iberoamericana and Vervuert.

Böhrt, Carlos, Silvia Chávez, and Andrés Torres. 2008. *Puentes para un Diálogo Democrático – Proyectos de Constitución y Estatutos: Compatibilidades y Diferencias.* La Paz: Friedrich Ebert Stiftung.

Boix, Carles. 1998. *Political Parties, Growth and Equality.* Cambridge, U.K.: Cambridge University Press.

Bradley, David H., and John D. Stephens. 2007. Employment performance in OECD countries: A test of neo-liberal and institutionalist hypotheses. *Comparative Political Studies* 40, no. 12 (December): 1486–510.

Braga, José Carlos de Souza. 2000. *Temporalidade da Riqueza: Teoria da Dinâmica e Financeirização do Capitalismo.* Campinas: IE/UNICAMP.

Brant, Roberto. 2003. A reforma da previdência: Comentários. In *Governo Lula: Novas Prioridades e Desenvolvimento Sustentado*, ed. João Paulo dos Reis Velloso, 183–88. Rio de Janeiro: José Olympio.

Bresser Pereira, Luiz Carlos. 2007. *Macroeconomia da Estagnação*. São Paulo: Pereira Editora 34.

———. 1993. Economic reforms and economic growth: Efficiency and politics in Latin America. In *Economic Reforms in New Democracies: A Social Democratic Approach*, Luiz Carlos Bresser Pereira, José Maravall, and Adam Przeworski, 15–76. New York: Cambridge University Press.

Burbach, Roger. 2009. Et Tu, Daniel? The Sandinista Revolution betrayed. *NACLA Report on the Americas* 42, no. 2 (March/April): 33–7.

Buxton, Julia. 2008. European Views of the Bolivarian Progressive Social Image. Paper delivered at the conference Ten Years of Venezuelan Foreign Policy: Impacts in the Hemisphere and the World. Summit of the Americas Center, Florida International University, Miami, FL, 29 May.

———. 2001. *The Failure of Political Reform in Venezuela*. Aldershot, U.K.: Ashgate.

Calderón, Fernando, and Eduardo Gamarra. 2004. Crisis, inflexión y reforma del sistema de partidos en Bolivia. *Cuaderno de Futuro* no. 19, Informe Sobre Desarrollo Humano – PNUD.

Cameron, Maxwell. 2009. Latin America's left turns: Beyond good and bad. *Third World Quarterly* 30, no. 2: 331–348.

Canache, Damarys. 2004. Urban poor and political order. In *The Unraveling of Representative Democracy in Venezuela*, eds. Jennifer L. McCoy and David J. Myers, 33–49. Baltimore, MD: Johns Hopkins University Press.

Carey, John. 2003. Presidentialism and representative institutions. In *Constructing Democratic Governance in Latin America*, eds. Jorge Domínguez and Michael Shifter, 11–42. Baltimore, MD: Johns Hopkins University Press.

———. 1999. Partidos y coaliciones en el Congreso Chileno. *Política y Gobierno* 6, no. 2 (September): 365–406.

Carneiro, Ricardo, ed. 2006. *A Supremacia dos Mercados e a Política Econômica do Governo Lula*. São Paulo: UNESP.

CASEN (Encuesta de Caracterización Socioeconómica Nacional). 2006. *La Situación de la Pobreza en Chile. Série Analísis de Resultados de la Encuesta de Caracterización Socioeconómica Nacional*. Santiago de Chile: MIDEPLAN. http://www.mideplan. cl/casen/cpublica_2006.html. Accessed 12 December 2008.

Cason, Jeffrey. 2006. Hopes dashed? Lula's Brazil. *Current History* 105, no. 688 (February): 74–8.

Castañeda, Jorge. 2006. Latin America's left turn. *Foreign Affairs* 85, no. 3 (May): 28–43.

———. 1993. *Utopia Unarmed: The Latin American Left after the Cold War*. New York: Knopf.

———, and Marco Morales, eds. 2008. *Leftovers: Tales of the Latin American Left*. New York: Routledge.

Castañeda, Tarcisio. 1990. *Para Combatir la Pobreza: Política Social y Descentralización en Chile durante los '80*. Santiago de Chile: Centro de Estudios Públicos.

CEDLA (Centro de Desarrollo Laboral y Agrario). 2006. *Legitimando el Orden Neoliberal: Los 100 Primeros Días de Gobierno de Evo Morales*. La Paz: CEDLA.

CEP (Centro de Estudios Públicos). 2009. Estudio Nacional de Opinión Pública N. 59, Mayo-Junio 2009. http://www.cepchile.cl/dms/lang_1/doc_4397.html. Accessed 20 June 2009.

CEPAL (Comisión Económica para América Latina y el Caribe). 2008. *Panorama Social de América Latina*. Santiago de Chile: CEPAL.

Chasquetti, Daniel. 2007. Uruguay 2006: Éxitos y dilemas del gobierno de izquierda. *Revista de Ciencia Política* (volumen especial): 249–63.

Chávez, Hugo, Martha Harnecker, and Chesa Boudin. 2005. *Understanding the Venezuelan Revolution: Hugo Chávez Talks to Marta Harnecker*. New York: Monthly Review Press.

Cleary, Matthew. 2006. Explaining the left's resurgence. *Journal of Democracy* 17, no. 4 (October): 35–49.

Coimbra, Marcos. 2007. Lula continua muito bem. *Estado de Minas*, 1 July. http://www.voxpopuli.com.br/artigos/MC/MC20070701.pdf. Accessed 24 September 2008.

Collier, Paul. 2007. *The Bottom Billion: Why the Poorest Countries Are Failing and What Can Be Done about It*. New York: Oxford University Press.

Conaghan, Catherine, and Carlos de la Torre. 2008. The permanent campaign of Rafael Correa: Making Ecuador's plebiscitary presidency. *International Journal of Press/Politics* 13, no. 3: 267–84.

Conde, Alfredo. 2009. Se alzó Barrio Adentro. *Zeta* (Caracas) 1716, July 23.

Coppedge, Michael. 2003. Venezuela: Popular sovereignty versus liberal democracy. In *Constructing Democratic Governance in Latin America*, eds. Jorge Domínguez and Michael Shifter, 165–92. Baltimore, MD: Johns Hopkins University Press.

————. 1994. *Strong Parties and Lame Ducks: Presidential Partyarchy and Factionalism in Venezuela*. Stanford, CA: Stanford University Press.

Coronel, Gustavo. 2006. *Corruption, Mismanagement, and Abuse of Power in Hugo Chávez's Venezuela*. Washington, DC: Cato Institute.

Coronil, Fernando. 1997. *The Magical State: Nature, Money, and Modernity in Venezuela*. Chicago: University of Chicago Press.

Corporación Latinobarómetro. 2008. *Informe 2008*. Santiago: Corporación Latinobarómetro (November).

————. 2007. *Latinobarómetro Report 2007*. Santiago: Corporación Latinobarómetro (November).

————. 2006. *Informe Latinobarómetro 2006*. Santiago: Corporación Latinobarómetro.

————. 2005. *Latinobarómetro Report 2005*. Santiago: Corporación Latinobarómetro.

Corrales, Javier. 2008. Polarization, oil and regime change in Venezuela. In *Revolution in Venezuela*, eds. Jon Eastman and Thomas Ponniah. Durham, NC: Duke University Press. Book manuscript.

————. 2006. Hugo Boss. *Foreign Policy* 152 (January/February): 32–40.

————. 2005. In search of a theory of polarization. *European Review of Latin American and Caribbean Studies* 79 (October): 105–18.

————. 2000. Reform-lagging states and the question of devaluation: Venezuela's response to the exogenous shocks of 1997–98. In *Exchange Rate Politics in Latin America*, eds. Carol Wise and Riordan Roett, 123–58. Washington, DC: Brookings Institution.

————, and Michael Penfold. 2007. Venezuela: Crowding out the opposition. *Journal of Democracy* 18, no. 2 (April): 99–113.

Corte Departamental Electoral de Santa Cruz. 2008. http://www.corteelectoralsc. com/computo2008/. Accessed 15 August 2008.

Couto, Cláudio, and Paulo Baia. 2006. Lula's Administration: The Limits of Change. Paper delivered at the 26th International Congress of the Latin American Studies Association, San Juan, Puerto Rico, 15–18 March.

Cox, Cristián. 2006. Policy Formation and Implementation in Secondary Education Reform: The Case of Chile at the Turn of the Century. Education Working Paper #3. Washington, DC: World Bank.

Cox, Gary, and Scott Morgenstern. 2002. Epilogue: Latin America's reactive assemblies and proactive presidents. In *Legislative Politics in Latin America*, eds. Scott Morgenstern and Benito Nacif, 446–68. New York: Cambridge University Press.

Crabtree, John, and Laurence Whitehead, eds. 2008. *Unresolved Tensions: Bolivia, Past and Present*. Pittsburgh, PA: University of Pittsburgh Press.

Crisp, Brian. 2000. *Democratic Institutional Design: The Powers and Incentives of Venezuelan Politicians and Interest Groups*. Stanford, CA: Stanford University Press.

Dahl, Robert. 1971. *Polyarchy: Participation and Opposition*. New Haven, CT: Yale University Press.

Dávila, Mireya. 2005. Health Reform in Contemporary Chile: Does Politics Matter? Master's thesis, Department of Political Science, University of North Carolina, Chapel Hill.

De la Torre, Carlos, and Enrique Peruzzotti, eds. 2008. *El Retorno del Pueblo: Populismo y Nuevas Democracias en América Latina*. Quito: FLACSO & Ministerio de Cultura.

Dietz, Henry A., and David J. Myers. 2007. From thaw to deluge: Party system collapse in Venezuela and Peru. *Latin American Politics and Society* 49, no. 2 (Summer): 59–86.

Di John, Jonathan. 2009. *From Windfall to Curse? Oil and Industrialization in Venezuela, 1920–2005*. University Park: Pennsylvania State University Press.

Diniz, Aline, Peter Kingstone, and Jonathan Krieckhaus. 2008. The limits of economic reform in Brazil. In *Democratic Brazil Revisited*, eds. Peter Kingstone and Timothy J. Power, 137–60. Pittsburgh, PA: University of Pittsburgh Press.

Di Tella, Rafael, Javier Donna, and Robert MacCulloch. In press. Oil, macro volatility and crime in the determination of beliefs in Venezuela. In *Venezuela: Anatomy of a Collapse*, eds. Ricardo Hausmann and Francisco Rodríguez. Book manuscript.

Domínguez, Jorge. 2008. Three decades since the start of the democratic transitions. In *Constructing Democratic Governance in Latin America*, 3rd ed., eds. Jorge Domínguez and Michael Shifter, 323–52, 398–400. Baltimore, MD: Johns Hopkins University Press.

Dornbusch, Rüdiger, and Sebastian Edwards, eds. 1991. *The Macroeconomics of Populism in Latin America*. Chicago: University of Chicago Press.

Draibe, Sônia M. 2004. Federal leverage in a decentralized system: Education reform in Brazil. In *Crucial Needs, Weak Incentives: Social Sector Reform, Democratization, and Globalization in Latin America*, eds. Robert R. Kaufman and Joan M. Nelson, 376–406. Washington, DC: Woodrow Wilson Center Press.

———. 2003. A política social do governo FHC e o sistema de proteção social. *Tempo Social – Revista de Sociologia da USP (São Paulo)* 15, no. 2 (November): 63–101.

Drake, Paul. 1978. *Socialism and Populism in Chile, 1932–1952*. Urbana: University of Illinois Press.

Echevarría, Oscar. 1995. *La Economía Venezolana, 1944–1994*. Caracas, Venezuela: Editorial Arte/Fedecámaras.

Eckstein, Susan, ed. 2001. *Power and Popular Protest: Latin American Social Movements*. Berkeley: University of California Press.

ECLAC (United Nations Economic Commission on Latin America and the Caribbean). Various years. Statistics.

_____. 2007. *Social Panorama of Latin America 2007*. Santiago, Chile: United Nations ECLAC.

_____. 2003. *Preliminary Overview of the Economies of Latin America and the Caribbean*. Santiago de Chile: United Nations ECLAC.

(*El*) *Economista*. 2007. Gobierno basa presupuesto 2008 en venta barril de petróleo a solo 35 dólares. 18 October.

EFE. 2009. Chile Tuvo Superávit Fiscal de 5.2% del PIB en 2008. 30 January. http://www.soitu.es/soitu/2009/01/30/info/1233336213_442614.html. Accessed 20 June 2009.

EIA (Energy Information Administration). 2009. Venezuela. Country Analysis Briefs (January). http://www.eia.doe.gov/cabs/Venezuela/Background.html. Accessed 1 August 2009.

_____. 2007. Venezuela: Country Analysis Briefs. http://www.eia.doe.gov/emeu/cabs/Venezuela/Oil.html. Accessed 27 July 2008.

Ellner, Steve. 2008. *Rethinking Venezuelan Politics: Class, Conflict and the Chávez Phenomenon*. Boulder, CO: Lynne Rienner.

Espinasa, Ramón. 2009. *The Performance of the Venezuelan Oil Sector 1997–2008: Official vs. International and Estimated Figures*. Coral Gables, FL: University of Miami, Center for Hemispheric Policy.

Espinosa, Consuelo, Marcelo Tokman, and Jorge Rodríguez. 2005. Finanzas públicas de la reforma. In *Reforma de la Salud en Chile: Desafíos de la Implementación*, ed. Universidad Andrés Bello. Santiago de Chile: Editorial Universidad Andrés Bello.

Etchemendy, Sebastián, and Candelaria Garay. 2008. Between Moderation and Defiance: The Kirchner Government in Comparative Perspective (2003–2007). A paper delivered at the conference Latin America's Left Turn: Causes and Implications, Harvard University, 4–5 April.

Evans, Peter. 1995. *Embedded Autonomy: States and Industrial Transformation*. Princeton, NJ: Princeton University Press.

Fahri, Maryse. 2006. O impacto dos ciclos de liquidez no Brasil: Mercados financeiros, taxa de câmbio, preços e política monetária. In *A Supremacia dos Mercados e a Política Econômica do Governo Lula*, ed. Ricardo Carneiro, 173–205. São Paulo: UNESP.

Fairfield, Tasha. 2007. The Politics of Taxing Latin American Elites. Paper delivered at the 27th International Congress of the Latin American Studies Association, Montreal, Canada, 5–8 September.

Faría, Hugo J. 2008. Hugo Chávez against the backdrop of Venezuelan economic and political history. *Independent Review*, 12, no. 4 (Spring): 519–35.

_____. 2007. Socialismo Democrático contra Socialismo Totalitario. http://www.hacer.org/current/Vene221.php. Accessed 13 December 2007.

Ffrench-Davis, Ricardo. 2002. *Economic Reforms in Chile from Dictatorship to Democracy*. Ann Arbor: University of Michigan Press.

Flores Macías, Gustavo. 2008. The Political Economy of the Left in Latin America: Explaining Governments' Reactions to Neoliberal Reforms. Ph.D. dissertation (draft), Georgetown University.

Flynn, Peter. 2005. Brazil and Lula, 2005: Crisis, corruption and change in political perspective. *Third World Quarterly* 26, no. 8 (December): 1221–67.

Folha de São Paulo. 2007a. Blog do Josias: Brasil é 7° em desempenho do PIB na América do Sul. 28 December. http://www1.folha.uol.com.br/folha/dinheiro/ult91u358618.shtml. Accessed 28 December 2007.

———. 2007b. Leia a íntegra do pronunciamento do Presidente Lula. 27 December. http://www1.folha.uol.com.br/folha/brasil/ult96u358580.shtml. Accessed 27 December 2007.

Forbes. 2007. Brazil raises 2007 GDP, inflation forecasts. 27 December. http://www.forbes.com/reuters/feeds/reuters/2007/12/27/2007-12-27T104058Z_01_N27360354_RTRIDST_0_BRAZIL-ECONOMY-INFLATION-URGENT.html. Accessed 27 December 2007.

Franco, Gustavo. 2006. *Crônicas da Convergência: Ensaios sobre Temas já Não Tão Polêmicos*. Rio de Janeiro, Brazil: Top Books.

Frank, Volker. 2004. Politics without policy: The failure of social concertation in democratic Chile, 1990–2000. In *Victims of the Chilean Miracle: Workers and Neoliberalism in the Pinochet Era, 1973–2002*, ed. Peter Winn, 71–124. Durham, NC: Duke University Press.

Franko, Patrice. 2007. *The Puzzle of Latin American Economic Development*. Lanham, MD: Rowman and Littlefield.

Freedom House. 2009. Freedom in the World 2009. New York: Freedom House. http://www.freedomhouse.org/template.cfm?page=445. Accessed 20 June 2009.

———. 2008a. Freedom in the World. http://www.freedomhouse.org. Accessed 9 October 2008.

———. 2008b. Freedom in the World – Nicaragua. New York: Freedom House. http://www.freedomhouse.org/template.cfm?page=22&year=2008&country=7459. Accessed 18 June 2009.

Fuentes, Claudio. 2004. *El Costo de la Democracia. Nueva Serie*. Santiago de Chile: FLACSO.

———. 1999. Partidos y coaliciones en el Chile de los '90. In *El Modelo Chileno: Democracia y Desarrollo en los Noventa*, eds. Paul Drake and Iván Jaksic, 191–222. Santiago de Chile: LOM Ediciones.

Fundación Milenio. 2006. *Espejismos y Realidades: Análisis del Plan Nacional de Desarrollo*. La Paz, Bolivia: Fundación Milenio.

Funk, Robert L. 2006. Un destape chileno: Reformas políticas y cambio social durante el gobierno de Ricardo Lagos. In *El Gobierno de Ricardo Lagos: La Nueva Vía Chilena Hacia el Socialismo*, ed. Robert Funk, 37–46. Santiago de Chile: Ediciones Universidad Diego Portales.

Galasso, Emanuela. 2006. With Their Effort and One Opportunity: Alleviating Extreme Poverty in Chile. Washington, DC: Inter-American Development Bank. http://www.iadb.org/res/pub_desc.cfm?pub_id=S-1. Accessed 4 May 2009.

Gamarra, Eduardo. 2008. Bolivia: Evo Morales and democracy. In *Constructing Democratic Governance in Latin America*, 3rd ed., eds. Jorge Domínguez and Michael Shifter, 124–51. Baltimore, MD: Johns Hopkins University Press.

———. 1997. Hybrid presidentialism and democratization: The case of Bolivia. In *Presidentialism and Democracy in Latin America*, eds. Scott Mainwaring and Matthew Soberg Shugart, 363–93. Cambridge, U.K.: Cambridge University Press.

Garretón, Manuel Antonio. 2005. Coping with opacity: The financing of politics in Chile. In *The Financing of Politics: Latin American and European Perspectives*, eds. Eduardo Posada-Carbó and Carlos Malamud, 160–88. London: Institute for the Study of the Americas.

Geddes, Barbara. 1995. The politics of economic liberalization. *Latin American Research Review* 30, no. 2 (June): 195–214.

Gibbs, Terry. 2006. Business as unusual: What the Chávez era tells us about democracy under globalization. *Third World Quarterly* 27, no. 2 (March): 265–79.

Goldfrank, Benjamin. 2008. The Left and Participatory Democracy: Scaling Up or Scaling Back? A paper delivered at the conference Latin America's Left Turn: Causes and Implications, Harvard University, 4–5 April.

Gonçalves, Reinaldo, and Luiz Filgueiras. 2007. *A Economia Política do Governo Lula*. Rio de Janeiro, Brazil: Contraponto Editora.

Government of Bolivia. 2006. *Plan Nacional de Desarrollo*. La Paz, Bolivia: Ministry of Development Planning.

Government of Chile. 2007. Acuerdo por la Calidad de la Educación. http://www. minsegpres.gob.cl/portal/documentos/documentos/otros_documentos/ 200711131451580_acuerdocalidaddelaeducacion/documentoLista/0/documento/ 200711131451580.acuerdocalidaddelaeducaciOn.pdf. Accessed 23 September 2008.

Gray Molina, George. 2009. The Other Revolution: Accelerating Equalizing Changes in Bolivia. Working paper, Center for Inequality, Ethnicity and Human Security (CRISE), University of Oxford. Oxford: CRISE.

———, and Alvaro Araníbar. 2006. La Economía Boliviana en 2006: Una Buena Coyuntura para "Salir de la Estructura." Working paper, Human Development Report, 2006. La Paz: United Nations Development Programme.

———, and Mark Purser. In press. The Puzzle of Divergent Convergence: Human Development Trends 1970–2007. Working paper, Human Development Report 2010. New York: UNDP.

———, and Fernanda Wanderley. 2007. Explaining Growth Pockets in a Low-Growth Economy. Working paper, Center for International Development (CID), Harvard University Seminar on Bolivian Growth and Poverty Reduction, 15–16 November 2006.

———, and Ernesto Yáñez. 2009. The dynamics of inequality in the best and worst of times, Bolivia, 1997–2007. In *The New Dynamics of Inequality in Latin America*, eds. Luis Felipe López-Calva and Nora Lustig. Washington, DC: Brookings Institution.

Green, Duncan. 2003. *Silent Revolution: The Rise and Crisis of Market Economics in Latin America*. New York: Monthly Review Press.

Grimm, Michael, Kenneth Harttgen, Stephan Klasen, Mark Misselhorn, Teresa Munzi, and Timothy Smeedy. 2009. Inequality in Human Development: An Empirical Assessment of 32 Countries. Social Indicators Research. Published online 10 June. http://ir. iss.nl/eserv.php?pid=iss:185&dsID=fulltext.pdf

Grindle, Merilee. 2003. Shadowing the past? Policy reform in Bolivia, 1985–2002. In *Proclaiming Revolution: Bolivia in Comparative Perspective*, eds. Merilee Grindle and Pilar Domingo, 318–44. Cambridge, MA: Harvard University Press. David Rockefeller Center for Latin American Studies.

Haggard, Stephan, and Robert R. Kaufman. 1995. *The Political Economy of Democratic Transitions*. Princeton, NJ: Princeton University Press.

Haggard, Stephan, and Steven B. Webb, eds. 1994. *Voting for Reform: Democracy, Political Liberalization, and Economic Adjustment*. New York: Oxford University Press.

Hagopian, Frances. 1998. Democracy and political representation in Latin America in the 1990s. In *Fault Lines of Democracy in Post-Transition Latin America*, eds. Felipe Agüero and Jeffrey Stark, 99–143. Miami, FL: North-South Center Press.

Hall, David. 2007. Public Sector Finance for Investment in Infrastructure: Some Recent Developments. Paper submitted for the UN CSD meeting, May.

Hartlyn, Jonathan, and Juan Pablo Luna. 2007. Constitutional Reform in Latin America: Intentions and Outcomes. Paper delivered at the 27th International Congress of the Latin American Studies Association, Montréal, Canada, 5–8 September.

Hausmann, Ricardo, and Francisco Rodríguez. In press. Why did Venezuelan growth collapse? In *Venezuela: Anatomy of a Collapse*, eds. Ricardo Hausmann and Francisco Rodríguez.

Hirschman, Albert. 1991. *The Rhetoric of Reaction*. Cambridge, MA: Harvard University Press.

Hochstetler, Kathryn. 2008. Organized civil society in Lula's Brazil. In *Democratic Brazil Revisited*, eds. Peter Kingstone and Timothy Power, 33–56. Pittsburgh, PA: University of Pittsburgh Press.

Houtzager, Peter, Arnab Acharya, and Adrián Lavalle. 2007. Associations and the Exercise of Citizenship in New Democracies: Evidence from São Paulo and Mexico City. Working paper no. 285. Brighton, U.K.: Institute of Development Studies.

Hsieh, Chang-Tai, Daniel Ortega, Edward Miguel, and Francisco Rodríguez. 2008. The Price of Political Opposition: Evidence from Venezuela's Maisanta. Working paper no. 08–14. Chicago: University of Chicago.

Huber, Evelyne. 2009. The new left versus neoliberalism in Latin America. In *Democratic Deficits: Addressing Challenges to Sustainability and Consolidation around the World*, eds. Gary Bland and Cynthia Arnson, 67–82. Washington, DC: Woodrow Wilson Center.

———. 1995. Assessments of state strength. In *Latin America in Comparative Perspective*, ed. Peter Smith, 163–93. Boulder, CO: Westview.

———, and John D. Stephens. 2001. *Development and Crisis of the Welfare State*. Chicago: University of Chicago Press.

———. 1998. Internationalization and the social democratic model. *Comparative Political Studies* 31, no. 3 (June): 353–97.

Human Rights Watch. 2008. *Venezuela – A Decade under Chávez: Political Intolerance and Lost Opportunities for Advancing Human Rights in Venezuela*. New York: Human Rights Watch.

———. 2007. Venezuela: Proposed Amendments Threaten Basic Rights. 29 November. http://hrw.org/doc/?t=americas&c=venezu. Accessed 13 December 2007.

Hunter, Wendy. 2007. The normalization of an anomaly: The Workers' Party in Brazil. *World Politics* 59, no. 3 (April): 440–75.

———, and Timothy Power. 2007. Rewarding Lula: Executive power, social policy, and the Brazilian elections of 2006. *Latin American Politics and Society* 49, no. 1 (April): 1–30.

_____, and Natasha Borges Sugiyama. 2009. Democracy and social policy in Brazil: Advancing basic needs, preserving privileged interests. *Latin American Politics and Society* 51, no. 2 (summer): 28–58.

IBGE (Instituto Brasileiro de Geografia e Estatística). Various years. http://www.ibge. gov.br.

IBOPE (Instituto Brasileiro de Opinião Pública e Estatística). 2007. Avaliação do governo Lula se mantém estável. Notícias, Opinião Pública, IBOPE Inteligência, 6 July.

_____. 2001. National Survey, March.

IDB (Inter-American Development Bank). 2009. Latin American and Caribbean Macro Watch Data Tool. http://www.iadb.org/res/lmw.cfm?s=1806. Accessed 20 June 2009.

_____. 2008. Country Indicators. http://www.iadb.org/countries/.

_____. 2005. *The Politics of Policies: Economic and Social Progress in Latin America, 2006 Report.* Washington, DC: Inter-American Development Bank; Cambridge, MA: Rockefeller Center for Latin American Studies.

IEDI (Instituto de Estudos para o Desenvolvimento Industrial). 2008. *A Política de Desenvolvimento Produtivo.* São Paulo: IEDI.

Ihrig, Jane, and Jaime Marquez. 2003. An Empirical Analysis of Inflation in OECD Countries. International Finance Discussion Papers, Board of Governors of the Federal Reserve System, no. 765, May.

IMF (International Monetary Fund). World Economic Outlook Database. Data retrieved 8 July 2009, from www.imf.org.

_____. 2009. *World Economic Outlook Update: Contradictory Forces.* Washington, DC: IMF.

Infolatam. 2009. Venezuela: Gobierno afirma que la nómina de PDVSA ha crecido 266.66%. *Infolatam: Noticias y Análisis de América Latina.* 19 July. http://www. infolatam.com/entrada/venezuela_gobierno_afirma_que_la_nomina_-15067.html. Accessed 1 August 2009.

_____. 2008. Chile obtiene el mayor superávit fiscal en 20 años. *Infolatam: Noticias y Análisis de América Latina.* 30 January. http://www.infolatam.com/entrada/chile_ obtiene_el_mayor_superavit_fiscal_-6918.html. Accessed 19 December 2008.

IPEA (Instituto de Pesquisa Econômica Aplicada). 2007. *Boletim de Políticas Sociais: Acompanhamento e Análise.* Edição especial 13.

_____. 2006. Sobre a recente queda da desigualdade de renda no Brasil. Nota Técnica 8 (August). http://www.ipea.gov.br/sites/000/2/livros/desigualdaderen danobrasil/NotaTecnica.pdf. Accessed 24 September 2008.

IPEADATA (Instituto de Pesquisa Econômica Aplicada, Base de Dados). Various years. Statistics (Secretaria de Planejamento de Longo Prazo). http://www.ipeadata.gov.br.

Iwakami Beltrão, Kaizô, and Sonoê Sugahara. 2003. Previdência dos servidores públicos: O impacto financeiro de teto de contribuição. In *Governo Lula: Novas Prioridades e Desenvolvimento Sustentado*, ed. João Paulo dos Reis Velloso, 217–64. Rio de Janeiro, Brazil: José Olympio.

Jatar, Ana Julia. 2006. *Apartheid del Siglo XXI.* Caracas, Venezuela: Publicaciones Monfort.

Jessop, David. 2008. The coming recession and oil. *BBC News*, October 28. http://www. bc.co.uk/caribbean/news/story/2008/10/081028_jessop_pct27.shtml. Accessed 24 December 2008.

Kakwani, Nanak, Marcelo Neri, and Hyun Son. 2006. Linkages between Pro-poor Growth, Social Programmes and Labor Market: The Recent Brazilian Experience.

Paper submitted for the Fifth General Meeting of the Poverty and Economic Policy Research Network, Addis Ababa, 18–22 June.

Karl, Terry. 1997. *The Paradox of Plenty*. Berkeley: University of California Press.

———. 1987. Petroleum and political pacts: The transition to democracy in Venezuela. *Latin American Research Review* 22, no. 1 (February): 61–94.

Kaufman, Robert. 2007. Political economy and the "New Left." In *The "New Left" and Democratic Governance in Latin America*, ed. Cynthia Arnson, 24–30. Washington, DC: Woodrow Wilson Center.

———, and Barbara Stallings. 1991. The political economy of Latin American populism. In *The Macroeconomics of Populism in Latin America*, eds. Rüdiger Dornbusch and Sebastian Edwards, 15–43. Chicago: University of Chicago Press.

Kelly, Janet, and Pedro A. Palma. 2004. The syndrome of economic decline and the quest for change. In *The Unraveling of Representative Democracy in Venezuela*, eds. Jennifer L. McCoy and David J. Myers, 202–30. Baltimore, MD: Johns Hopkins University Press.

Kendrick, Frank. 2009. Nicaragua under the Second Coming of the Sandinistas. Council on Hemispheric Affairs, Washington, DC. http://www.coha.org. Accessed 5 February 2009.

Kingdon, John W. 1995. *Agendas, Alternatives and Public Policies*. 2nd ed. New York: Longman.

Kingstone, Peter. 2003. Democratic governance and the dilemma of Social Security reform in Brazil. In *Latin American Democracies in the New Global Economy*, ed. Ana Margheritis, 221–40. Miami, FL: North-South Center Press.

Kingstone, Peter, and Joseph Young. 2009. Partisanship and policy choice: What's left for the left in Latin America? *Political Research Quarterly* 62, no. 1 (March): 29–41.

Knaudt, Rubens Barbery. 2006. ¿Por que los 2/3? *Los Tiempos*, 8 December.

Kornblith, Miriam. 2006. La revocatoria de mandato en Venezuela: Contexto, contenidos y balance de su aplicación. Paper delivered at the 26th International Congress of the Latin American Studies Association, San Juan, Puerto Rico, 15–18 March.

———. 2005. Elections versus democracy. *Journal of Democracy* 16, no. 1 (January): 124–37.

Lange, Peter, and Geoffrey Garrett. 1991. Political responses to interdependence: What's "left" for the left? *International Organization* 45, no. 4 (Autumn): 539–64.

Lanzaro, Jorge. 2008. La socialdemocracia criolla. *Nueva Sociedad* 217 (September–October): 40–58.

Latin American Regional Report. 2007. Brazil and Southern Cone. December.

Lehoucq, Fabrice. 2008. Bolivia's constitutional breakdown. *Journal of Democracy* 19, no. 4 (October): 110–24.

Leiras, Marcelo. 2007. Latin America's electoral turn: Left, right, and wrong. *Constellations* 14, no. 3: 398–408.

Lemke, Christiane, and Gary Marks, eds. 1992. *The Crisis of Socialism in Europe*. Durham, NC: Duke University Press.

Lenz, Rony. 2005. Políticas públicas en salud: Experiencias y desafíos en Chile, 1990–2010; una mirada económica. In *La Paradoja Aparente*, ed. Patricio Meller, 287–362. Santiago de Chile: Aguilar Chilena Ediciones.

Levine, Daniel. 1978. Venezuela since 1958: The consolidation of democratic politics. In *The Breakdown of Democratic Regimes: Latin America*, eds. Juan J. Linz and Alfred Stepan, 82–109. Baltimore, MD: Johns Hopkins University Press.

————. 1973. *Conflict and Political Change in Venezuela*. Princeton, NJ: Princeton University Press.

Levitsky, Steven, and Kenneth Roberts, eds. In press. *Latin America's Left Turn*. Baltimore, MD: Johns Hopkins University Press.

Levitsky, Steven, and Lucan Way. 2006. Competitive Authoritarianism: The Origins and Evolution of Hybrid Regimes after the Cold War. Paper delivered at the 102nd annual meeting of the American Political Science Association, Philadelphia, PA, 30 August–3 September.

Lijphart, Arend. 1984. *Democracies*. New Haven, CT: Yale University Press.

Lindblom, Charles. 1982. The market as a prison. *The Journal of Politics* 44, no. 2 (May): 324–36.

Lindert, Kathy, Emmanuel Skoufias, and Joseph Shapiro. 2006. Redistributing Income to the Poor and the Rich: Public Transfers in Latin America and the Caribbean. Working paper. Washington, DC: World Bank.

Lopreato, Francisco. 2006. Política fiscal: Mudanças e perspectivas. In *A Supremacia dos Mercados e a Política Econômica do Governo Lula*, ed. Ricardo Carneiro, 207–29. São Paulo, Brazil: UNESP.

Lora, Eduardo, ed. 2007. *The State of State Reform in Latin America*. Washington, DC: Inter-American Development Bank/Stanford University Press.

Lula da Silva, Luiz Inácio. 2002. Letter to the Brazilian People. http://www.pt.org.br.

Luna, Juan Pablo. 2006. Programmatic and Non-Programmatic Party-Voter Linkages in Two Institutionalized Party Systems: Chile and Uruguay in Comparative Perspective. Ph.D. diss., Department of Political Science, University of North Carolina, Chapel Hill.

Lustig, Nora. 2009. Poverty, Inequality and the New Left in Latin America. Washington, DC: Woodrow Wilson Center. Update on the Americas No. 5 (October).

Macedo e Silva, Antonio. 2006. A montanha em movimento: Uma notícia sobre as transformações recentes da economia global. In *A Supremacia dos Mercados e a Política Econômica do Governo Lula*, ed. Ricardo Carneiro, 51–96. São Paulo, Brazil: UNESP.

Madrid, Raúl. 2008. The rise of ethnopopulism in Latin America. *World Politics* 60, no. 3 (April): 475–508.

Mainwaring, Scott, and Timothy Scully, eds. 2010. *Democratic Governance in Latin America*. Stanford, CA: Stanford University Press.

Mainwaring, Scott, and Mariano Torcal. 2005. Party System Institutionalization and Party System Theory after the Third Wave of Democratization. Kellogg Institute, University of Notre Dame. Working paper #319.

Mantega, Guido. 2007. The Brazilian Economy in 2007. London. January. http://www.fazenda.gov.br/portugues/documentos/2006/p290107.pdf.

Maravall, José María. 1995. *Los Resultados de la Democracia*. Madrid: Alianza Editorial.

Marinakis, Andrés. 2007. Desempolvando el salario mínimo: Reflexiones a partir de la experiencia en el Cono Sur. In *Para Qué Sirve el Salario Mínimo?* eds. Andrés Marinakis and Juan Jacobo Velasco, 2–20. Santiago de Chile: Oficina Internacional del Trabajo.

Márquez, Patricia, and Ramón Piñango, eds. 2004. *En Esta Venezuela*. Caracas, Venezuela: IESA.

Martin, Nathan D., and David Brady. 2007. Workers of the less developed world unite? A multilevel analysis of unionization in less developed countries. *American Sociological Review* 72, no. 4 (August): 562–84.

Martínez, Juan, and Javier Santiso. 2003. Financial markets and politics. *International Political Science Review* 24, no. 3 (September): 363–95.

Martins Biancareli, André. 2006. Países emergentes e ciclos internacionais. In *A Supremacia dos Mercados e a Política Econômica do Governo Lula*, ed. Ricardo Carneiro, 97–129. São Paulo, Brazil: UNESP.

Mayorga, Fernando. 2002. *Neopopulismo y Democracia: Compadres y Padrinos en la Política Boliviana (1988–1999)*. La Paz, Bolivia: Plural Editores.

McKinley Jr., James C. 2008. Nicaraguan councils stir fear of dictatorship. *The New York Times* 4 May: 6.

Medinacelli, Mauricio. 2007a. Aspectos económicos de los nuevos contratos. In *El Nuevo Ciclo de los Hidrocarburos*, ed. Fundación Boliviana para la Democracia Multipartidaria, 19–27. La Paz, Bolivia: FBDM.

———. 2007b. *La Nacionalización del Nuevo Milenio: Cuando el Precio Fue un Aliado*. La Paz, Bolivia: Fundemos.

Melo, Marcus. 2008. Unexpected successes, unanticipated failures: Social policy from Cardoso to Lula. In *Democratic Brazil Revisited*, eds. Peter Kingstone and Timothy J. Power, 161–84. Pittsburgh, PA: University of Pittsburgh Press.

———. 2005. O sucesso inesperado das reformas de segunda geração: Federalismo, reformas constitucionais e política social. *Dados* (Rio de Janeiro) 48, no. 4 (October/December): 845–89.

Meneguello, Rachel. 2005. Government popularity and public attitudes to social security reform in Brazil. *International Journal of Public Opinion Research* 17, no. 2 (summer): 173–89.

Mercadante, Aloizio. 2006. *Brasil: Primeiro Tempo; Análise Comparativa do Governo Lula*. São Paulo, Brazil: Planeta do Brasil.

(*El*) *Mercurio*. 2009. Los anuncios de Bachelet: Bonos, subsidios y planes de reforma. 22 May.

———. 2008. PSU 2008: Crece la brecha educacional entre colegios municipales y particulares pagados. 21 December. http://blogs.elmercurio.com/cronica/2007/12/21/psu-2008-crece-la-brecha-entre.asp. Accessed 23 September 2008.

Mesa-Lago, Carmelo, and Alberto Arenas de Mesa. 1998. The Chilean pension system: Evaluation, lessons, and challenges. In *Do Options Exist? The Reform of Pension and Health Care Systems in Latin America*, eds. María Amparo Cruz-Saco and Carmelo Mesa-Lago, 56–84. Pittsburgh, PA: University of Pittsburgh Press.

Michels, Robert. 1959/1915. *Political Parties*. New York: Dover.

Milanovic, Branko. 2005. Can we discern the effect of globalization on income distribution? Evidence from household surveys. *World Bank Economic Review* 19, no. 1 (May): 21–44.

Ministério do Desenvolvimento Social e Combate à Fome. Statistics. Accessed 8 July 2009 from http://www.mds.gov.br.

Modelo Importado do Brasil. 2009. *Veja* 2115 (3 June): 66–8. http://veja.abril.com.br/030609/p_066.shtml. Accessed 23 June 2009.

Moffett, Matt. 2009. Prudent Chile thrives amidst downturn. *Wall Street Journal*. May 27.

Molina, Fernando. 2007. *El Retorno de la Izquierda Nacionalista*. La Paz, Bolivia: Eureka.

Montúfar, César. 2008. Two Perspectives on Ecuador: Rafael Correa's Political Project. Andean working paper. Washington, DC: Inter-American Dialogue (August).

Mosley, Layna. 2003. *Global Capital and National Governments*. Cambridge, U.K.: Cambridge University Press.

Müller, Katharina. 2009. Contested universalism: From Bonosol to Renta Dignidad in Bolivia. *International Journal of Social Welfare* 18, no. 2 (April): 163–72.

Muñoz Gomá, Oscar. 2007. *El Modelo Económico de la Concertación, 1990–2005: Reformas o Cambio?* Santiago de Chile: FLACSO.

Myers, David. 2004. The normalization of Punto Fijo democracy. In *The Unraveling of Representative Democracy in Venezuela*, eds. Jennifer McCoy and David Myers, 11–32. Baltimore, MD: Johns Hopkins University Press.

Naím, Moisés. 1993. *Paper Tigers and Minotaurs*. Washington, DC: Carnegie Endowment for International Peace.

————, and Ramón Piñango, eds. 1984. *El Caso Venezuela: Una Ilusión de Armonía*. Caracas, Venezuela: IESA.

Nelson, Joan. 1989. *Fragile Coalitions: The Politics of Economic Adjustment*. New Brunswick, NJ: Transaction.

Nelson, Roy. 2009. *Harnessing Globalization: The Promotion of Nontraditional Foreign Direct Investment in Latin America*. University Park: Pennsylvania State University Press.

Nêumanne, José. 2008. Enchendo o bolso do rico e a barriga do pobre. *O Estado de São Paulo*, 20 February: A2.

Norden, Deborah. 1998. Party relations and democracy in Latin America. *Party Politics* 4, no. 3 (October): 432–4.

North, Douglas, William Summerhill, and Barry Weingast. 2000. Order, disorder, and economic change: Latin America versus North America. In *Governing for Prosperity*, eds. Bruce Bueno de Mesquita and Hilton Root, 23–9. New Haven, CT: Yale University Press.

O'Donnell, Guillermo. 1994. Delegative democracy. *Journal of Democracy* 5, no. 1 (January): 55–69.

OECD (Organisation for Economic Co-operation and Development)/HRDC (Human Resources Development Canada). 2000. *Literacy in the Information Age: Final Report of the International Adult Literacy Survey*. Paris: OECD; Statistics Canada.

Olavarría Gambi, Mauricio. 2005. *Pobreza, Crecimiento Económico y Políticas Sociales*. Santiago: Editorial Universitaria.

Oliveira, Gesner. 1995. The Brazilian Economy under the Real: Prospects for Stabilization and Growth. Paper presented at the 19th International Congress of the Latin American Studies Association, Washington, DC, 28–30 September.

Ondetti, Gabriel. 2007. An ambivalent legacy: Cardoso and land reform. *Latin American Perspectives* 34, no. 5 (September): 9–25.

Oporto, Henry. 2007. *Plan Nacional de Desarrollo: Entre Mitos y Utopías*. La Paz, Bolivia: Fundación Nuevo Norte.

Ordenes, Jorge V. 2006. Los dos tercios. *Los Tiempos*, 26 December.

Orellana, Lorgio. 2006. *El Gobierno del MAS no es Nacionalista ni Revolucionario: Un Análisis del Plan Nacional de Desarrollo*. La Paz, Bolivia: CEDLA.

Ortega, Daniel, and Francisco Rodríguez. 2008. Freed from illiteracy? A closer look at Venezuela's Misión Robinson literacy campaign. *Economic Development and Cultural Change* 57, no. 1 (January): 1–30.

Paes de Barros, Ricardo, Miguel Nathan Foguel, and Gabriel Ulyssea. 2007. *Desigualdade de Renda no Brasil: Uma Análise da Queda Recente.* 2 vols. Brasília, Brazil: IPEA. http://www.ipea.gov.br/sites/ooo/2/livros/desigualdaderen danobrasilv2/Livrocompleto.pdf. Accessed 23 September 2008.

Paiva, Paulo. 2006. Lula's political economy: Changes and challenges. *Annals of the American Academy of Political and Social Sciences* 606 (July): 196–215.

Paula, João Antonio de. 2005. *Adeus ao Desenvolvimento: A Opção do Governo Lula.* Belo Horizonte, Brazil: Ed. Autêntica.

Paz Arauco, Verónica. 2008. El Desafío Urgente: Actuar ante la Asimetría Departamental. Documento de trabajo, Informe de Desarrollo Humano. La Paz, Bolivia: PNUD.

Penfold-Becerra, Michael. 2007. Clientelism and social funds: Empirical evidence from Chávez's Misiones programs. *Latin American Politics and Society* 49, no. 4 (Winter): 63–84.

Peres, Wilson. 2006. El lento retorno de las políticas industriales en América Latina y el Caribe. *Revista de la CEPAL* 88 (April): 71–88.

Pérez Martí, Felipe. 2008. Revisión, rectificación y reimpulso económico. In *Reimpulso Productivo,* ed. Ministerio del Poder Popular para la Comunicación y la Información. Caracas, Venezuela: Ministerio del Poder Popular. Book manuscript.

Perticará, Marcela. 2004. Chile Solidario. Presentation delivered at the Third Meeting of the Social Policy Monitoring Network, Buenos Aires, Argentina, November. http://www.iadb.org/res/pub_desc.cfm?pub_id=p-276.

Petkoff, Teodoro. 2008. A Watershed Moment: Venezuela. Andean working paper. Washington, DC: Inter-American Dialogue.

———. 2005. Las dos izquierdas. *Nueva Sociedad* 197 (May–June): 114–28.

Petras, James. 2000. *The Left Strikes Back: Class and Conflict in the Age of Neoliberalism.* Boulder, CO: Westview.

Pierson, Paul. 2004. *Politics in Time: History, Institutions, and Social Analysis.* Princeton, NJ: Princeton University Press.

Pinheiro, Armando Castelar, and Fabio Giambiagi. 2005. *Rompendo o Marasmo.* Rio de Janeiro, Brazil: Editora Campus.

Ponce, Aldo. 2007. From Traditional Populism to Multiple Political Strategies: The Transformation of the Latin American Left and Its Determinants. Paper presented at the 27th International Congress of the Latin American Studies Association, Montréal, 5–8 September.

Portes, Alejandro, and Kelly Hoffman. 2003. Latin American class structures. *Latin American Research Review* 38, no. 1 (February): 41–82.

Power, Timothy. 2001. Blairism Brazilian style? Cardoso and the "Third Way" in Brazil. *Political Science Quarterly* 116, no. 4 (winter): 611–36.

Prata, José. 2006. *Um Retrato do Brasil: Balanço do Governo Lula.* São Paulo, Brazil: Fundação Perseu Abramo.

Pribble, Jennifer. 2008. Protecting the Poor: Welfare Politics in Latin America's Free Market Era. Ph.D. diss., Department of Political Science, University of North Carolina, Chapel Hill.

———. 2006a. Interview no. 1: High official from the Lagos Government. Santiago de Chile, 22 September.

———. 2006b. Interview no. 4: Union Leader (Chile). Santiago de Chile, 9 June.

———. 2006c. Women and welfare: The politics of coping with new social risks in Chile and Uruguay. *Latin American Research Review* 41, no. 2 (June): 84–111.

Pritchett, Lant. 1997. Divergence, big time. *Journal of Economic Perspectives* 11, no. 3 (summer): 3–17.

Przeworski, Adam. 1991. *Democracy and the Market: Political and Economic Reforms in Eastern Europe and Latin America*. New York: Cambridge University Press.

———. 1985. *Capitalism and Social Democracy*. Cambridge, U.K.: Cambridge University Press.

———, Michael E. Alvarez, José Antonio Cheibub, and Fernando Limongi. 2000. *Democracy and Development: Political Institutions and Well-Being in the World, 1950–1990*. New York: Cambridge University Press.

Ramírez Gallegos, Franklin. 2006. Mucho más que dos izquierdas. *Nueva Sociedad* 205 (September–October): 30–44.

Rawlings, Laura. 2005. A new approach to social assistance: Latin America's experience with conditional cash transfer programs. *International Social Security Review* 58, no. 2–3 (April–September): 133–61.

———, and Gloria Rubio. 2005. Evaluating the impact of conditional cash transfer programs. *World Bank Research Observer* 20, no. 1 (spring): 29–55.

(La) Razón. 2009. El 2008, la inflación cerró en 11,85%, 7 January.

Roberts, Kenneth. In press. *Changing Course: Parties, Populism, and Political Representation in Latin America's Neoliberal Era*. Cambridge, U.K.: Cambridge University Press.

———. 2008. ¿Es posible una socialdemocracia en América Latina? *Nueva Sociedad* 217 (September–October): 86–98.

———. 2007. Latin America's populist revival. *SAIS Review* 27, no. 1 (winter–spring): 3–15.

———. 1998. *Deepening Democracy? The Modern Left and Social Movements in Chile and Peru*. Stanford, CA: Stanford University Press.

———. 1995. Neoliberalism and the transformation of populism in Latin America. *World Politics* 48, no. 1 (October): 82–116.

Rocca, Carlos. 2003. Reforma da previdência e mercado de capitais. In *Governo Lula: Novas Prioridades e Desenvolvimento Sustentado*, ed. João Paulo dos Reis Velloso, 189–215. Rio de Janeiro, Brazil: José Olympio.

Rodríguez, Francisco. 2008. An empty revolution: The unfulfilled promises of Hugo Chávez. *Foreign Affairs* 87, no. 2 (March–April): 49–62.

Rodríguez Veltzé, Eduardo. 2008. Presupuesto judicial y justicia de paz. *La Razón* (La Paz), 20 May.

Rodríguez-Clare, Andrés, and Alberto Melo. 2007. Productive development policies and supporting institutions in Latin America and the Caribbean. In *The State of State Reform in Latin America*, ed. Eduardo Lora, 317–54. Stanford, CA: Stanford University Press.

Rogers, Tim. 2007. Nicaragua. *Mesoamerica* (December): 7–8.

Romero, Aníbal. 1997. Rearranging the deck chairs on the Titanic: The agony of democracy in Venezuela. *Latin American Research Review* 21, no. 1 (February): 7–36.

Romero, Evanan. 2008. The Petro Politics of Venezuela. Paper presented at the conference Venezuela: Oil, Politics, and Foreign Policy, Center for Hemispheric Policy, University of Miami, Miami, FL, 22 October.

Romero, Salvador. 2003. *Geografía Electoral de Bolivia*, 3rd ed. La Paz, Bolivia: Fundemos.

Ruiz Rodríguez, Leticia. 2006. El sistema de partidos chilenos: ¿Hacia una desestructuración ideológica? In *Chile: Política y modernización democrática*, ed. Manuel Alcántara Sáez and Leticia Ruiz Rodríguez, 73–110. Barcelona: Ediciones Bellaterra.

Sallum, Brasilio, Jr., and Eduardo Kugelmas. 2003. Gobierno de Lula ¿Continuidad, avance o retroceso? In *La Argentina de Kirchner y el Brasil de Lula*, ed. Chacho Álvarez, 19–35. Buenos Aires: CEPES.

Samuels, David. 2004. From socialism to social democracy: Party organization and the transformation of the Workers' Party in Brazil. *Comparative Political Studies* 37, no. 9 (November): 999–1024.

Sandbrook, Richard, Mark Edelman, Patrick Heller, and Judith Teichman. 2007. *Social Democracy in the Global Periphery*. Cambridge, U.K.: Cambridge University Press.

Sassoon, Donald. 1996. *One Hundred Years of Socialism*. New York: New Press.

Scaglione, Matías. 2008. Behind the discourse: Economic policy and performance in Chávez's Venezuela. *Lateinamerika Analysen* 19: 55–94.

SERNAM (Servicio Nacional de la Mujer). 2008. Aumentó Participación de las Mujeres en Mercado Laboral. Press release, 31 January. http://www.sernam.cl/opencms/opencms/sernam/modules/noticias/news_0088.html.

Serrano, Claudia, and Dagmar Raczynski. 2004. Programas sociales innovadores de superación de la pobreza en Brasil y Chile. In *Equidad y Protección Social*, ed. Clarisa Hardy, 15–44. Santiago de Chile: LOM Ediciones, Fundación Chile 21.

Shugart, Matthew Soberg, and John Carey. 1992. *Presidents and Assemblies: Constitutional Design and Electoral Dynamics*. New York: Cambridge University Press.

Siavelis, Peter. 2009. Chile's presidential election and the Marco Enríquez-Ominami factor: Insight from Patricio Navia's *El Díscolo. Americas Quarterly* 19 November. http://www.americasquarterly.org/chile-elections-ominami-factor. Accessed 6 March 2010.

———. 2005. Electoral system, coalitional disintegration and democracy in Chile. *Latin American Research Review* 40, no. 1 (February): 56–82.

Silva, Eduardo. 2009. *Challenging Neoliberalism in Latin America*. Cambridge, U.K.: Cambridge University Press.

Silva, Fabricio Pereira da. 2009. Izquierdas Latinoamericanas: ¿Una Tipología es Posible? Paper for 21st World Congress of Political Science, International Political Science Association, Santiago de Chile, 12–16 July.

Smith, Benjamin. 2006. The wrong kind of crisis: Why oil booms and busts rarely lead to authoritarian breakdown. *Studies in Comparative International Development* 40, no. 4 (winter): 55–76.

Smith, William C., and Roberto Korzeniewicz. 2000. Poverty, inequality, and growth in Latin America: Searching for the high road to globalization. *Latin American Research Review* 35, no. 3 (October): 7–54.

———, eds. 1997. *Politics, Social Change, and Economic Restructuring in Latin America*. Miami, FL: North-South Center Press.

Sola, Lourdes. 2008. Politics, markets, and society in Lula's Brazil. *Journal of Democracy* 19, no. 2 (April): 31–45.

Stefanoni, Pablo. 2007. Empate catastrófico en Bolivia: Sin avances en la Asamblea Constituyente. *Le Monde Diplomatique*, 24 October.

———, and Hervé do Alto. 2006. *La Revolución de Evo Morales: De la Coca al Palacio*. Buenos Aires, Argentina: Claves para Todos.

Stephens, John. 1986. *The Transition from Capitalism to Socialism*. 2nd ed. Urbana: University of Illinois Press.

Stephens, Klara. 2008. Women and Work in Chile: Policy Puzzles. Honors thesis. Department of Political Science. Chapel Hill: University of North Carolina.

Tavares Soares, Laura, Emir Sader, Rafael Gentili, and Cesar Benjamin. 2004. *Governo Lula: Decifrando o Enigma*. São Paulo, Brazil: Viramundo.

Tejero Puntes, Suhelis. 2008. Sector público absorbe a 41,400 trabajadores por estatizaciones. *El Universal* (Caracas), 2 June.

Tesouro Nacional, Ministério da Fazenda. Statistics. Accessed 8 July 2009 from www. tesouro.fazenda.gov.br.

Titelman, Daniel. 2000. Reformas al sistema de salud en Chile: Desafíos pendientes. In *Serie CEPAL: Financiamiento del Desarrollo*, 1–41. Santiago de Chile: United Nations Economic Commission for Latin America and the Caribbean.

Toranzo Roca, Carlos. 2008. Let the mestizos stand up and be counted. In *Unresolved Tensions: Bolivia, Past and Present*, eds. John Crabtree and Laurence Whitehead, 35–50. Pittsburgh, PA: University of Pittsburgh Press.

Torres Filho, Ernani Teixeira, Fernando Pimentel Puga, and Marcelo Machado Nascim. 2007. Investimento deve crescer mais de 10% ao ano em 2008–2011. *Visão do Desenvolvimento* (BNDES) 43, 20 December.

Touraine, Alain. 2007. Entre Bachelet y Morales ¿Existe una izquierda en América Latina? *Nueva Sociedad* 205 (September–October): 46–55.

Tribunal Constitucional (Bolivia). 2008. Declaración del Tribunal Constitucional al Pueblo de Bolivia. 17 May.

Trinkunas, Harold. 2004. The military: From marginalization to center stage. In *The Unraveling of Representative Democracy in Venezuela*, eds. Jennifer McCoy and David Myers, 50–70. Baltimore, MD: Johns Hopkins University Press.

UDAPE (Unidad de Análisis de Políticas Sociales y Económicas), INE, IBCE, and CANEB. 2006. *Empleo Exportador en Bolivia*. La Paz, Bolivia: UDAPE.

UNDP (United Nations Development Programme). 2008. *La Otra Frontera: Informe Temático de Desarrollo Humano de Bolivia*. La Paz, Bolivia: UNDP.

———. 2005. *La Economía Más Allá del Gas: Informe Temático de Desarrollo Humano de Bolivia*. La Paz, Bolivia: UNDP.

———. Various years. *Human Development Report*. New York: UNDP.

UNESCO (United Nations Educational, Scientific and Cultural Organization), Institute for Statistics, Global Education Database. Data retrieved 8 July 2009 from www.uis .unesco.org.

(*El*) *Universal*. 2008. Analysts: Venezuela needs that price of oil exceeds USD 90 to pay expenses. 14 October. http://english.eluniversal.com/2008/10/14/en_eco_esp_analysts:-venezuela_14A2068487. Accessed 24 December 2008.

U.S. Social Security Administration. 1999. *Social Security Programs throughout the World*. Washington, DC: U.S. Social Security Administration.

Uthoff, Andras. 1995. *Reformas a los Sistemas de Pensiones en América Latina y el Caribe*. Santiago de Chile: CEPAL.

Vargas Llosa, Alvaro. 2007. The return of the idiot. *Foreign Policy* 160 (May/June): 54–61.

Veneconomía. 2008. Perspectivas Económicas, Políticas y Sociales de Venezuela, 2008–2013. Caracas, Venezuela: Veneconomía.

———. Various years. Daily Report. Caracas, Venezuela: Veneconomía.

Versión Final (Maracaibo). 2008a. Arsenales son más importantes que obras sociales. 20–26 June: 12–13.

———. 2008b. La aplanadora mediática. 6–12 June: 4–5.

Villasmil, Ricardo, Francisco Monaldi, Germán Ríos, and Marino González. 2004. *Venezuela. Global Development Network: Understanding Reform Country Studies*. Caracas, Venezuela: IESA.

Weber, Max. 1971. *Gesammelte Politische Schriften*, 3rd ed. Tübingen: J.C.B. Mohr.

Weisbrot, Mark. 2008. *An Empty Research Agenda: The Creation of Myths about Contemporary Venezuela*. Washington, DC: Center for Economic and Policy Research, Issue Brief, March.

Weisbrot, Mark, and Luis Sandoval. 2006. *Bolivia's Challenges*. Washington, DC: Center for Economic and Policy Research. http://www.cepr.net/documents/bolivia_challenges_2006_03.pdf

Weisbrot, Mark, Luis Sandoval, and David Rosnick. 2006. Poverty rates in Venezuela: Getting the numbers right. *International Journal of Health Services* 36, no. 4 (November): 813–23.

Weyland, Kurt. 2009. The rise of Latin America's two lefts: Insights from rentier state theory. *Comparative Politics* 41, no. 2 (January): 145–64.

_____. 2007. *Bounded Rationality and Policy Diffusion: Social Sector Reform in Latin America*. Princeton, NJ: Princeton University Press.

_____. 2004. Threats to Latin America's market model? *Political Science Quarterly* 119, no. 2 (summer): 291–313.

_____. 2002. *The Politics of Market Reform in Fragile Democracies*. Princeton, NJ: Princeton University Press.

_____. 1998. The Brazilian state in the new democracy. *Journal of Interamerican Studies and World Affairs* 39, no. 4 (winter): 63–94.

_____. 1996. Neopopulism and neoliberalism in Latin America: Unexpected affinities. *Studies in Comparative International Development* 31, no. 3 (fall): 3–31.

Wibbels, Erik. 2006. Dependency revisited: International markets, business cycles, and social spending in the developing world. *International Organization* 60, no. 2 (April): 433–68.

Wilpert, Gregory. 2007. *Changing Venezuela by Taking Power: The History and Policies of the Chávez Government*. London: Verso.

_____. 2003. Venezuela's New Constitution. 27 August. http://www.venezuelanalisis.com. Accessed 5 December 2008.

Winn, Peter, ed. 2004. *Victims of the Chilean Miracle: Workers and Neoliberalism in the Pinochet Era, 1973–2002*. Durham, NC: Duke University Press.

World Bank. 2008. Doing Business. http://www.doingbusiness.org. Accessed 5 December 2008.

_____. 2008. *Migration and Remittances Factbook*. Washington, DC: The World Bank.

_____. Various years. *World Development Indicators*. Washington, DC: The World Bank.

Zaratti, Francesco. 2007. Repercusiones de la nacionalización y el futuro de los hidrocarburos en Bolivia, tras la firma de los nuevos contratos petroleros. In *El Nuevo Ciclo de los Hidrocarburos*, ed. Fundación Boliviana para la Democracia Multipartidaria, 35–48. La Paz, Bolivia: FBDM.

Zavaleta Reyles, Diego. 2008. The debate over what is indigena and what is mestizo. In *Unresolved Tensions: Bolivia, Past and Present*, eds. John Crabtree and Laurence Whitehead, 51–60. Pittsburgh, PA: University of Pittsburgh Press.

Index